D1713322

Some Pathways in Twentieth-Century History

Reginald Charles McGrane

Some Pathways in Twentieth-Century History

Essays in Honor of Reginald Charles McGrane

Edited by

Daniel R. Beaver

Published for the University of Cincinnati by
The Wayne State University Press Detroit 1969

Published simultaneously in Canada
by The Copp Clark Publishing Company
517 Wellington Street, West
Toronto 2B, Canada.
Library of Congress Catalog
Card Number: 69-11348

Published with the help of
the Charles Taft Memorial Fund
of the University of Cincinnati

Contents

Introduction

It is with profound pleasure that I write an introduction to this *Festschrift* in honor of Professor Reginald C. McGrane—fellow historian, colleague at the University of Cincinnati, and friend.

When this great teacher and writer—who made history interesting even to generations of engineering students—retired as professor emeritus in 1959, he had completed nearly half a century of service to his beloved "UC." And in 1963 he continued his service to his Alma Mater by publishing a history of the University, a publication distinguished not alone by diligent research and adroit selection but by a style so readable as to set it favorably apart from a host of similar books.

The most effective testimony to his inspirational skill as teacher and scholar is the sizable number of his students who have become distinguished historians in their own right. Nine of these former students, holding appointments at half a dozen universities and in two leading federal offices, have, in gratitude and affection, contributed essays to this volume intended to honor their mentor. Their interests and those of his other historian students—and consequently Professor McGrane's own influence—are truly both broad and significant. For this, our whole nation may well be thankful.

That this *Festschrift* should have been conceived at the University of Cincinnati and edited by one of its alumni and professors is eminently fitting. May the volume be as well received as were Professor McGrane's own lectures and writings.

WALTER C. LANGSAM, *President*
UNIVERSITY OF CINCINNATI
December 5, 1968

Editor's Preface

An editor is by tradition compelled to write a preface. Although I can add little to the splendid biography written by Harry Stevens which introduces these memorial essays, perhaps a few impressions of my own will highlight Reginald McGrane's influence upon some of us who knew him well.

We called him "The Boss." He spent most of his academic life at the University of Cincinnati teaching undergraduate engineering students. He never conducted a doctoral seminar at the University. He never had a student write a Ph.D. dissertation under his direction. Because he insisted that the lectern was not a pulpit, he founded no cult. His interest was in sound historical method and he encouraged his students and other associates in the profession to break their own paths; thus these essays lack the common theme characteristic of similar enterprises. Only Harry Stevens, among the nine men who contributed to this volume, followed McGrane into nineteenth-century American history. Alfred Sumberg marked out a field in the progressive era. Thomas McCormick, Francis Loewenheim, and William Franklin devoted themselves to international affairs. Richard Leighton and Daniel Beaver chose the study of military history. Henry Winkler and C. William Vogel became immersed in the study of British life and institutions. Yet all have been influenced substantially by knowing Reginald McGrane—the man's scholarly vigor, his detachment, his disdain for a piece of shoddy work, his biting criticism have had a lasting impact.

Shortly before McGrane retired as head of the department at the University of Cincinnati, I stopped into his office for a chat. He did not often relish such interruptions, but this time he was in an expansive mood. The talk wandered from world affairs to local politics and eventually came to the importance of history. I asked him what he had learned in nearly half a century of writing and teaching. He replied in that epigrammatic way of his: "A little tolerance." There is really no more to say.

A volume such as this is a labor of love. The contributors gave much of their own time editing and proofreading the manuscript. Kathy J. Kiefer, a graduate student in history at the University, typed the final draft with accuracy and dispatch. My wife Margery Schubert Beaver and my good friend Barbara J. Triplett checked the galley and page proof and prepared the index. The work could not have been undertaken without the encouragement of the Taft Committee at the University of Cincinnati. A substantial grant from the Taft Fund made publication possible.

DANIEL R. BEAVER
UNIVERSITY OF CINCINNATI
December, 1967

Reginald Charles McGrane

Harry R. Stevens
OHIO UNIVERSITY

When Reginald Charles McGrane completed his teaching in 1959, he had fulfilled one of his most cherished concepts: the opportunity afforded by the American community for individual success. He was born at Cincinnati, Ohio, July 28, 1889, the only child of John J. and Laura J. (Lawhead) McGrane. His father, not a prosperous man, had taken part in the Alaska Gold Rush of the late 1890s and in 1900 or 1901 was living in Denver, where he had a tobacco shop on the edge of the business center and furnished rooms two blocks away. He died soon afterwards. The boy remembered both his father and his grandmother with affection and respect, and later dedicated his first book to their memory.

Following his father's death, McGrane lived with his mother, whom he adored, in the West End of Cincinnati. She had been on the stage; later, in his teaching, he often used language and metaphors referring to the theater. From an early age he had a strong desire to get an education, and in 1904 entered Hughes High School. His courses included four years each of English, Latin, and mathematics, and three years of science, but only one year (when he was a freshman) of history. During this time he worked in a drug store, coming home to study far into the night with a wet towel around his head to keep himself awake. When he graduated with high grades in all his work, he turned to the University of Cincinnati as the best bargain available in higher education and entered as a freshman in 1908.

At the University his interest in history was kindled by Professor Merrick Whitcomb, who had come from the University of Pennsylvania to Cincinnati in 1900. McGrane described him as a scholar, the author of several volumes, a cultured gentleman, and one of the most popular lecturers on the campus. Whitcomb was McGrane's first history teacher and probably the great inspiration of his career. His particular interest lay in the Renaissance, and it was his assignment of Cellini's *Autobiography* that led McGrane to decide to major in history. He thought it would be pleasant to spend the rest of his life reading such interesting books as he had found the *Autobiography* to be.

Another of his early teachers was Isaac Joslin Cox. Like Whitcomb, Cox was a graduate of the University of Pennsylvania. He had begun teaching at Cincinnati in 1904. His academic interest lay in the eighteenth- and early nineteenth-century frontier between Spanish America and the United States.

McGrane was much impressed by the faculty of the University in his day. It was small, but numbered a group of outstanding men (later sometimes referred to as "the old guard"): Whitcomb, Frank W. Chandler (whom McGrane afterwards described as "the genial dean") in the field of comparative literature and modern drama, Louis T. More in physics, Nevin M. Fenneman in geology, Philip Ogden in Romance languages, Frederick C. Hicks in economics, and others whom he regarded as both scholarly and "tough," and McGrane tried to pattern himself along their lines. Although highly diverse, they had in common a deep dislike for the elective system then being introduced in many colleges.

As a student, McGrane did exceptionally well. He won the Colonial Dames prize for the best work in United States history. He was elected in 1912 to membership in Phi Beta Kappa and, as a result of his participation in forensics, to membership in Tau Kappa Alpha. He was the principal founder in 1910 of the local chapter (Alpha XI) of a social fraternity, Pi Kappa Alpha, and remained a loyal and active alumnus. The alumni association of the fraternity later named him as their "man of the year." Through the fraternity he made some of his closest friendships, such as that with Herbert F. Koch, who became a banker but also had an interest in history. He took part in the flag rush as an undergraduate, but only once. The student demonstration was a four-hour battle between the Freshman and Sophomore classes for retention of their class flag and capture of the enemy's. McGrane had been excused from physical education for physical reasons but when the "phys. ed." instructor saw him in the melee, he told him to cut it out or take the course. McGrane was of rather slight build and suffered most of his life from serious illnesses, some of them brief, others, such as asthma, persistent, but his constitution was basically strong.

He graduated with a bachelor's degree in 1912 and at once entered the Graduate School of the University of Cincinnati. It offered four fellowships, one of them the Daughters of the American Revolution Fellowship in American history, which carried a stipend of $100 per year. McGrane held the D.A.R. Fellowship in 1912–13 and studied under the supervision of Professor Cox, whose assistant he was. Cox wrote of him: "He is always faithful and prompt in the performance of his task, anxious to do well whatever he undertakes, and able to work accurately and rapidly. I never had a student cover so much ground in a given time as he, or do it so well. He seems to revel in work."

He investigated the boundary controversy between Ohio and Michigan, and at the same time studied a manuscript and pamphlet collection concerning the American Southwest in the 1790's. The two studies resulted in his first historical publications, both appearing in 1913 (see bibliography). His first scholarly work was distinguished by the major features that marked all his work for more than half a century: careful and extensive research, critical appraisal of the sources, a firm grasp of underlying realities, clear organization, lucid and economical statement, succinct and soundly based conclusions, and relevance to current public issues.

McGrane received the degree of Master of Arts in 1913 and was encouraged to do further graduate work by the award of an assistantship at the University of Wisconsin. On the way to Madison, he spent the summer working at the University of Chicago under Professor William E. Dodd. At Wisconsin he studied with Victor Coffin, A. L. P. Dennis, Dana C. Munro, and Frederic Logan Paxson, and was in charge of a division of the large introductory course in European history.

He wanted to write a dissertation on South African history, a field that always held his interest. Languages seemed to be no problem (as an undergraduate he had done well in Greek, and he regarded himself quite justly as competent in modern languages, although some felt that his pronunciation was deficient). But he found that he would have to travel abroad to pursue this interest, and he had no money. Paxson, whom he always regarded very highly (and with whom he had a life-long friendship), suggested in his seminar the possibilities of working in the Jacksonian field; McGrane turned to American history, for which the sources were more conveniently at hand, and began to work on the subject that became his dissertation.

By February, 1914, he decided to return to the University of Chicago. He received a fellowship there and, after finishing his work at Madison, transferred to Chicago where he did most of his work under the direction of Professor Dodd. A North Carolinian, Dodd had been educated at Leipzig and had been teaching at Chicago since 1908. McGrane seems to have been a frequent visitor in Dodd's home. He also studied with Andrew C. McLaughlin, whom he probably admired most among his graduate school teachers. Dodd's interpretative lectures contrasted with the rigorous analytical discipline of McLaughlin's constitutional history, and McGrane learned much from both. McLaughlin's method was especially attractive to the young man, and later he made extensive use of it in his own teaching.

At Chicago he formed a number of enduring friendships, perhaps the most important to him being that with Theodore Henley Jack, a fellow graduate student. A native of Alabama, eight years older than McGrane, Jack already had several years of experience in teaching before he came to Chicago in 1914. He was later professor of history at Emory University and then president (1933–52) of Randolph-Macon Woman's College in Lynchburg, Virginia. Their friendship endured more than half a century until President Jack's death in 1965.

Within a few weeks of his arrival at Chicago, McGrane took the initiative in reviving the long-languishing Graduate History Club, and he soon had the pleasure also of seeing a third historical study published: his edition of William Clark's journal of General Anthony Wayne's campaign, which appeared in the first volume of the *Mississippi Valley Historical Review.* He was assistant to McLaughlin in American history (McLaughlin afterwards wrote, "He has shown unusually good sense and appreciation of the task. . . . I am very much interested in Mr. McGrane's welfare, and perhaps I am unduly influenced by that fact"), and in the spring quarter he was in addition placed in charge of a section of the European history survey.

His main job, of course, was to write a dissertation, which he did under the direction of Dodd. He submitted "The Panic of 1837"; it was approved; on September 15, 1915, he was awarded the degree of Doctor of Philosophy.

Professor Whitcomb, who had kept an eye on him during his two-year absence, called McGrane back to the University of Cincinnati as soon as he had his degree. He returned with an appointment as instructor and began his teaching career in association with his two former teachers, Whitcomb and Cox. He shared in the teaching of a two-semester survey course of European history from the Middle Ages; the rest of his thirteen-hour program was made up of a general course in English history, a course in England since 1815, and a course in ancient history. He seems to have had no opportunity to teach his major field, American history, for three years. When the opportunity came, it was at another university.

During his first year of teaching, he worked assiduously on his research and prepared a timely paper on "The Veto Power in Ohio." It was announced for presentation at the ninth annual meeting of the Mississippi Valley Historical Association in Nashville, April 27–29, 1916. Unfortunately he was not able to attend the meeting, and the paper was read only by title. It was published later in the Association's *Proceedings for 1915–1916.*

Yet those efforts clearly did not occupy all of his time. In July, he married Lenore R. Foote, a librarian at the Cincinnati Public Library, and they spent the first weeks of their married life at the

New York Public Library where McGrane worked in several manuscript collections. By this time, he had also carried on research in manuscripts at the Library of Congress. During the latter part of the year, he presented two papers at historical meetings. The first involved a trip to Indianapolis where he read "Speculation in the Thirties" at the opening session of the tenth general meeting of the Ohio Valley Historical Association on October 4. It was published in that Association's *Proceedings* in due time. At the closing session of this meeting, he heard the address given by former president William Howard Taft, of whom he became a great admirer. At the American Historical Association meeting in Cincinnati at the end of the year, McGrane read a paper in which he developed an unusually dramatic topic that he had dealt with in his dissertation. While it was summarized in the *American Historical Review,* he already had more elaborate plans in mind; the paper, however, did not appear in its original form but after further research was included in one of his books.

During 1917, McGrane provided a much valued service to his colleague Cox by reading both manuscript and printer's proofs of Cox's *West Florida Boundary Controversy, 1798–1813,* published in the following year. In the summer of 1918, at the suggestion of his friend Dr. Laura A. White (formerly a fellow graduate student at the University of Chicago), he was invited to teach at the University of Wyoming where she was head of the history department. He gave two courses, one on English diplomacy from the Congress of Vienna to the outbreak of the war in Europe in 1914, and the other, which he now offered for the first time, on recent American history. He enjoyed the summer in Laramie and used to speak of it afterwards.

The University of Cincinnati promoted him to an assistant professorship from September 1, 1918. A month later, the new Students' Army Training Corps was established at Cincinnati at the request of a committee of the War Department; and a course on war aims (the only course in the program that was a general requirement) was offered by the history department under the direction of Professor Whitcomb. Since it was still a department of only three members, it seems likely that McGrane had a share in the program. He remembered, when writing his history of the University, that the operations of the SATC were never sufficiently settled to make a fair evaluation possible, and that after the signing of the armistice on November 11, 1918, interest in the work definitely waned.

With all this activity, it is difficult to see how McGrane found time at all for his first major work. The papers of Nicholas Biddle, president of the Second Bank of the United States, had been deposited in the Library of Congress in 1913. McGrane was given permission to work in this important collection and, later, in other family papers at the home of Edward Biddle in Philadelphia and at the Biddle family homestead, Andalusia, where Charles Biddle was most helpful. He made good use of all three collections in the preparation of *The Correspondence of Nicholas Biddle Dealing with National Affairs, 1807–1844.* Among other acknowledgments he mentioned his debt to the Biddles, to Professor Dodd, and to his associates Whitcomb and Cox. The book was published in 1919 and brought him immediate recognition. It was widely and favorably reviewed. He was aware of the importance of professional book reviews since he himself had already begun to write reviews for both the *American Historical Review* and the *Mississippi Valley Historical Review.*

He was invited at this time to participate in a session of the American Historical Association annual meeting held in December, 1919, at the Hotel Hollenden in Cleveland. This was again a joint meeting of the American Historical and the Mississippi Valley Historical Associations. At the opening session, December 29, under the chairmanship of Milo M. Quaife, five men were scheduled to present papers, but many of the men expected were absent as a result of illness, and only McGrane and one other man appeared. McGrane delivered a paper on the "American Position on the Revolution of 1848 in Germany." It was based principally on research in the Donelson and Clayton manuscripts at the Library of Congress, the United States *House* and *Senate Executive Documents,* and the *National Intelligencer.* A year later it was published under the original title in the *Historical Outlook.*

Changes in both organization and faculty of the University of Cincinnati in 1919 and 1920 brought about a redirection of McGrane's academic responsibilities that was to have far-reaching consequences. The College of Engineering and the College of Commerce were merged in 1919 to form the College of Engineering and Commerce. Dean Herman Schneider then began a comprehensive reconstruction of the curriculum. He wished to provide the engineering students with more work in the humanities than was customary at that time, and established courses for them in English and history. Because of an earlier unfortunate experience in bringing an instructor from another college to teach history to the engineering students, he wanted to have a teacher on the faculty of his own college. McGrane, who had published a significant book and was professionally alert and active, got the appointment in September, 1920, and was promoted to the rank of professor. He shared the work in the humanities with Professor Clyde W. Park who gave instruction in English.

Other changes occurring at the same time altered his relationships throughout the University. His beloved teacher Whitcomb who had been absent on leave for two years, 1919–21, died October 12, 1923, soon after the opening of the fall term in the third year following his return to the campus. He was sixty-three years old and had been professor of history at the University twenty-three years. In 1919, Isaac J. Cox left Cincinnati to go to Northwestern University, where he remained until his retirement in 1941. In the fall of 1920, when McGrane moved to the College of Engineering and Commerce, the University brought Dr. Beverley W. Bond, Jr. from Purdue as an associate professor, and the next year Dr. George A. Hedger, a native of Utah and graduate of Cornell, whose interest lay in recent British foreign policy, was added to the staff. McGrane came to admire Hedger greatly and was probably closer to him personally than to any of his other colleagues. He was distressed by Hedger's apparent lack of any religious faith or concern, but the two men maintained a most friendly relationship throughout their academic association.

Early in 1921, McGrane and Dean Schneider had a confrontation. H. G. Wells's *Outline of History* had been published in the United States late in the fall of 1920. It drew immediate and widespread attention and was the center of a vigorous controversy in academic circles as well as among the general public. Schneider read it and told McGrane that was to be his textbook. Although McGrane was usually very deferential to the Dean, this time he stood firm, and said if he could not pick his book and determine the content of his courses Dean Schneider could find another man. He won.

In the spring of 1921, McGrane published another article, an outgrowth of the work on his dissertation, but also a study of timely interest, "The Rise and Fall of the Independent Treasury." It appeared in the *Historical Outlook* in May.

During the early part of the year, and perhaps extending back into the previous year, McGrane was disturbed by an apparent disintegration and loss of fundamental purposes in college education, even a change of attitude and behavior on the part of college deans and presidents. In a carefully reasoned analysis he traced the evils to the elective system.

He promptly mentioned "the sophisticated freshman" who avoided courses at "the preposterous hour" of eight o'clock, instructors whose ties jarred his nerves, and teachers who were "so inhumane as to demand a little work." He observed that "competition for popularity with the student body means the unconscious lowering of educational standards," and a little later he cautioned, "so long as college presidents and deans listen to the gossip of the corridors, [and] the fraternity house, [or watch] the enrollment of students in the classes of a single professor . . . so long will the present evil continue and grow."

To this denunciation he added constructive proposals:

> Regular prescribed courses are formulated in all professional and technical schools; and the more advanced of these schools as they introduce the so-called "cultural subjects"—such as history, political science, and economics—are even listing them among the required curriculum. Nothing is left to the choice of the student; and there is little doubt that the graduates of these schools are better trained and more serious because they have been forced to learn more thoroughly one subject. They have been taught the fallacy of snap judgment, they have been kept in daily touch with the big movements in their several fields; and the result is that they come from these institutions with an appreciation for sound learning and a receptive mind toward current issues.

With a final blast at the seekers of football glory and fraternity prestige and at the "lounge lizard," he finished his article and sent it off to an editor. "The Bane of Our Colleges" was published in *School and Society* on September 10, 1921.

The tone and language are completely different from anything else McGrane ever published, and suggest strongly (although there are no direct allusions) that he was personally involved and had been subject to some disagreeable experience. The remedy he offered was of course not taken up, but he worked out an alternative solution for himself within the next few years that proved to be most effective. He created his own methods of teaching and established his own personal discipline and leadership.

In 1919, McGrane encouraged his wife to enter the University and work toward a college degree. He guided her selection of courses and her choice of a major, which was political science. She was graduated in 1923, having like her husband been elected to membership in Phi Beta Kappa.

Both McGrane and his wife were interested in government and politics, and Mrs. McGrane was one of the founders of the "Charter Party," a movement in Cincinnati for civic reform. The municipal reform movement in opposition to the long-established "boss" government of George B. Cox and his lieutenant Rud Hynicka was a combination of dissident Republicans and Democrats who beginning in 1922 sought to improve the government of the city by radical changes in its form and administration. In close association with Murray Seasongood, Henry Bentley, and Russell Wilson, the McGranes contributed to the election victory of 1924 that brought a new charter and a city manager form of government. Over the next decade they maintained their active participation.

McGrane gave much greater attention during this decade to his work as a teacher. In addition to his regularly scheduled courses, England and the British Empire, Nineteenth Century Europe, and American Diplomacy, he initiated in 1921 a course in American Economic History that soon became one of his most outstanding offerings. Eventually he wrote his own textbook with a distinctive interpretation revolving about the panics. His history of American diplomacy was first offered in the Graduate School that same year.

His great course in the College of Engineering, however, was Contemporary Problems. It was first offered in 1928, although it seems in some ways to have been an outgrowth of a course in recent American history that he had been teaching for nine years previously. He devised the course with the thought that a senior student ought to be familiar with the problems of the world he was entering. Each year he would select some eight or a dozen major national issues and work the course around them with full topical treatment of their development. Thus he created a specialized course in recent United States history that appealed strongly to the practical-minded engineers. He was acutely conscious that both students and faculty in the College of Engineering were job-minded and tended to regard history as a frill. He largely overcame this attitude by his skillful presentation of material and by his demonstration that it could be one of the businessman's most useful tools. He made himself one of the most popular instructors in the College; many graduates sing his praises.

During the 1920's, McGrane was responsible not only for engineering students but for those in the School of Applied Arts. He had the assistance of a junior, who usually remained only a year or two and taught ancient history and the British empire; McGrane himself taught the introductory course in medieval and modern civilization as well as his regular program and sometimes a course on problems in economic history. In 1926–27 his assistant (as an instructor) was William A. Russ, who shared the work in two of the courses before going on to De Pauw University and later to Susquehanna University; at the same time he was aided by John Oddy. It was Oddy who taught ancient and medieval history to the architecture students in Applied Arts, and his recollections of this period are illuminating:

I first met Reginald McGrane one *hot* Tuesday following Labor Day in 1926 in his office located in the old Applied Arts School . . . I was fresh from Harvard where I was specializing in ancient history and classical archaeology. My impressions of Cincinnati and its climate had best be forgotten, but my feeling[s] toward Mr. and Mrs. McGrane were very special ones indeed as they accepted me with warm hospitalit[y] such as I had never experienced in the East. A greener acolyte than one Oddy never sprouted, and I sit here today humbled and gratified when I reflect on the frankness, kindness, and human understanding with which Mr. McGrane guided me through that first year. I am now at the end of my teaching career, and whatever I have been where good accomplishment is concerned, has been due to the contributions of these men: George Dutcher, W. Scott Ferguson, and Reginald McGrane. The second year I returned with my new wife and our associations with the McGranes became still closer. We were now introduced to a third member of the household, Reginald's mother, a very independent woman.

By this time I had a much deeper understanding of Reginald McGrane and the forces that had contributed to a remarkably strong character that refused any slightest compromise with superficiality. Toward the bluffer, the cheat, and the *poseur* he was merciless. A quicker and more violent temper I have seldom encountered. From those with whom he associated he demanded loyalty, for of all qualities this was the one in which he greatly excelled—loyalty to friends, to family, to students, to scholarship. With his evaluation of loyalty there was no compromise. He extended his friendship to few, but to those few so favored to enjoy it, here was a friendship from which one came to expect and get whatever was needed physical, moral, intellectual, or financial. To these friends his purse, his home, his mind, his heart were open.

During these years McGrane received a number of invitations to move to other colleges, all of which he declined. For one thing, his mother, to whom he was much attached, would not have wanted to leave Cincinnati. But he accepted several other appointments as visiting lecturer or professor in summer sessions. In addition to the summer in Wyoming, in the early 1920's he taught at Northwestern University (where his former teacher Isaac J. Cox was chairman of the history department), and returned to teach there in 1938. In 1923, he taught at American University, in Washington, D.C. and in 1925 at the University of Nebraska during the first part of the summer, rushing off to Austin to teach at the University of Texas for the second part. Nebraska called him back to teach once more in 1926.

The summer appointments involved a special problem since the College of Engineering operated on a twelve-month calendar. In its "co-operative plan," two groups of students alternated in six-week cycles between study on the campus and work on an outside job, and the faculty usually had to be on hand almost the entire year. McGrane resolved this by turning his work over to someone else while he was away, and justified his absence by carrying on his research wherever he went. He had done this from the close of his first year of teaching. Two men who took over his work on certain occasions have offered additional perspectives. One recalls that when McGrane lost half a year of teaching in 1928–29 as a consequence of scarlet fever, he carried McGrane's work in addition to his own; and then adds: "[it] was little enough as return for what he had done and was still doing for me. I used to go daily to the [hospital] where I was dressed in an *all*-covering white garment and taken to see [him] to get information, advice, and encouragement." The other mentions that when he was married in June, 1937, McGrane insisted he take two weeks off from his teaching and met all his classes so that the young couple could have a proper honeymoon.

McGrane's research was more productive than ever. He prepared a paper on "Ohio and the Greenback Movement" which he read at the May 2, 1924 meeting of the Mississippi Valley Historical Association in Louisville. It was published a year later in the Association's *Review*. Meanwhile he completely rewrote his thesis (the formal abstract was published in 1926), incorporating material from the Biddle manuscripts, and early in 1925 published *The Panic of 1837: Some Financial Problems of the Jacksonian Era*. It was soon recognized as a classic monograph, and forty years later was republished by the University of Chicago Press.

Within the year he published a third book, *William Allen: a Study in Western Democracy*. In preparing this volume on one of Ohio's most distinguished but least-known political leaders (Allen is one of the two Ohio men commemorated in the National Statuary Hall), he worked with family papers in Chillicothe and enjoyed, as with previous writing, the encouragement and criticism of Dodd and the thoughtfulness, scholarly interest, and suggestions of his colleague George Hedger. He also took occasion to express his appreciation for the help of Nathaniel R. Whitney, professor of finance at the University from 1920 to 1923 and afterwards economist with Procter & Gamble. Although the book was not as widely reviewed as *The Panic of 1837*, it received honorable mention for the Justin Winsor Prize in 1925.

From time to time McGrane took a short and usually unsuccessful vacation. He and Mrs. McGrane would visit the East coast, staying generally at Asbury Park, New Jersey, where they found the atmosphere congenial; McGrane (it is said) would spend the first day on the beach getting terribly sunburned and be ill for the rest of the time. In the early 1930's, the McGranes, who had a car, took the Oddys, who did not, on frequent trips that were long remembered. McGrane also loved picnics, but he seems to have had little idea how to participate and often wound up in some discomfort.

His longer travels, which he enjoyed greatly, whether they were used for teaching summer school or as a vacation, he tried to make as utilitarian as possible by getting to a research library or, at least in later years, by having his wife take colored slides of buildings, statues, and other monuments to exhibit to his students.

During the latter part of the decade, he worked extensively on articles for the *Dictionary of American Biography,* his earliest ones appearing in the fourth volume, published in 1930. Most of his essays were contained in the volumes published between 1930 and 1933. In view of the editorial work demanded by this massive enterprise and its corresponding deadlines for the submission of material, it is clear that the research and writing of the articles preceded their publication by rather a long time. McGrane's articles, each based on an examination of widely scattered and often ephemeral sources, involved painstaking investigation in many libraries and private collections. When the work was completed with the publication of the twentieth volume in 1936 (including McGrane's essay on Eugene Zimmerman), he had written thirty-five articles. Outstanding among them were those on George Barnsdale Cox, Thomas Ewing, Joseph Benson Foraker, Charles Hammond, John McLean, George Hunt Pendleton, and Allen Granberry Thurman.

At this time, McGrane also began to write historical and other articles for the *Encyclopedia Americana,* a responsibility he carried for more than twenty years. Among his earlier essays were the ones on the vice presidency of the United States and the speakership of the House of Representatives, and in later years the articles on Andrew Johnson, James Monroe, and Zachary Taylor. His book reviews continued to appear regularly in professional historical journals.

In 1928 he was invited to the University of Chicago to teach during the summer quarter, an invitation that was renewed for the two succeeding summers. In three quarters he offered successively the three terms of work that constituted an introductory course in the history of the United States; and at an advanced level he offered in the first summer the Jacksonian Era; in the second, Emergence of an Insurgent Northwest 1837–57; and in the third, Jeffersonian Democracy, 1800–20. Almost forty years later, in a chance conversation with a stranger, one of the students in the first of his advanced courses recalled verbatim the opening words of his first lecture, and went on to say that it was in this class that McGrane had suggested the topic on which she eventually wrote her dissertation and based her entire scholarly career of writing and publication. The second advanced course was one of McGrane's happiest interpretations; it became a widely accepted synthesis elaborated on, restated, and objected to by many later historians.

At the business session of the annual spring meeting of the Mississippi Valley Historical Association, held in Vincennes, Indiana, April 26, 1929, McGrane was elected to a three-year term on the editorial board of the *Review*.

Throughout the 1920's, one of the most conspicuous public questions concerned the payment of the European war debts. The problem of international public finance was vexing, and it is not surprising that McGrane should have been interested in it. His work on the economic history of the 1830's and 1840's, as well as his teaching of American Economic History and of Contemporary Problems dealt with it in more than an incidental way. He wrote:

> The acrimonious disputes over the collection of private and intergovernmental debts has attracted universal attention. The problems confronting foreign investors in the collection of debts due them and the defalcation and repudiation by whole communities of their obligations have led to frequent references in the press to similar occurrences in the past. Among the long forgotten unpaid debts to which attention has been called are those of certain American states.

It was in the hope "that a recital of the circumstances surrounding the origin of these American state debt controversies might throw some light upon the problems of lenders and borrowers" that McGrane undertook his next study. He was awarded a John Simon Guggenheim research fellowship in the spring of 1930. With this support, after finishing his quarter at Chicago, he and Mrs. McGrane traveled to Europe where he spent the year working in financial records in London and Amsterdam. He was given access to the archives of Frederick Huth and Company in England and Hope and Company in the Netherlands, as well as other records, and spent the better part of the year working in them, although in England he had a very serious time with influenza. He met and talked with a number of men prominent in both public and private finance in both countries, and came to hold them in high esteem; and he took pleasure in being able to quote or cite them, especially Sir Josiah Stamp, in his later teaching.

To his great satisfaction, the research fellowship was renewed for 1931–32, and he was able to continue his investigations in Ottawa during the second year. When he arrived in Canada, he had an attack of appendicitis that was nearly fatal. Nevertheless, as soon as he was able he continued his work, reading in the Baring Papers and other materials in the Canadian Archives. He presented some of his evidence and conclusions at the meeting of the American Historical Association in Toronto in December, 1932. His paper was published in the *American Historical Review* under the original title, "Some Aspects of American State Debts in the Forties." A few months later he presented additional findings in a paper read at the meeting of the Mississippi Valley Historical Association in Chicago in April, 1933.

When he returned to his teaching at the University, McGrane was awarded a grant by the trustees of the Charles Phelps Taft Memorial Fund that enabled him to complete the work on his manuscript. With continued interest, encouragement, and suggestions from his colleagues—among those he singled out for special mention were Frederick C. Hicks, William W. Hewett, and Wilbur P. Calhoun of the Economics Department, and George A. Hedger, John Oddy, and Charles R. Wilson of the History Department—he finished *Foreign Bondholders and American State Debts;* it was published by the Macmillan Company in 1935. At the same time he contributed an essay, "The Apologia of American Debtor States," to *Essays in Honor of William E. Dodd, by His Former Students at the University of Chicago* which treated a special aspect of his subject.

Within a few months after the appearance of those works on September 1, 1936, McGrane was appointed both Professor of American History and a Fellow in the Graduate School of the University. The unexpected expansion of the Graduate School that began in the early 1930's provided an opportunity for him to offer, starting in 1933–34, specialized courses in the Jeffersonian and Jacksonian periods and seminar training in American history. Now he had a greater opportunity to reach beginning graduate students with a primary interest in history, as well as advanced undergraduate history majors, and to work though in a very different way toward the aims he had endorsed so vigorously in the fall of 1921: better trained and more serious students, with an appreciation for sound learning and receptive minds. It was not through changes in the institution and its rules governing required courses and electives but through his own personally developed methods of instruction and the example he gave that he reached a broader group of young men and women and gave clearer focus to their academic efforts.

Throughout the decade, McGrane generally attended the annual meetings of both the American and the Mississippi Valley Historical Associations, and in the latter organization he served on various committees, including for a while the executive committee. In April, 1934, the Mississippi Valley Historical Association accepted an invitation from the University of Cincinnati and the Historical and Philosophical Society of Ohio to hold its next meeting at Cincinnati. At that meeting, which was held in the Sinton-St. Nicholas Hotel, McGrane presided at the opening session on April 25, 1935. When the American Historical Association met in Providence in December, 1936, he presented a highly provocative paper, "America's Entry into the World War: Twenty Years of Interpretation." He observed that when peace and war are at stake "we cannot afford the luxury of bad history," but that for twenty years we had had a great deal of it. Professors Samuel F. Bemis (who had shared a session with McGrane at the American Historical Association meeting in 1919) and William T. Langer, and Mr. Harley A. Notter (who had been assisting Ray S. Baker in his work on Woodrow Wilson) took part in a lively discussion that followed. The event was unusual enough to reach the pages of the New York *Times*.

McGrane at this time also wrote a number of articles for the *Dictionary of American History*, a five-volume work published in 1940 under the editorship of James T. Adams, and as usual he continued to review for professional journals.

His advancement in the University probably carried increases in salary (all university salaries had been drastically cut during the preceding years), and it was no doubt expected that he would devote a larger part of his time to research and writing. First he moved to a more commodious residence. Since 1922, he and Mrs. McGrane had been living in the Brookline Apartments, a brick building on Ludlow Avenue facing Burnet Woods and only a short walk through the park from the Engineering College. Early in 1937 he built a large and attractive new home at 860 Clifton Hills Terrace. There on the second floor he had an admirable study where he was able to work in pleasant surroundings. Here he and Mrs. McGrane were able to display their interesting collection of old silver, assembled in England and elsewhere, and to enjoy the antics of their dachshund. McGrane had a succession of dachshunds, becoming attached to each in turn. When he went abroad one summer, he hired a couple to live in the house and take care of the dog. Mrs. McGrane enjoyed the garden they now had for the first time, and took pleasure in her flowers, especially her Dutch tulips. He admired them for her sake. He never gardened himself; once, when a colleague shamed him into mowing the grass, it was almost more than he could endure doing. They moved into the new home in the fall of 1937. McGrane's mother lived with them there for the remaining weeks of her life.

Toward the end of the 1930's, McGrane was pleased with the opportunities to bring to the University several of his friends as speakers for the Taft Memorial Lectures and other occasions, among them William E. Dodd, at that time ambassador to Germany. Dodd always stayed with him when he brought him to Cincinnati, and was entertained there in 1937.

One further aspect of his work during the 1930's requires mention. His colleague John Oddy wrote of it later:

> I always had the feeling that he kept the student at arm's length, and I am certain he regarded with great disfavor my relations with the student group which I tended to entertain more than faculty associates. After all that was the way I had been brought up. But as you know to the student he gave the best of his intellectual self and demanded the same in return. The pride and joy of his teaching was his course in American history . . . offered as a required credit to Senior chemical, electrical and mechanical engineers—already young men of twenty-two or three years of age who had four years of schooling and experience behind them. It was a large group, and if I have ever seen a more attentive and respectful class, I don't know where or when. Those en-

gineers adored him because of the quality of what he gave and the natural enthusiasm with which it was given. He presented the material in this course with a spontaneity and devotion that students I am sure never forgot. I came to know this group rather well because in 1928–29 . . . and again in 1930–31 . . . I lectured to them and after forty years of teaching, I can say that a finer group I have never met. The course was a joy to give and these young men a joy to teach. Prof[essor] McGrane's lecture cards (he used to use about six [three by five] cards for each lecture, on which he would jot down the points he intended to develop) were always available to me if ever I felt the need of them (or could read them—his handwriting was exceedingly difficult to make out).

Another side of his relationship with his students is described by one of his junior colleagues who shared his office in 1939–40. A young man rushed into the office one day in great agitation, waving a paper and exclaiming "Mr. McGrane, Mr. McGrane! I don't care what you do to me! You can do anything you want to! But I want you to know! This paper you gave me a C minus on—three years ago you gave it a B plus!" McGrane looked up at him calmly and said, "Young man, that just shows you how my standards have gone up in three years."

McGrane suffered more than one heavy loss during the 1930s; only one need be mentioned here. In the financially desperate years of the Depression the University not only reduced all salaries but dismissed several members of the faculty in order to save money. John Oddy, who had worked with McGrane seven years, was one of the victims in 1933. He has written: "Over my strong opposition Mr. McGrane moved h. & h. to keep me there. . . . He failed in his efforts, but I was relieved under most generous terms for which I always consider he was responsible. Again it was his sense of loyalty."

When it was possible to make another appointment, the position was given to C. William Vogel who, like McGrane, was a native of Cincinnati and a graduate of the University of Cincinnati. Vogel taught there as an instructor in history from 1930 to 1932, and did further graduate work at Harvard, where he received his doctorate. He was an assistant professor at Miami University during the year 1935–36, and then returned to the University of Cincinnati to join McGrane in his work in the College of Engineering and Commerce. His major fields lay in modern European and recent British history. During the year Vogel was at Harvard finishing his work, McGrane brought in another of his former students, Henry R. Winkler, to carry on the work.

For his next undertaking McGrane turned to those men, and to George Hedger, Charles R. Wilson then of Colgate University, and four of his colleagues in the College of Engineering and Commerce, Professors Francis A. Bird, Bradley Jones, Hans P. Leipman, and Charles A. Joerger, from whom he drew assistance, criticism, and suggestions. This undertaking was the writing of a textbook for the course in American Economic History which he had been teaching almost annually since 1921; it is characteristic that he expressed his thanks also to the students of the College of Engineering and Commerce. "Both the organization and content of the book," he wrote, "have benefited as the result of their reactions."

Designed primarily for undergraduates, the textbook was unusual in several respects, most notably in its chronological organization structured around the successive panics. Like his other works, it is permeated by his philosophical outlook. His general statements are not random observations but matters of conviction. He wrote in the preface: "Each generation desires to solve its problems in its own way . . . . Each generation has a right to establish its own law; but in reaching a decision upon perplexing questions the experiences of former generations with almost identical problems should be of help."

In addition to the customary substance of economic history, he introduced in the text sketches of business and industrial leaders, with their economic and social philosophies, and the specific programs they urged or their solutions to critical problems. He matched them with similar accounts of reformers and their alternative philosophies and plans, particularly at the decisive stages in successive periods of economic expansion and depression. The problems that had to be dealt with by one generation after another were thus analyzed and defined and the student himself was confronted by the questions of the times. The narrative was not a mere chronological sequence but the story of a dynamic process carried forward by men in a constantly changing environment. Economic development was shown as taking place not in isolation but with a close relationship to society and government. He closed his preface significantly with a quotation from the historian David S. Muzzey:

> Our destiny is not the making of money but the making of America. Our heritage of political ideals is a far richer possession than our heritage of material resources; for if the ideals be lost or obscured, all the treasures of field, factory, and mine cannot avail to save us from the fate of Nineveh or Rome.

It was a theme to which he returned later.

For some years McGrane had been deeply concerned about the possibility of another major war and felt a personal anxiety for the consequences that American involvement in such a war could bring to his country and to the people closest to him. As the international scene had grown darker, his feelings became more acute, his sense of personal distress and of a personal obligation for the safety and survival of those he loved, the values and institutions he cherished, became more intense.

The United States was already at war when *The Economic Development of the American Nation* was published in 1942, and reference to the war is made in the closing lines. With many of his students already in service, McGrane was deeply affected and sought to give them what aid and encouragement he could. More than one remember the generous and helpful letters he wrote at this time and doubtless his personal counsel. During the gloomy months following Pearl Harbor, he wanted to be of greater service than he felt opportunities permitted, and for a time (according to a colleague) he was most difficult to get along with. He seemed to believe that the University itself would be closed. It was not. Instead, beginning early in 1943, a series of four new programs was created, and McGrane was placed in full charge of organizing history instruction for the army contingent that came into being under the Army Specialized Training Program. When this program ended in June, 1944, he went to Washington, D.C. and spent a year working for the War Production Board. His title was Analyst and his work was classified. From it came another book, *The Facilities and Construction Program of the War Production Board and Predecessor Agencies May 1940 to May 1945.*

Except for the period after 1930, when he was engaged in the work on his Guggenheim research fellowship, this was the only time McGrane was absent from the University during his entire teaching career. He never had a sabbatical leave; and he maintained that he did not believe in released time. He felt that he could do all the scholarly work one needed to do along with routine obligations. Of course, he did; but some of his friends felt that he did it to the neglect of most other human activities and associations.

During the war years, McGrane did not neglect his professional responsibilities. The publication of historical books was curtailed, and many of those who might have written them were otherwise engaged. McGrane served as a member of the John H. Dunning Prize Committee of the American Historical Association from 1942 to 1945 and was chairman of the committee from 1945 to 1947.

With the close of the war in 1945, he returned to the University and was immediately confronted by the large number of war veterans attending college under special legislation. Their numbers increased greatly in the following terms, and a drastic reorganization of courses and curriculum was imperative to cope with the problem. One major change was the formation in 1946 of a new College of Business Administration at the University, emerging from a former department of the College of Engineering and Commerce. McGrane devised new courses to meet the needs of the College, sought and found instructional staff, and handled not only his own previously established courses but the development, almost down to the last detail, of the content, structure, methods, and position of the new work as well.

The increase in numbers of students in colleges occurred throughout the country with a heavy demand for textbooks. McGrane's *Economic Development* was one of the popular books, and the publishers offered a second, revised edition in 1950.

Meanwhile Bond, who had become chairman of the department of history in the College of Liberal Arts in 1922, retired and became professor emeritus of the University in 1948. McGrane was thereupon appointed to the chairmanship of the department of history and, in addition to his former duties, undertook a consolidation of the department of history in the College of Engineering with that in the College of Liberal Arts. It was in some respects the crowning achievement of his life, and certainly a thing he had long wanted. He always seemed to feel some sense of inferiority about a position in a technical college, and was far more at home in what he regarded as the more respectable surroundings of an arts and sciences college. Ever since the University had opened a new library building in 1930, he had had a private office in it, in addition to the office he had in Baldwin Hall, the building in which the College of Engineering was housed. In his library office, he seemed to be more comfortable. Surrounded by his own books and research notes and papers rather than the paraphernalia of the teacher, McGrane generated the atmosphere of a master of his own realm; and he was readier to relax and joke in his distant way.

In 1948, he initiated a well thought-out reorganization of the departmental offerings to develop strength in three areas that he then considered most important for the students of the University: the United States, Great Britain, and Russia. The plan was based on his philosophy of preparing students for the public world they would soon be entering. He brought in Vogel from the College of Engineering in British history and in 1954 Jurgen H. Roetter from the University of Wisconsin in Russian history. The department already included Hilmar C. Krueger in the medieval field; Miriam Urban in modern Europe; and Joseph E. Holliday and George Engberg in American history. George F. Howe, also in American history, had been in Washington, D.C. from time to time, and left permanently in 1948; in that year McGrane brought Edward Anderson from Harvard and Garland G. Parker from Wisconsin to round out his American history staff.

He also encouraged the formation of a local chapter of Phi Alpha Theta, national history honor society, which he regarded as an excellent morale builder for history majors. It was installed on May 12, 1950, by Professor Lowell Ragatz and other members of the chapter at Ohio State University, assisted by George Engberg. Among the members of the Gamma Pi chapter at Cincinnati initiated on that occasion were McGrane himself and several others of the department faculty, students, and his friend Herbert F. Koch and other alumni. He went to Georgetown College in Kentucky May 27 to install a new chapter there. The Cincinnati chapter was active, holding regular meetings and a regional conference early in 1952, and established a scholarship key to be awarded to the history major in the Junior class who had the highest grades in the field.

About this time McGrane struck up quite a friendship with Arthur M. Schlesinger, who had previously visited the University, and invited him to Cincinnati twice to deliver the Taft Lectures. Schlesinger reciprocated, to his great pleasure, by inviting him to teach at Harvard in the summer of 1951, and a decade later to participate in ranking the American presidents, a poll conducted for the New York *Times* which published the evaluations July 29, 1962.

The dozen years following his new appointment were filled with additional responsibilities. Within the University, where McGrane had excellent working relations and warm personal ties with President Raymond Walters, he was chairman of the University Post-war (Planning) Committee (to which he had been appointed in 1946), and served as a member and chairman of the Library Committee, and as a member of several other committees. Beyond the University, he served until 1956 as member of the Anthony Wayne State Highway Commission (a quasi-historical board created by the Ohio Legislature in 1947). He was elected to the Executive Committee of the Mississippi Valley Historical Association (a three year term) at the Madison meeting in April, 1949; and in 1951 he was chairman of the local arrangements committee for the spring meeting of the Association held that year in Cincinnati. He was elected an honorary member of the Historical and Philosophical Society of Ohio, and from 1954 was a member of its editorial board. He was also elected in 1952 a member of the editorial board of *The Historian*, The Journal of Phi Alpha Theta.

After an absence of seven years from the pages of the *American Historical Review*, he reappeared as a book reviewer in 1950, and made other contributions in the following years; also in 1950 he started reviewing for the *Ohio Archaeological and Historical Quarterly*, *The Historian*, the *Historical and Philosophical Society of Ohio Bulletin*, and the *Mississippi Valley Historical Review*.

It was a highly productive time. With six articles in eight

years, from 1953 through 1961, he kept his hand busy in the smaller forms of historical writing; they appeared in the *Bulletin* of the Historical and Philosophical Society of Ohio, the *Virginia Magazine of History and Biography,* and *Museum Echoes,* the monthly publication of the Ohio Historical Society; and he wrote a biographical sketch for the Ohio Sesquicentennial Commission's volume, *The Governors of Ohio.* His contributions showed his enduring interest in economic questions, Jacksonian politics and Jacksonian America, and (long a private and personal matter) in American patriotism.

Soon after he had finished the revised edition of his textbook, McGrane was asked in 1952 by members of the Cincinnati Academy of Medicine to help them find a suitable person to study and write the hundred-year history of the Academy. The search proved to be a difficult one, as the qualifications demanded were highly specialized. Finally the Academy asked McGrane himself to do the work. He consented, and while engaged in the research he made many new friends and enjoyed the opportunities for association among men of the medical profession, for whom he came to have a great respect. In 1957 the Academy published his book, the *Cincinnati Doctors' Forum.* At a session of the Academy on February 5, with McGrane as the principal speaker, the members presented him with the first copy of the volume, and then by rising vote elected him an honorary member.

Historical work of quite a different character simultaneously was brought to him. A committee of the American Historical Association under the chairmanship of George F. Howe was engaged in the production of a massive and comprehensive historical bibliography. Eventually the committee, acting as a board of editors, produced *The American Historical Association's Guide to Historical Literature.* In this volume Walter C. Langsam, who had succeeded Walters as president of the University of Cincinnati in 1956, and McGrane were made the responsible editors for the section on recent history. McGrane did the work on this himself, not only in the United States but in England where he worked in the British Museum in the late 1950's.

McGrane's interest in his students, in the welfare of the history department, and in other educational work was in no way diminished by those labors. He persuaded his friend Herbert F. Koch to return to the University and take a master's degree in history; Koch was then given an appointment as instructor in the College of Business Administration. The two men also worked closely with Clyde W. Park and Dwight L. Smith in furthering the work of the Cincinnati Historical Society. McGrane strengthened his department by the addition of new faculty almost annually. He continued to teach in the evening session of the University (from which he held his initial appointment in 1923) until the year of his retirement.

One of McGrane's special innovations in the University was the organization of the Business Men's Club and Lecture Series. The Lecture-Discussion series, as it was called, was set up at least as early as 1926–27, and continued for many years. Once a month he brought men of national distinction to Cincinnati, and in the choice of lecturers he played an important part. He was indeed mentioned as "the staff of life" as far as this group was concerned.

McGrane long believed that it was improper to use the classroom to advocate partisan political views. He was very careful not to reveal his own political inclinations in class, and took great pleasure in leaving his students guessing. The teacher, he felt, had such an advantage over those entrusted to him for instruction that the use of that advantage for party interest would be unfair.

Mrs. McGrane maintained the active interest in government and politics that she had shown since graduating from the University. In addition to her membership in the Woman's Club and the Woman's Literary Club of Cincinnati, she was a member and twice president of the Cincinnati League of Women Voters. Her brochure, *The Ohio Primary*, was published soon after the passage of the primary election law in Ohio, and in 1948 she wrote for the League of Women Voters a much-valued pamphlet, *Know Hamilton County*. Eventually both Professor and Mrs. McGrane lost their early enthusiasm for the Charter Party, turned from it and became Republicans about the time of the 1932 presidential campaign. McGrane much later modified his rule of personal conduct on political matters when many of the members of the faculty became more blatantly partisan, and took the job of faculty adviser to the student Republican club.

After World War II, the McGranes began to take a new attitude toward vacations. Through John Oddy, whom they saw in Boston, and whenever an eastern meeting of the American Historical Association brought them together, they took a cottage at Roque Bluffs, near Calais, Maine, and enjoyed visits there for several summers. Eventually McGrane said that he wished he had known Maine sooner so that he could have bought a cottage there. His idea of such a place was, however, spartan. A wood stove and a reading lamp were furniture enough. In 1951, after teaching summer school, he and his wife traveled on the continent, and he gave more time than usual to observations of the current scene and less to research. Two years later, he spent the summer working at Oxford and in the British Museum on research in his favorite Jacksonian period, but managed to make a side trip to little-visited spots in Wales. Still later in the decade, another summer in England was once more given over almost wholly to research.

His tentative approach to vacations had its counterpart in a new attitude toward recreation. When Cincinnati had a professional hockey team, he and Mrs. McGrane went to the games quite regularly. Later, in Spain, he went to see a bullfight and apparently enjoyed it. He was quite proud of the way the engineering students took him to the opening football game. But after one experience at such a game, when he nearly caught pneumonia from sitting exposed in the stands, he decided to give it up and never attended again. His interest in such activities was at most peripheral. His life was one of study and teaching.

In 1959, McGrane taught summer school for the last time, and at the end of August retired from teaching. The occasion was marked by several social gatherings, among them an entertainment in his honor given by the Department of History. Reviewing the past and looking toward the future, he drew a new pattern for his life. He had enjoyed his European travels, above all in England, and wanted to continue them. He pictured a fuller home life. Plans for writing a long-contemplated biography of Martin Van Buren, a history of the University of Cincinnati, and other projects were a part of the pattern, but they were sidelines. First would come another of the favorite trips starting late in the summer. They would spend the fall in the Mediterranean. The trip started as planned. But in Spain Mrs. McGrane was taken ill. A hurried return to the United States brought the opportunity for additional medical aid, but it was not successful. McGrane did not recover from the loss.

Conscientiously he turned to the history of the University; it became his principal occupation for almost three years. President Walters had wanted a comprehensive history to be written, and his successor, President Langsam, pressed the matter, hoping to have it prepared in advance of the sesquicentennial (1969) of the oldest component of the institution. Two others had been approached with the proposal, but nothing had been accomplished until McGrane assumed the responsibility. Painstakingly typing the entire manuscript himself (Mrs. McGrane had typed all his previous manuscripts from the time of their marriage), he completed the work and *The University of Cincinnati: A Success Story in Urban Higher Education* was published in 1963.

He had already begun to withdraw from most of his former friends and associates, and he lived as a recluse in the home which he and Mrs. McGrane had shared for so many years. He was surrounded there by his books and notes. From time to time he tried to work on a manuscript. He told a visitor that the biography of Van Buren could not be finished without further research but he refused to travel to the libraries where he could do the work. The memories associated with the previous visits when his wife had accompanied him and helped him, he explained, would be too painful. The fiftieth anniversary of his graduation from the University he shared with a few surviving classmates who attended the reunion, and with two or three who called on him at home. He particularly enjoyed at that time a visit from President and Mrs. Theodore H. Jack. He was deeply pleased with the spontaneous recognition that was offered to him for his achievements in teaching and scholarship, with such formal acknowledgment as the republication of *The Panic of 1837*, and with the loyal admiration of students and colleagues. But later even the values of his past achievements, both of scholarship and of personal association, seemed to lose much of their former importance for him. Reginald McGrane died July 26, 1967, after a long illness. He will be remembered with affection and gratitude by those who were his students and associates.

"A Fair Field and No Favor": The Structure of Informal Empire

Thomas McCormick
UNIVERSITY OF PITTSBURGH

One year after the armistice with Spain, America sent forth into the world the then-famous, now-denigrated Open Door notes. In and of themselves, they established no new policy lines. Both Grover Cleveland's response to the Sino-Japanese War and William McKinley's stance during peace talks with Spain make it abundantly clear that the Open Door in China was already cardinal American policy long before the 1899 notes made their way into the great power chanceries.

What the promulgation of the Hay Doctrine did accomplish was to pass the sceptre of Open Door champion from Great Britain to the United States. For a half century, the British had successfully used an open door policy to create and sustain their economic (and diplomatic) supremacy in the Chinese Empire; the Americans, in the role of "hitch-hiking imperialists," simply tagged along passively, gathering the commercial leavings. Now, as Britain's power waivered—and with it her commitment to the Open Door —the United States made a concerted effort to adopt and adapt the nineteenth-century policy to the impending and expansive needs of a twentieth-century industrial America.

This dramatic departure and its timing have long been the

source of interpretative controversy. For example, George F. Kennan—in an oversimplified, lay version of A. Whitney Griswold's work—has viewed the Open Door notes as a rather haphazard product, sold by an English member of the Chinese Customs Service indirectly to a somewhat disinterested and quickly disillusioned secretary of state.[1] On the other hand, Charles S. Campbell, Jr. in his short but classic study, has stressed the midwife role played by special business interests in bringing the policy to life.[2] Yet each analysis, in its own way, has trivialized an event of enormous importance. One grossly overestimates the influence of a quite peripheral figure, whose ideas were wholly unoriginal (and well known to every journeyman diplomat) and whose efforts no way affected the timing of the Open Door notes. The other bases its provocative interpretation upon a far too narrow segment of the national community. Both inadequately appreciate that the Open Door policy accurately reflected the widely-shared assumptions and analyses of most social elements in America (including many without special vested interests); that both individual and group pressures were at best minor catalytic factors. Both, by focusing on the particular, miss the really substantive thing about the Open Door policy—that it represented America's basic response to the methodological question of how to expand: instead of closed doors, open markets; instead of political dominion, economic hegemony; instead of large-scale colonialism, informal empire. In short, a most interesting hybrid of anti-colonialism and economic imperialism.

On October 19, 1898, President McKinley told a Citizens' Banquet of Chicago that "territorial expansion is not alone and always necessary to national advancement" and the "broadening of trade." [3] Before another year had passed, his State Department was to be found feverishly at work trying to transform this unilateral sentiment into a universally-accepted tenet—at least so far as the Chinese Empire was concerned. Behind this belated effort to make the Open Door a multilateral vehicle were two seemingly contradictory factors: a sense of power and a sense of impotence.

Latter-day critics of the Open Door policy have managed to evade one central truth—that the policy was one of strength as well as weakness. A less confident nation might easily have joined in the partitioning scramble in China, content to have an assured but fragmentary slice of the market. But America wanted more, much more than that—and was certain of her ability to acquire it. When Brooks Adams wrote in 1899 that "East Asia is the prize for which all the energetic nations are grasping," few of his readers doubted who would win that prize.[4] When William McKinley told Congress in that same year that "the rule of the survival of the fittest must be . . . inexorable" in the "rivalry" for "mastery in commerce," most of his listeners were doubtless sure who would be the fittest.[5] In each instance, the certitude grew from one root—that sense of American economic supremacy born in the export revival of 1897, nourished by the retooling and refinancing of American industry, and confirmed by the return of full prosperity. Viewed from this vantage, the Open Door became appropriate means for the most advanced and competitive industrial nation(s) to grab the lion's share of the China market, instead of settling for a pittance. No one saw this more clearly or said it more forcefully than the influential *Bankers' Magazine* when it exclaimed that "without wars and without military aggression that nation will secure the widest and best markets which can offer the cheapest and best goods"; that

> if China was open to trade with all the world . . . the United States and England need not be afraid of any competitors. But Russia, Germany and France . . . are more or less at a disadvantage when they meet either English or American goods. They therefore do not take the philosophical view at all.[6]

The analysis was anything but an isolated one. In the private sector, for example, the Riverside, New York Republican Club assured Secretary of State John Hay that "the Chinese market . . . rightfully belongs to us and that in free and untrammelled competition we can win it." [7] The old warhorse, Joseph C. Wheeler, musing on his belief that "eight thousand miles of ocean could not stay the destinies of mankind," prophesied to President McKinley that the ultimate volume of American exports to China would reach $5.4 billion a year.[8] The International Commercial Congress, an *ad hoc* meeting of Eastern manufacturers and merchants, wrote Far Eastern expert, William W. Rockhill, that "no other market in the world offers such vast and varied opportunities for the further increase of American exports" [9] as does China. The National Association of Manufacturer's journal, *American Trade,* reported authoritatively that "millions after millions are being invested in Southern mill property, solely in the faith of a continuation of a trade . . . in the Chinese empire." [10] Later, *The Nation* nicely summarized such general sentiments by predicting that "An open door and no favor infallibly means . . . the greater share and gain in the commercial exploitation of China." [11]

Likewise, public officials expressed optimism about America's open door penetration of the China market. Cushman K. Davis, chairman of the Senate Foreign Relations Committee, proclaimed that our position in the Orient was now such "that we can commercially [do] what we please," and predicted that the China trade "would put 18 millions of people on the Pacific coast within not many years and give its cities a preponderance like that of Tyron. . . ." [12] Henry L. Wilson, secretary of agriculture and informal adviser on foreign affairs, reported his impression that "the people of the West regard the Pacific as an American lake which should be covered with ships carrying the American flag" and added, "I don't know but they are about right." [13] Administration trade expert, Worthington C. Ford, noted (with some mental reservations) that "the commercial future" of the China trade "is wonderful to think of"—a view based on an independent analysis that China could both double its population and living standards, "and this without any revolutionary change. . . ." [14] Finally, even the cautious John Hay, in a public letter that coincided with the dispatch of Open Door notes, exclaimed that "in the field of trade and commerce we shall be the keen competitors of the richest and greatest powers, and they need no warning to be assured that in that struggle, we shall bring the sweat to their brows." [15]

In view of subsequent developments, such glowing optimism about the future of the China trade appears naive, misguided, and grotesquely overdrawn. It was much flap about nothing. Nevertheless, the *potential* for trade expansion was real, and remained real (enough so to exercise vast impact upon American policy-makers for the four decades that preceded Pearl Harbor). Indeed, in 1899, there were signs, however small, that the penetration of the China market was already underway. For one thing, in the relative sense, manufactured products began to account for more than 90 per cent of American exports to China—a fact of some significance to those preoccupied with *industrial* overproduction. By 1906, 96 per cent of all United States exports to China were finished products, as compared to 27 per cent for Europe. Moreover, the absolute volume of manufactured exports experienced a sharp rise, albeit beginning from a small base. It multiplied four times between 1895 and 1899, from $3,200,000 to $13,100,000. Seven years later, despite a Chinese boycott and persistent obstacles from both Russia and Japan, the total had reached nearly $42,000,000. Particularly blessed were the iron and steel industry and cotton textile enterprises, both key elements in the American economy. The latter, for example, grew from less than $2,000,000 in 1895 to almost $10,000,000 in 1899, and reached $30,000,000 by the Panic of 1907, accounting for 56.5 per cent of all American cotton textile exports.[16] The figures lent an air of credence to one Southern group's assessment that the China trade is everything.[17] All these facts were, to be sure, small straws in the wind, and easily written off in retrospect. But in the expansionist psychology of the 1890's, they were eagerly seized upon to bolster the widespread expectation that given equal, open door access, the United States could and would win economic dominion in China.

If American commercial ascendancy made the Open Door policy a fruitful one, then American weaknesses also made it a nearly unavoidable one.

Political power was the prime deficiency. The Far East was no Latin America, where, after 1895, American hegemony was seldom challenged and usually acknowledged. In China, the United States faced all the handicaps of the latecomer to a game already in play, in which the full lineup of great powers was engaged. To be sure, the United States now had the capacity to play a significant role in Chinese affairs, and its words and acts now carried substantially more weight, thanks to the Spanish-American War. As the American ambassador to France reported to McKinley: "we did in three months what the great powers of Europe had sought in vain to do for over a hundred years . . ." and "the most experienced statesmen here envy our transcendent achievements and see clearly the future benefits."[18] Nevertheless, heightened power and all, the United States was in no position to issue any Olney corollaries for the Chinese Empire; to make American word fiat; to manipulate with relative impunity and success. Here more subtle methods would be demanded.

The instances are many and well-known of America's continuing inability to control events in the Western Pacific. Significantly, these failures came despite "the President's most serious consideration" of Chinese instability; despite Secretary Hay's "serious attention" to the famous petition of cotton textile spokesmen, exhorting that something be done to keep the door open in North China; despite his assurances to Paul Dana of the New York *Sun* that "we are keenly alive to the importance of safeguarding our great commercial interests in that Empire. . . ."[19] For all this accumulated anxiety, America's newly-won status in the Pacific could not prevent Germany's acquisition of Spain's old insular empire in Micronesia.[20] It could not prevent Japan from occupying Marcus Island, a cable point upon which the American Navy had tentative designs, or from establishing an extraterritorial settlement in Amoy, which was important for its geographic relationship to Manila.[21] It could do little to stop Russia's apparent drift toward trade discrimination in Manchuria.[22] It could do nothing, one way or another, about the rumored, impending war between Russia and Japan.[23] Finally, it could not block Italy's far-reaching demands for a sphere of influence in Sanmen Bay and Chekiang Province—demands that ominously had the support of Great Britain; demands that threatened to set off another whole round of partitioning in China; demands that led the New York *Times* to conclude that the disintegration of China (and the open door) was "inevitable," and the Chicago *Inter-Ocean* to guess that "the end may be at hand."[24] All the administration did was to watch, wait, and hope—a policy (better, a stance) that augured ill for the future.

Financial weakness, another marked American liability, was in part an extension of political weakness. Simply put, American commercial expansion could not encompass financial expansion. In the realm of investments (chiefly railroads and mines), no open door existed and no American syndicate seemed likely to compete on equitable grounds with its European peers. None of this was exactly new, of course. The move toward a "modified" open door, one that concerned only commerce, not investment, had begun in 1895 and, as already noted, accelerated sharply in 1898. But it did not reach its climactic peak until the Anglo-Russian agreement of April, 1899. In effect, Great Britain promised not to compete for railroad concessions north of the Great Wall, while Russia made a similar pledge for the Yangtze basin. All that remained between them for open competition was a buffer zone between the Russian and British spheres, and much of this was already covered by the earlier Anglo-German agreement.[25]

As for American investors, this tightly constricted area of activity left them with little more than hope of a junior partnership with the British. This would be by no means inconsequential, and in early 1899 there was some hope along these general lines.[26] On February 1, the American China Development Company and the British and Chinese Corporation agreed, on paper, to share in each other's future concessions.[27] One day later, the New York *Times* reported that yet another British syndicate had agreed to give American capital a one-quarter share of investment in the railroads and mines of Szechuan Province.[28] Yet, in point of fact, British support was seldom vigorous and American financiers fared poorly indeed in competition with their politically and financially subsidized opponents. Prime example was the glaring failure of the American China Development Company to secure the Hankow-Canton concession, despite initially high hopes. The syndicate's inability to meet the rigorous Chinese terms was probably the major reason for the contract loss, but the company in its frustration blamed it on inadequate governmental support. In the end, the concession "went thataway" while the Department of State and the American China Development Company engaged in futile backbiting as to why.[29] Overall, the episode was more souring than cathartic, and played no small role in the administration's later attitude toward American investment in China.

A *realistic* foreign policy is an exact blend of means and ends —one that knows what is vital to the national interest, whether that interest can be fulfilled within the framework of national power and ideology, and precisely how. By 1899, the makers of American foreign policy had long since defined marketplace expansion into China as vital to the survival of the political economy and the social fabric. But they had to adopt means that would make the best use of American commercial power, while minimizing American liabilities: a still inadequate power base and financial frailty.

In terms of viable choices, there were but three, and the McKinley administration considered them all. One obvious alternative was to accept the disintegration of China as inevitable, or even beneficial, and join in the partitioning.[30] In 1899, there were repeated rumors that the United States would take precisely that course. The New York *Times,* during the Sanmen Bay crisis, reported that the administration had already determined to have Pechili Province for an American sphere, while at the same time the actions of the American consul in Amoy seemed designed to convert that port and its environs into an American entrepôt.[31] But the rumors were untrue, and the American consul's efforts were repudiated, both for the same reason: the administration felt that partitioning was an ineffectual vehicle for American trade expansion.[32] For one thing, it would intensify anti-imperialist criticism, while adding bureaucratic and military burdens that McKinley wished to avoid, a view shared with his anti-imperial critics. For another, American sales and arteries of distribution were largely centered in spheres controlled by Russia and Germany and to relocate these in an American sphere would be expensive and time consuming; it would be far better to keep open existing channels if possible. And finally, to re-emphasize an earlier point, a small slice of the pie, which is all partitioning could offer, held little attraction for men who wanted and thought they could get the major share of the market.

The second possibility was to make common cause with other open door supporters, presumably England and Japan, and use force if necessary to keep trade entrees open.[33] In an informal way, this was the method that Theodore Roosevelt later tried, and it did have the merit of reflecting one vital truth: that in the last analysis, only force could make the open door work. But this technique also raised basic objections that ultimately made it an impractical choice for the administration. To begin with a truism, no military alliance, especially one with the English, was likely to enhance the political popularity of the McKinley administration. Moreover, such a formal commitment would deprive the United States of complete freedom of action—something that cut across the grain of not only nineteenth-century traditionalism but McKinley's own pragmatism, for President McKinley, far more than his Anglophile secretary of state, disliked tying American national interests too rigidly to the foreign policies of countries whose own shifting interests might not always coincide with ours. Certainly, he already had sufficient evidence (and more was to come) of British and Japanese ambivalence toward the Open Door policy: enough to make them seem somewhat uncertain allies. And finally, there was one more basic objection to this second alternative. Any policy predicated upon the *possible* use of force might eventually require its *actual* use, and the use of force in China, save against the Chinese themselves, was deemed out of the question. A Far Eastern war would be an unpopular war. Such a war might lead to the very consequence one wished to avoid—the fragmentation of China—a war that might spread and ignite the general world holocaust that all the great powers feared and rightly so at the turn of the century. No, this would not do. What the United States wanted was not force, but coexistence and economic competition for open markets, an "eat-your-cake-and-have-it-too" policy of both peace and market domination. That America could have both was, again, the certain fallacy of informal, marketplace expansionism and the insoluble dilemma that American policy-makers vainly struggled with for the first half of the twentieth century.

Whatever, the administration chose to reject the second alternative as well as the first. There was, to be sure, some informal, tripartite consultation and cooperation, and some public figures (generally outside the government) did refer to an "Open Door Entente" of Great Britain, Japan, and the United States. But such collusion never aimed at the use of force, and moreover, it was generally an on-and-off-again sort of thing: a tactical stratagem employed when it was advantageous to American interests and ignored when it was not, which was frequently.

The third alternative—the one embodied in the Open Door notes—was to gain common agreement among an inclusive concert of powers that China would be exempted from imperial competition, just as some talk today of insulating Africa from the Cold War. This course of action obviously begged the whole question of force, and has been rightly criticized on that ground. But on the other hand, this line was hardly the legalistic-moralistic anachronism that some have made it seem to be. On the contrary, as we shall see, it tried to make use of two very real and interrelated factors: 1) the *de facto* balance of power that existed between the Russo-French entente and the emerging Anglo-Japanese bloc; 2) the intense fear of possible world war that preoccupied the foreign offices of Europe. In such a framework of balance and fear, two things were likely to be true and they were. One, the policies of each power were likely to be flexible and even a bit tentative, for rigidity could be disastrous. Certainly British action had a chameleon quality to it, and students of Russian policy in the Far East at this century's turn find it so baffling and contradictory that there is doubt that one existed. Similarly, any changes in the *status quo* were likely to be cautious ones, undertaken on a *quid pro quo* basis, lest imbalance lead to conflict. Under these circumstances, if some third force dramatically insisted that the *status quo* (the open door and Chinese sovereignty) be universally accepted, and if that added variable had the credible capacity to upset the delicate equilibrium of power, as the United States certainly had in Europe's eyes after 1898, then a good chance existed that the powers would acquiesce in such a proposal. The acquiescence might indeed be more rhetorical than real, but it would and did offer useful leverage in exploiting Europe's fears and in occasionally manipulating the apothecary's scale of power.

Such were the realities that produced the Open Door notes. Neither partitioning nor military alliance offered practical means to realize the desired American ends; only the neutralization of China by consensus held any glimmer of hope. That such hope was illusory—that indeed it *had* to be illusory—is worth analyzing later at length. But for the moment, it ought to be emphasized that given America's commitment to economic penetration in China, given the peculiar combination of American strengths and weaknesses, the Open Door policy was the most *realistic* one at hand.

In actual fact, the choice of a policy was less perplexing to the United States than the timing of its implementation. Hay, above all others, was concerned lest any effort at securing an open door consensus fail of prematurity. Part of his restraint reflected his nearly-paranoid view that "the senseless prejudices in certain sections of the 'Senate and people' compel us to move with great caution in the China matter." [34] Actually, Hay's fears were badly misplaced, as they were frequently. Indeed, public opinion could hardly have been more favorably disposed to a vigorous Open Door policy than it was in 1899.

Chief honors for crystallizing this favorable opinion belong to two Englishmen, Archibald R. Colquhoun and Lord Charles Beresford. Colquhoun's influence, of course, went beyond the general public, for he was a frequent correspondent of Hay's and in his letters he constantly kept before the Secretary of State the ominous and "growing influence of Russia in China"; the need to decide "which of the two policies" to "press for," the "open door" or the "sphere" (implicitly suggesting the former); and the hope "that action will be taken while there is time." [35] But Colquhoun also influenced wider circles of American opinion through his oft-quoted (and presumably oft-read) book, *China in Transformation,* published both in America and England in 1899. Within its pages, he stressed the Anglo-American community of interests in Asia, the increasing American need for foreign markets to absorb its industrial surplus, the primacy of the Russian threat, and the need to act quickly and vigorously in defense of the open door while the spheres were relatively small and confined to the coastal provinces.[36] Most Americans who read it, praised it and probably concluded that his thesis made sense.

Far more dramatic was the influence of Lord Beresford, regarded by most Americans as the leading foreign authority on the Chinese question. Like Colquhoun, Beresford had substantial influence upon Hay and probably upon McKinley and Rockhill as well. Also like Colquhoun, he reached an American reading audience through his article in *The North American Review*, "China and the Powers," and his renowned book, *The Break-Up of China*, in which he also espoused the Open Door policy, warned against the Russian threat to American trade, and urged that "a decision must be arrived at and action of some sort taken very soon." [37] But Beresford's impact upon the American public, and especially the business community, took on an added dimension with his trip through the United States in early 1899, following on the heels of his semiofficial survey in China itself. His cross-country trek was a triumphant tour de force: a warm visit with his old friend Hay; private talks with the President that left McKinley clearly impressed; conferences with Rockhill and key Congressional leaders; private chats with leading American businessmen; and widely-heralded speeches on the banquet circuit.[38] His talk before the Chicago Commercial Club led even the anti-British *Inter-Ocean* to exclaim that "his address . . . was a mine of information to businessmen who ought to look at the new possibilities in the East" and to admit that "the Beresford idea [the open door] has its advantages" over "the 'sphere of influence' policy." [39] Similarly, his speech to the members and guests of the American Asiatic Association in New York excited warm response from his elite audience, prompting ironmaster Abram S. Hewett, program cospeaker, to assure Beresford that "it is our desire to give the fullest possible expression . . . supporting the policy of the Open Door" and the "preservation of the integrity of the Chinese Empire." [40] Little wonder that Beresford departed firmly convinced of influential support for the open door, but still apprehensive about the administration's hesitancy to move immediately to support it.[41]

The magic of the Colquhoun-Beresford interpolation was not in creating any new public opinion base for a vigorous Open Door policy, for such a base already existed. What it did do was to promote added conviction and provide articulation for that opinion, by sanctifying it with the mantle of British expertise—something a great many key Americans traditionally if reluctantly held in awe. In any case and for whatever reasons, 1899 produced a bumper crop of written and spoken words in behalf of some dramatic effort to gain universal support for the open door in China.

Certainly, the chief opinion-shaping magazines both sensed and re-inforced the public demands for trade protection in China. *The Nation,* for example, reported that "powerful influences are now at work to bring about a change" in the administration's China policy, and added its own advice that something, even "a tacit . . . alliance with England," be done to keep "the Orient open to trade of all nations on equal terms." [42] The *Atlantic Monthly* similarly discovered "signs of a healthy and growing interest" in the China question, and urged "the utmost vigilance in behalf of our commercial privileges on the continent of Asia." [43] In like vein, *Harper's Weekly* and *The North American Review* approvingly printed articles by such influential men as John R. Proctor and John Barrett advocating an enlarged Monroe Doctrine to guarantee "the integrity of China" and an "open door" to forestall "our great and growing markets" from being "entirely lost to us." [44] Without belaboring the point, suffice it to add that the editors of business journals such as *Bankers' Magazine* and the *Journal of Commerce and Commercial Bulletin* reflected similar positions, as did the proceedings, writings, and petitions of the National Association of Manufacturers, the Philadelphia Commercial Museum, and the American Asiatic Association.[45] (Rather typical was the Southern Cotton Spinners' Association appeal to President McKinley for the "preservation of the integrity of the Chinese Empire, and the maintenance of an open-door policy in China with the commerce of all nations.") [46] Amazingly, even the learned *Annals of the American Academy of Political and Social Science* got into the act by devoting an entire supplementary issue to American foreign economic policy, chiefly in its relationship to Asia. Conceived as a debate to dramatize policy differences, the work was more revealing for the common ground it disclosed. Most stunning examples were the articles by Assistant Secretary of State John Bassett Moore and by arch anti-imperialist Carl Schurz: the first, an articulate defense of recent American policy, the other, a blistering attack upon it. Yet Moore could insist that the prime "object" of that policy was "to maintain an open door to the world's commerce," while Schurz could agree that the "golden key of industrial progress" lay in "open[ing] to our trade many doors." [47] Small wonder then, that one year later William Jennings Bryan found imperialism to be a dead issue. The Open Door notes had already killed it by offering an expansionist method that even "large policy" proponents and anti-imperialists could jointly support.

Capping this domestic surge of "keep-the-door-open" sentiment were the remarks of Jacob Gould Schurman, reported with such precision, though evaluated with some exaggeration, by Professor Griswold. Arriving in San Francisco on his return from service on the first Philippine Commission, the renowned educator and articulate anti-imperialist held a dramatic news conference in which he talked little about the Philippines and much about China. The essence of his words was that "the future of China was the one overshadowing question" in the Far East (and that all others, including Philippine affairs, were only important in their relationship to the Chinese problem); that China "should maintain its independent position, but the *doors* should be kept *open*"; that Russia was the chief enemy of American ambitions; and that the United States "should stand with [England and Japan] in preventing the dismemberment of China," a nearly perfect paraphrase of the Beresford position.[48] Overall, the interview received fair publicity and its impact was important. It was hardly in a league with Senator Redfield Proctor's speech on the Cuban Revolution in 1898, but it was nice and welcome frosting on the cake. It was enough to help ease temporarily John Hay's hypertension about the nature of American public opinion.

Hay's fear of precipitous action, his general caution and restraint, also grew out of his hope that a "watchful waiting" posture would eventually offer a more favorable international climate, and hence a more propitious time in which to act assertively, a time that would measurably increase the possibility of favorable, great power response to the American position. Thus, throughout the sporadic crises in China in early 1899 the Department of State remained relatively silent, apparently hoping for sunnier days. Whether this reflected wishful thinking or a realistic assessment of the balance of power can only be guessed at. Whatever the motivation, the wish fortunately proved father to the deed, for by August, 1899, even Hay could feel, with relative assurance, that the Far Eastern situation was unlikely to offer another so appropriate time in which to act.

The change to a more favorable international climate evolved slowly and climaxed suddenly. Initial good omens were evident even amidst earlier discord. The Sanmen Bay crisis passed as quickly as it came, rendering the obituary of the New York *Times* on the open door a bit premature. China simply refused the Italian demands; no third power came to the Mediterranean country's support; so Italy backed down, leaving fears of a new round of partitioning to another day.[49] The tension eased, and American relations in the Pacific began to undergo a marked change for the better with three key powers. Great Britain, for one, despite her acceptance of the "modified" open door concept, made it quite clear that she was willing to have one more go at preserving the commercial open door, provided the United States used its newly-won status to take the lead. Some Americans even saw the British tie-in with American railroad interests as a conscious scheme to keep the United States "on the spot" where "her presence in China might be relied upon to help in keeping the open door to trade for all comers on equal terms."[50]

At the same time, Japanese-American friction over the Amoy international settlement proved to be nonexistent, save in the overwrought imagination of the American consul, who received a reprimand from the Department of State as his reward.[51] On the contrary, relations between the two countries began to take on an amity of tone and an identity of interests that was to prove most useful during both the Open Door negotiations and the Boxer Rebellion. Finally, the hostility that had marked German-American relations in the Pacific in late 1898 rapidly gave way to a very real detente, highlighted by conciliatory talks on the Samoan problem, the establishment of the Chinese Customs Service in Shantung, and the publication of a German White Paper accepting the equal access principle in China.[52] Thus, by mid-1899, the Department of State believed that England, Japan, and probably Germany could be counted as safely in the open door camp. This fact would, in time, prove most useful in the tricky negotiations that followed the

Open Door notes. But the immediate utility of Anglo-Japanese-German support was rather limited, since the McKinley administration had no intention of using balance of power tactics to coerce the Russo-French entente into line. Instead, maneuver, manipulation, and persuasion were the order of the day, and the ultimate aim was the entente's (especially Russia's) voluntary and peaceful acceptance of the open door principle, even if in words only, for even words can be a useful tool in a diplomat's hands. What Hay still awaited was some small sign that Russia could be maneuvered into such a public commitment. But instead of a mere sign, Russia handed Hay almost the whole loaf and on a silver platter at that.

This quite unexpected but thoroughly welcomed gift came in mid-August in the form of a Czarist Ukase governing leased territory in China, an imperial decree glowingly characterized by the American Ambassador in St. Petersburg as "the open door in China" at least "in so far as Russia is concerned." To be sure, it was not the open door, in so far as America was concerned, for it said nothing about the vital question of railroad rates. Nevertheless, it seemed to make clear that "Russia has no intention to interfere with in any manner, or to control, Chinese customs duties"; that "no restriction is provided" on "foreign commerce and trade" in the Russian sphere. The *raison d'etre* of the Russian declaration remains still obscured; probably it reflected the temporary ascendancy of Count Sergei Witte's Far Eastern policy of peaceful, covert penetration, marked by steady but unadvertised ambitions. Whatever the reasons, the Russian move seemed to Charlemagne Tower, the American ambassador, a guarantee of the "future development of American trade and the certain increase of American mercantile prosperity."[53] To more doubting Thomases, like the editors of the New Orleans *Picayune,* the "concession [was] undoubtedly made to distract attention from the steady inroads Russia is making upon Chinese territory."[54] Or as the New York *Times* put it: "It is a sop to Cerberus, the watchdog whose three heads may be called England, Japan and the United States."[55] But to Hay, the nature of Russia's long-range intentions (assuming there were some) was immaterial; the real significance was quite immediate. The Russians, either wisely or unwittingly, had offered the United States a psychological entering wedge. They had opened the door just a crack, and no good salesman, particularly one so long-suffering as Hay, was going to miss a chance to get his foot in.

Buoyed by this happy turn of events, the Secretary of State discarded his normal restraint to act quickly and decisively, instructing his chief Far Eastern adviser, W. W. Rockhill, to prepare a memorandum on the administration's China policy.[56] Rockhill, along with his friend, Alfred E. Hippisley, a long-time English official in the Chinese Customs Service, had, in fact, badgered Hay for weeks for some dynamic move to insure international commitment to the open door, stressing the Russian threat to American textiles as the most compelling reason. But neither their analysis nor recommendations were new (much indeed reads like passages out of Beresford's book).[57] Hay had been exposed to them before from countless, influential sources; and he had long ago adopted them as his own. What had held the Secretary back was not the question of policy itself, but the question of timing. And even here the two "old China hands" exerted no influence; indeed, Rockhill, in despair, had already given up on the private pressure technique and had decided upon published articles as the only avenue of influencing policy.[58] One is almost forced to conclude that the Russian Ukase largely produced the Open Door notes, and that the chief importance of Rockhill and Hippisley lay in putting out a correspondence so fascinating, so voluminous, and so articulate that historians have been loathe to concede its monumental irrelevancy.

Hay's specific instruction to his assistant called for drafted notes to the great powers, aimed at a relatively "formal engagement" that "the recent extension of spheres of influence, etc., will not result in restricting our commercial freedom in China." [59] An elated Rockhill, certain that the Chinese "question seems now in very good shape," did his superior's bidding with alacrity.[60] Building upon Beresford's *The Break-up of China* for the "great weight" it carried with "the American public," he rested "the policy of the 'open door'" upon the single premise that "the mercantile classes of the United States" regarded it as "essential to the healthy extension of trade in China." Noting that "zones of interest" implicitly threatened this policy, he called upon the great powers to give formal guarantees of equal commercial access to both treaty and nontreaty ports, and assurance of uniform harbor dues and railroad rates in their spheres.[61]

One week later, on September 6, the Rockhill memorandum became the basis for the formal Open Door notes to England, Germany, and Russia. Copies later were sent to Japan, France, and Italy. A precise content analysis of the notes sends the reader away with three main impressions, some of them a bit at odds with current historical interpretation.

First, these first Open Door notes, while accepting the sphere of interest as "accomplished fact," did not ignore the relationship between Chinese integrity and the open door. On the contrary, the preamble to the British note stressed that the open door would help in "maintaining the integrity of China in which the whole western world is alike concerned."[62] All the notes prefaced the phrase "spheres of influence" with the modifying adjective, "so-called," a fact repeatedly brought to the attention of Russian negotiators.[63] And Rockhill's definitive article on "The United States and the Future of China" of May, 1900, undoubtedly cleared with Hay, insisted that the Open Door notes in no way questioned China's "outright sovereignty" in the "sphere of interest."[64] So it seems clear that the Department of State saw quite early that the open door was neither a legal nor practical possibility unless Chinese independence could be sustained.

Second, and not without contradiction, the Open Door notes treated China as a passive object by imposing a policy in which that country had no say, either in formulation or negotiation. In fact, the United States neglected even to inform China of its actions until international rumors provoked an official inquiry from the Chinese government. Even then, the essence of the Department of State's response was a rather pointed request "that no arrangements will be entered into by the Government of the Emperor which shall be to the disadvantage of American commerce."[65] Clearly, while the United States wanted an independent China, it did not wish one *too* independent, at least not independent enough to close the door on its own. It was a dilemma that post-1911 Chinese nationalism would do much to heighten.

Third, the notes only encompassed an open door of the "modified" variety: one with a strictly commercial orientation; one that ignored loans, railroad, and mining concessions, all on the simple grounds (stated in the Rockhill memorandum) that an open door in "privileges and concessions" was not feasible.[66] What they did attempt was to neutralize trade advantages inherent in railroad concessions by insisting that railroad rates on all lines, even those operated by foreigners within their spheres, be absolutely nondiscriminatory. Thus transportation cost would remain uniform while the market competitiveness of American goods would stand intact.

The Open Door negotiations themselves have yet to receive their proper attention either in terms of detailed narration or balanced evaluation. Sometimes dismissed as a colossal game of blind man's buff, they were, in fact, imaginatively conceived and generally well-executed under circumstances that would have taxed the patience, purposefulness, and expertise of the most experienced foreign office.

The original plan of the negotiations grew out of Rockhill's memorandum. Basically, it called for simultaneous negotiations with England, Germany, and Russia. It aimed for similar though not necessarily identical acceptances in principle of the American position. The prospect for approval from each seemed bright: from England because the open door was both traditional and profitable; from Germany because her interests were primarily financial rather than commercial, and thus would not be impaired by the American proposals; from Russia because the August 23 Ukase showed her to be either too conciliatory or too subtle to permit a public rejection of the equal access principle. Interestingly, Rockhill like Hippisley saw France's inflexible colonial policy as the major stumbling block to success and, on his advice, Hay postponed dispatch of the note to France, apparently hoping that an early Russian acceptance would bring her recalcitrant partner into line.[67]

Rockhill's stratagem proved altogether unrealistic. Instead of the anticipated, early success, it produced only an icy, diplomatic calm. England hesitated out of concern for her recent Hong Kong extension lease. Her consequent insistence that "leased lands" as opposed to general "spheres of interest" be exempted from the open door would have rendered that doctrine meaningless, since "the holdings of nearly all the great powers are in the form of leases," or so concluded Joseph Choate, American ambassador in London.[68] At the same time, Germany, given her diplomatic isolation in Asia, declined to go out on a limb, preferring to straddle the fence while testing the international winds. Clearly, she would make no move unless it was a safe one. Finally, Russia, despite Rockhill's optimistic predictions, proved utterly reluctant to bind herself to anything so vague, universal, timeless, and implicitly dangerous as the American Open Door policy. She had had her say in the Imperial Ukase and proclaimed to see no need for further declarations on the matter.[69] Moreover, like Germany, she was much interested in seeing how the other powers would respond before making any final policy decisions of her own.

It stands as a credit to Hay's pragmatism and independence that he substantially changed tactics, and with great success, when Rockhill's original conception proved abortive. His basic shift was to scuttle the idea of simultaneous negotiations in favor of a "falling dominos" technique: concentrate on each power one at a time; move down the line from the nation most likely to accept the American proposals to the one least likely to comply; use the accumulating acceptances as leverage to pry assent from the more regressive. Within this framework, he arranged his dominos somewhat differently than Rockhill might have done.

First, he advanced Japan, which had been passed over in the September 6 notes, to second position. He did so because the British suggested it; because it fit his own sense of identity with Japan; and because early Japanese acceptance, which he assumed would be forthcoming, would add another useful length to his diplomatic crowbar.[70]

Second, Hay brought France (Rockhill's imaginary nemesis) into the negotiations and placed her ahead of Russia in his mental spectrum, reflecting his own belief that France would prove more amenable than her Eastern ally. His own predilections partly account for this move, for he had long defined Russia as the chief obstacle to the open door, and the notes in his own mind had been directed primarily against that nation. But immediate developments also re-enforced his preconceptions, for while Russia coldly rebuffed American overtures, France in informal talks revealed a most friendly disposition. Indeed, in early November, American Ambassador Horace Porter in Paris reported that French Foreign Minister Théophile Delcassé, fearful that further partitioning might lead to war, saw the American suggestions as a possible basis for stabilization. Porter also added that he found a growing French respect for American power and an increased inclination to lend weight to American policies.[71]

By early November, Secretary of State Hay had evolved a rough scheme to concentrate first on England and Japan, and then pressure Germany, France, and Russia, individually, in succession. Italy made her way into the hopper as little more than an afterthought. The Japanese proved no obstacle whatsoever. The initial note to Japan leaves the strong feeling that informal talks had already been held on the subject, and that Japan had already given assurances in regard to commercial equality.[72] The subsequent lack of real negotiations on the matter bolsters this impression.

Anglo-American talks, however, still had to get around the sticky problem of the Hong Kong extension and British insistence on its "exempt" status. Ultimately, Rockhill forged the basic compromise formula by suggesting that a distinction be made between leases that carried economic privileges for the lessee, and those leased military stations that brought with them no special rights as regarding trading with China.[73] By excluding the latter from the Open Door proposals, the British by stretching a point might legitimately exempt the Hong Kong extension. Hay accepted the compromise in principle, but modified it by denying the British the right to make public and specific mention of their exemption lest such favored treatment open the door to endless exemptions by other powers.[74] His qualification proved no great obstacle, however, for it still permitted exemption by omission. Realizing this, the British, in their informal reply of December 1, accepted the open door for Weihaiwei and all future acquisitions, "lease or otherwise," while making no mention of the Hong Kong extension.[75] Ten days later, at Hay's urging, the British sent a more formal reply, one the American Secretary thought would "be of great assistance to us in our negotiations with other powers." [76]

The next other power was Germany, a nation sandwiched between the Anglo-Japanese bloc and the Russo-French entente, but nevertheless in a fulcrum position to make or break the American efforts. As Hay viewed it, Germany would remain quite noncommittal until the United States could achieve a clear preponderance of power in behalf of its China policy, then she would feel safe to give her own assent. Since the Secretary felt the Anglo-Japanese responses had already tipped the balance toward the United States, he decided to step up diplomatic pressure on the fence-straddler in early December. The startlingly quick result was an informal German declaration that "the politics of Germany in China are *de facto* those of the open door, and that Germany proposes to maintain the principle in the future." Nevertheless, she still hesitated to take an unequivocal, public stand, lest she "excite controversy" by appearing "to be drawn into a position where she must take sides" between "England on one" hand and "France and Russia on the other." [77] But under further American pressure, Germany did agree to accept the American note if all other powers did so, and gave permission "to have this information communicated to the other Powers." [78] Actually, the qualifying provision was not unlike that appended to the British acceptance, and its apparent evasiveness no more than a normal diplomatic safeguard, especially since everyone, including Hay, realized that the door could not be kept open short of overt force without consensus agreement. Either everyone played by the rules or everyone, in self-defense, did not. In any case, the German promissory note constituted a crucial turning point in the Open Door negotiations, for it put the entente (especially Russia) in a position where it either had to accept the American position, at least in principle, or else advertise its ulterior ambitions somewhat prematurely to its potential adversaries.

Negotiations with France were both frank and amicable as Hay had come to expect. French Foreign Minister Delcassé, without benefit of any American prodding, gave immediate assent to points one and two dealing with tariff rates in treaty and non-treaty ports. But he regarded the third point on equal railroad rates with some suspicion, fearful that its vagueness "as to industrial privileges" and to what constituted a "sphere" inferred an entering wedge to transform the modified, commercial open door into a financial one as well, one that might permit "people of all nations to secure vested rights, build railways, and possess and work mines, water powers, etc., in such spheres." [79]

For a short while, Delcassé considered offering a substitute open door proposal as the best means of clarification and delineation, but Germany's quasi-acceptance of the American proposals undercut that alternative.[80] Consequently, the French cabinet agreed to accept the open door "substantially in form presented" by the United States, but with reservations as to point three.[81] Specifically, France limited her pledge of "equal treatment" for "tariffs on railroads" solely to her "leased territory," which was relatively small, while making no mention of equal railroad rates in her "spheres of interest," which were relatively large.[82] Further American efforts to include coverage for "spheres" were unproductive, as Delcassé continued to insist that point three, in its full form, might be misconstrued to mean "an industrial parity" that would threaten projected French mines, wells, and railroads in the Chinese interior. Happily, though, he did offer an indirect, verbal assurance by pointing out that if France adhered to equal railroad rates in her leased territory, she could hardly do otherwise "in territory [she] did not possess or control." This informal commitment was enough to persuade Ambassador Porter that France was "naturally, on the side of preserving the open door," even in the area of "transportation facilities." [83] Hay also turned out to be a true believer and chose to regard the French reply as sufficiently satisfactory, a course made easier by the remoteness of French interests in south China from American ones further north, and by the hope that French affirmation would give him the decisive weapon to bring the reluctant Russians into line.

The postponement of talks with Russia did put the United States in a better negotiating position, but it did not put Russian decision-makers in a better frame of mind. Indeed, by early December, Russian diffidence had given way to overt hostility as Count Witte managed to convince his governmental colleagues that the Open Door notes were essentially an anti-Russian vehicle. The argument was a simple one. The key section of the American notes was that concerned with nondiscriminatory rates. Russia was the only power in China already in the process of railroad construction, and one, moreover, that possessed the treaty right (in the Li-Lobanov pact) to use differential railroad rates as a means of making an initial profit off its lines; therefore, the American proposals had Russia as its obvious target. This viewpoint, coupled with Hay's very real Russophobia, transformed the Russo-American bargaining chamber into an arena of mistrust and suspicion.[84]

From the very beginning, the railroad rate section lay squarely across the path of diplomatic accord. Neither Rockhill in Washington nor Tower in St. Petersburg obtained anything but firm refusals on that key point.[85] By December 11, it seemed clear to the latter that Russia did not "intend to make the complete declaration that we hope for." [86] In fact, two weeks later he quoted one Russian official as saying: "Well, we have built the railroads, and I think it quite probable that we shall give some preference to our own people." To make matters worse, he unearthed a plan to apply Russian tariffs at Dalmy on goods which Russian officials designated as bound ultimately for Russia proper (by implication, making Manchuria a Russian protectorate).[87]

In this unhappy state, Hay felt obliged to play upon Russian isolation by mustering as much bluff and bluster as possible. On December 19, he had Rockhill threaten Russian Ambassador Count A. P. Cassini with a presidential message to Congress, which would declare "that his proposals had been accepted by all the Great Powers" except Russia, an event that "would be extremely prejudicial to the friendly relations between the two nations." [88] The probe was not without salutary results, since it apparently persuaded Russia to resume serious negotiations, this time in St. Petersburg, where Hay hoped that Foreign Minister M. N. Mouraviev would prove more tractable than Cassini.[89]

When no miracles ensued, Hay simply kept pounding away, seeking to convince Russia that America regarded the matter of such vital importance that she would not relent until Russia, like the other nations, took some definite stand. So at Hay's urging to "try energetically" again, Tower, in a December 28 interview with Mouraviev, repeated the American position with as much bluntness as diplomatic niceties permitted.[90] One: "American trade, which concerns the welfare of the whole American people, must depend much upon the breadth or narrowness of the policy to be adopted now by the great European Powers." Two: "A refusal upon the part of Russia to adhere to these propositions would produce the most painful and unfortunate impression in the United States."[91]

Apparently patience had its rewards. American belligerency probably had little effect on Russian foreign policy, but American persistence probably did. Russian Far Eastern policy, under Witte's influence, had vast, ambitious designs, but all were predicated upon the use of subtle, gradual techniques. Either ignoring repeated American inquiries or rejecting them outright would most certainly arouse foreign suspicion and antagonism toward Russia, and, given her obvious military-economic shortcomings and her lessened influence in Peking, such a development could be disastrous to her long-term goals.

For whatever reasons, Russia bent a bit. To Tower's great surprise, Mouraviev expressed general sympathy with the Open Door principle, and insisted that Russia objected only to the vagueness of American proposals and hesitated only out of a desire not "to bind herself to something which she does not perfectly understand." Promising "renewed consideration," he closed with the teasing comment that "whatever France does, Russia will do."[92]

The fruits of Russian reconsideration came five days later. Like the French, the Russian reply accepted the first two articles on tariff duties; unlike the French, it said nothing about railroad rates in either leased lands or sphere zones.[93] It neither accepted nor rejected point three, but its silence was ominous—enough to provoke Rockhill's oft-quoted remark that "it has what we call in America a string attached to it."[94] But prudence reigned supreme in the Department of State, and rightly so. No one knew better than Hay and Rockhill that "none of the European Powers were prepared to . . . get arrayed in hostile camps against each other on this subject." Any negative interpretation of the Russian response would only prompt a mass retreat from their conditional commitments. So Hay chose to regard the Russian answer in a favorable light, stressing its pledges and ignoring its omissions.[95]

He also determined to make the most of the Russian declaration by interpreting it as broadly and as favorably as he could without inciting outright contradiction from St. Petersburg. Seizing on Mouraviev's casual remark on Russian emulation of French policy, Hay proposed to publish the Russian and French replies in joint form. Thus, in "agreement by association," Russia would appear to have accepted at least a modified version of section three. But this ingenious gambit fell before Russia's unexplained reversal: that she "would not be bound by the reply of France, that the Russian Government has acted entirely for itself and not in concert with France." Foiled here, the Department of State nevertheless managed to secure one smaller but still valuable concession from Mouraviev (and one often ignored in later accounts): namely, explicit permission to proclaim "the Russian reply as a favorable one." [96] Using this for all it was worth, Hay, on March 20, 1900, sent a published circular note to the powers concerned that all their replies had been favorable and would be considered "final and definitive." [97] The descriptive terms were useful ones. They claimed no total and exact acceptance of the American proposals; they simply suggested that each power had had its final say on the matter, and that the United States and each power involved regarded each respective response as "favorable." If the American circular seemed to imply more, so much the better. But on its own explicit terms, it engaged in no amateurish bluff; it invited no contradiction from any power, least of all from Russia.

The domestic adulation heaped upon Hay's Open Door notes in early 1900 is well known.[98] So is the latter-day scorn of most historical scholars. But both idolators and critics have worshipped and reviled the wrong shrine because they have approached the notes within a frame of reference which was quite alien and irrelevant to its formulators. They have made the cardinal error of viewing the Open Door notes as a grand search for an immediate, impenetrable, permanent panacea that would insure, in and of itself, the perpetual commercial ascendancy of America in China. Looked at in this unrealistic fashion, the notes became either everything or nothing. They either insured that "anything produced in the United States will *permanently* find its way into *all* parts of the Celestial Empire" [italics added], or else they produced only "evasive and noncommittal" responses, empty and vague words, a jumble of legalistic, high-flown phrases—a monument to the American penchant for substituting slogans, scraps of paper, and good intentions for the tried and tested behavioral patterns of *realpolitik*.[99]

The fact stands, however, that the Hay circular was not an end in itself and should not be evaluated as such. It was simply an effort, albeit, a dramatic one, to structure a framework within which the more traditional dynamics of diplomacy could operate. Russia's promises might be "as false as dicer's oaths," as Hay clearly understood, but such public commitments still offered a handy instrument which American tacticians could use to force open door opponents to employ more indirect and less effective means for fulfilling their ends, thus limiting their freedom of choice and action; to exploit Europe's fear of world conflagration by offering it a peaceful substitute to the imperial rat race; to convince disbelievers of the earnestness of American intentions and, in the aftermath of the war with Spain, the credibility of American power.[100] All these techniques and others could be and were tried, for the China market, with its vast potential, was worth the effort.

If the attempt failed, *c'est la vie*. The China market, despite its vast potential, was not worth a war or the risk of war, a reality that contemporary suprarealists, in their make-believe world of omnipresent national interests, have side-stepped in order to continue their sterile debate over the means to undefined ends.

William Howard Taft and the Ohio Endorsement Issue, 1906-1908

Alfred D. Sumberg
AMERICAN ASSOCIATION OF UNIVERSITY PROFESSORS,
WASHINGTON, D.C.

On December 11, 1907, President Theodore Roosevelt repeated the statement he made after his election in 1904 barring a third term. "Under no circumstances," he had said, would he be "a candidate for or accept another nomination." Now in 1907 he announced: "I have not changed and shall not change the decision thus announced."[1]

Republicans accepted the President's statement and then faced up to the difficult task of choosing a nominee for the presidential election of 1908. Two factors played a key role in their final decision. One was Roosevelt himself who insisted on the right to select his successor, and the other was the victory of the forces supporting Secretary of War William H. Taft in the struggle for control of party leadership in Taft's native Ohio. Taft's victory in Ohio over the formidable Joseph B. Foraker gave Roosevelt substantial evidence that in supporting Taft he would be backing a candidate capable of winning both the nomination and the election.

Roosevelt played a key role in the selection of a candidate. He saw the opportunity to pick a strong candidate who would win the election and continue Republican control of the presidency.

But he made it clear that he intended to support for the nomination a person who could lead the liberal wing of the party, unite Republicans, and maintain the President's policies, particularly the philosophy of expanded federal responsibilities.

Roosevelt's first choice for the nomination was Secretary of State Elihu Root.[2] But Roosevelt decided that, while Root would make an excellent president, he would have difficulty winning both the nomination and the election. Roosevelt and Root agreed that the latter would be rejected by both the convention and the electorate because he was a corporation lawyer and many of his clients were Wall Street corporations. Root himself was reluctant to use the President's personal preference to advance his candidacy and believed he was too old (he was sixty-two in 1907) for the presidency. There is evidence, furthermore, that Root's health was not good in 1907. While Roosevelt seemed anxious to see his fellow New Yorker in the White House, both he and Root finally agreed not to pursue the matter further.[3]

When Roosevelt realized that Root would not be a suitable candidate, he turned more enthusiastically to Taft. Taft's record of governmental service since his graduation from the Cincinnati Law School in 1880 was impressive. He had served successively as assistant prosecutor of Hamilton County, collector of internal revenue for the First Ohio District, assistant solicitor of Hamilton County, judge of the Superior Court of Cincinnati, solicitor-general of the United States, United States circuit judge for the Sixth Circuit, president of the Philippines Commission, and secretary of war. His experiences had given him a reputation as a capable jurist and administrator.

The relationship between Roosevelt and Taft was one of mutual admiration. Roosevelt sought Taft's friendship and advice and appointed him to positions of responsibility. Both had served in Washington during the administration of Benjamin Harrison and they had become friends at that time.[4] In 1901 and 1903 Roosevelt expressed his respect for Taft's abilities.[5] "I wonder if you realize how much I respect and admire you," he told Taft.[6] When Taft joined the cabinet in 1904, Roosevelt called him "a high-minded and disinterested man." [7] In May, 1905, Roosevelt wrote at length about Taft to his English friend, Sir George Otto Trevelyan. Roosevelt told the English historian that Taft had been his acting secretary of state during John Hay's illness as well as his secretary of war. Taft was a great help, he reported, in both international affairs and domestic problems. "He has no more fear in dealing with the interests of great corporate wealth than he has in dealing with the leaders of the most powerful labor unions; and if either go wrong he has not the slightest hesitation in antagonizing them." Roosevelt reported further to Trevelyan on Taft's characteristics. "To strength and courage, clear insight, and practical common sense, he adds a very noble and disinterested character." Taft had stood by him "like a trump" in "some horrid matters" pertaining to corruption in the national government.[8] During 1907 and 1908, Roosevelt saw Taft in his own image. Again he told Trevelyan that "he [Taft] and I view public questions exactly alike." "In fact," said Roosevelt, "I think it has been very rare that two public men have ever been so much at one in all the essentials of their beliefs and practices."[9]

In spite of Roosevelt's admiration, Taft was a most reluctant candidate for the nomination. He did not wish to involve himself further in politics but preferred instead a place on the Supreme Court. Furthermore, he was not convinced that he could win the nomination. He lacked Roosevelt's experience in day-to-day politics and he believed that his decisions involving organized labor while on the bench would disqualify him from any consideration by Republicans.[10]

If Taft appeared to be unavailable, why did he become a candidate for the presidential nomination? The answer lies in the influence of the Taft family, political conditions in Ohio and Cincinnati, support promised to him by Roosevelt, and Taft's own conviction that his public life was at an end if he did not seek the presidency.

Taft's family had always played an important role in his public career. He inherited from his father, Alphonso Taft, his commitment to government service and his independent attitude in politics. From his mother, Louise Taft, he inherited a strong will and a determined desire to do well that which he set out to accomplish. His wife, Helen Herron Taft, and his brothers, Charles P., Horace D., and Henry W., held strong reins over him. Taft consulted regularly with his family about political matters.

Louise Taft and Helen Taft had always disagreed about the type of work Taft should do. Whereas Louise Taft believed that her son should remain in the judiciary and that his destiny was the Supreme Court, Helen Taft opposed a judicial career and regarded the Supreme Court as a "fixed groove." She approved her husband's acceptance of the presidency of the Philippines Commission and the cabinet post because these "were in line with the kind of work" she wanted him to pursue and the "kind of career" she wanted for him and expected him to have. After Taft joined the cabinet, his wife seems to have begun a campaign to convince him and Roosevelt that he would be a capable successor to the popular President.[11]

Mrs. Taft tended to be firm in her attitudes toward her husband's future and she was critical of those who were skeptical of Taft's ability to win the nomination. She helped to formulate the strategies of the preconvention campaign and she was most insistent that her husband be a more active candidate. Not only did she speak frankly to her husband and to her brother-in-law, Charles P. Taft, but also urged Roosevelt to undertake a more active role in behalf of his Secretary of War.[12] In early March, 1906, when Roosevelt offered a Supreme Court position to Taft, she told him that if he accepted the appointment he would be making "the great mistake" of his life. Taft declined the appointment in a letter which reflected the advice of his brothers, Henry and Horace. Mrs. Taft also discussed the situation personally with Roosevelt and apparently was quite frank with the President. Taft's letter and Mrs. Taft's visit did not set well with Roosevelt. He told Taft that this was "pre-eminently a matter in which no other man can take the responsibility of deciding for you what is right and best for you to do." In his reply to the President, Taft firmly rejected the Supreme Court position.[13]

Charles P. Taft, publisher of the Cincinnati *Times-Star,* was responsible for introducing William Taft's name into the intraparty struggle in Ohio and Cincinnati in 1906. Even before Taft had decided finally to become a candidate for the nomination, Charles

P. Taft had used his brother's position in the Roosevelt administration to criticize the control over the state Republican party held by Senator Joseph B. Foraker and over Cincinnati Republicans by George B. Cox.[14] Secretary Taft felt much the same way about Ohio and Cincinnati politics, but only rarely did he challenge the party's leadership. Once he had concluded, however, that his destiny was the presidential nomination, he was anxious to subdue the obstacles in his way. In 1906, 1907, and 1908, both Foraker and Cox were obstacles to his winning the nomination. For this reason, then, Taft permitted his brother to use his name and position to advance the cause of reform in Ohio and Cincinnati politics. The consequences of the work accomplished by Charles P. Taft proved beneficial to William H. Taft's campaign.

Ohio's Republican party had long suffered from factionalism. "Cincinnati and the lake shore," historian Frederic L. Paxson has observed, "have struggled to control the machines, now through alliance, now through outright war." [15] The result was that Ohio Republicans rarely had one leader. In the period of 1890–1904, Mark Hanna of Cleveland and Joseph Foraker of Cincinnati clashed, combined, and then clashed again in their attempts to control the Republican party of Ohio.[16] When Hanna died in 1904, Foraker failed to unite Ohio Republicans under his leadership. The Hanna organization was inherited by General Charles W. F. Dick, who had been four times a congressman, secretary of the National Republican Committee, and one of Hanna's closest associates.[17] Dick succeeded to not only the leadership of the Hanna organization but also Hanna's seat in the United States Senate. Tranquillity between Foraker and Dick lasted for only a brief period after Hanna's death. They conflicted over dispensation of federal patronage in Ohio. By 1906, however, the two men had come to an agreement on patronage.[18] The most important factor that helped to unite the leaders of the two Ohio factions was the attack of an insurgent group led by Congressman Theodore E. Burton of Cleveland and Harry M. Daugherty, a Columbus attorney. The insurgents emphasized their support of Roosevelt's reform policies.[19] By 1906, Ohio seethed with a bitter contest over control of the state Republican party.

The political picture in Ohio was complicated by the unreliability of the Republican "boss" of Cincinnati, George B. Cox. Cox had started out in the Foraker camp in 1895, but in 1897 he had shifted over to Hanna.[20] In 1903, he supported Hanna's candidate for governor, Myron T. Herrick, and upon Hanna's death in 1904 Cox joined with Charles Dick against Foraker.[21] In 1905, Cox suffered political defeats on both the state and city levels. In 1906–1907, however, Cox sought to regain his strength within the state Republican organization. Foraker and Dick, both of whom recognized that Cox's political machine in Cincinnati and Hamilton County was still an important influence on state politics, made strenuous attempts to obtain Cox's support against the new insurgent group led by Burton and Daugherty. Cox wavered in 1907 between the two groups in the hope of cementing an alliance that would give him more permanent stability in his control of Cincinnati politics.

Several factors influenced the conflict over control of the state Republican organization. One factor was the fact that Foraker's term of office expired in 1908. If Foraker could be dropped from the Senate, the pro-Roosevelt faction in Ohio would be much happier. Furthermore, if Foraker were forced to give up his seat in the Senate, he would lose his strength as one of the Republican bosses of Ohio. This would weaken the Dick machine as well. A second factor revolved about the Democratic victory in the gubernatorial election of 1905. Foraker and Dick blamed Taft for the loss. Even though Taft had served as chairman of the Republican State Convention in 1905, he campaigned throughout the state against "boss control." Speaking in Akron in October, he said that if he were voting in Cincinnati in November, he would "vote against the municipal ticket nominated by the Republican organization, and for the state ticket." [22] Myron T. Herrick, the incumbent and favorite of Foraker, Dick, and Cox, lost the governorship and Taft was blamed immediately.[23]

The state convention of 1906 was designed to help the Foraker-Dick alliance recoup its losses of 1905. Specifically, both Foraker and Dick intended to use the convention to strengthen their hold upon Ohio Republicans, eliminate the Burton-Daugherty insurgents, and rebuke Secretary of War Taft for his unfaithfulness in 1905. The character of the conflict was revealed on August 16 when Burton addressed the Tippecanoe Republican Club of Cleveland. In his talk, Burton advised that Foraker and Dick be endorsed for their services in the Senate at the forthcoming convention, "but that the need of praise to be accorded President Roosevelt be made so much more cordial that the difference could be noted by the dullest." The purpose of a less cordial endorsement was to weaken the Foraker-Dick organization and eliminate any consideration of Foraker for the presidential nomination in 1908 or for re-election as a senator in 1908. Dick replied to Burton on August 23. The junior Senator, who was under attack for his opposition to the Philippine Tariff Act, which Taft favored, defended his own record and announced that he would stand for re-election as chairman of the state executive committee at the convention in September. Foraker answered Burton on August 27 by defending his opposition to the Hepburn Rate Act and his support for a bill proposing joint statehood of Arizona and New Mexico, by calling for Dick's re-election to the chairmanship, and by declaring that the convention delegates, not Burton, should decide the matter of endorsement of the two senators.[24]

A further factor that influenced plans for the 1906 Republican State Convention was the endorsement of a presidential nominee. There was no state convention planned for 1907; the next one would meet probably in May 1908. It was customary for state conventions to endorse presidential candidates one or even two years before the national convention. In view of the fact that Ohio Democrats had endorsed William Jennings Bryan already, there was much speculation about the possible endorsement of a candidate by Ohio Republicans. In early September, rumors persisted that a compromise had been worked out. It was reported that the insurgent group would agree to the Foraker-Dick leadership and, in turn, both Foraker and Dick would support a resolution recommending Taft as Ohio's choice for the Republican nomination in 1908. Senator Dick hinted at the arrangement when he reported that Roosevelt recognized their leadership in Ohio Republican affairs. He said also that he believed "the delegates favorable to a senatorial indorsement will be a majority at the Dayton convention."[25]

Senator Dick's prediction proved accurate. Ohio Republicans gathered at Dayton on September 11–12 and gave Foraker and Dick a total victory. Dick was re-elected chairman of the state executive committee. Foraker, who appeared on the scene unexpectedly, won over the delegates to his position with a dramatic speech. In an atmosphere tense with sharp political conflict, Foraker lashed out at Roosevelt and at those Ohio Republicans who disagreed with him. He was incensed over the attempts to discredit him because of his differences with the President over the railroad rate policy. Foraker's talk had the expected result. It clinched the leadership of the Ohio Republicans for the senators. Yet it went one step further. Rumors prevailed in Dayton immediately after Foraker's talk that the senior senator would be endorsed by the convention delegates not for the senatorship but rather for the presidential nomination. The prospect of such an endorsement created panic among the insurgent group.[26]

On the morning of September 12, Foraker and Dick were successful in securing their control of the party. The platform was acceptable to them but not to Congressman Burton. His attempts to include a tariff revision plank and one calling for the direct election of United States senators were defeated. The platform endorsed Roosevelt but failed to mention Taft's presence in the cabinet, contrary to the platform adopted in 1905. In an obvious attack upon Burton, the platform condemned a "hostile House of Representatives" that was thwarting Roosevelt's aims and policies. Finally, the two senators were approved and endorsed "most heartily and without reserve." [27]

In spite of the serious rumors about the possible endorsement of Foraker for the presidential nomination, the platform contained no such resolution. The story was current after the convention that Foraker had rejected the endorsement because it was too early, he believed, for the delegates to take up the matter of the presidential election of 1908. Even without a presidential endorsement, Foraker's place in Ohio Republican affairs was more firmly entrenched.[28] Both he and Dick now held a tight rein over the Ohio Republican party. That rein was tightened in November by the sweeping victory in the general election of the state candidates chosen at the convention. The Cincinnati *Enquirer* observed that

> The result demonstrates beyond question that Senators Foraker and Dick have been indorsed by the people without reserve . . . . It establishes their complete mastery of the Republican party in Ohio, and assures to Senator Foraker, without serious opposition, indorsement in the next Republican state convention to succeed himself, and in addition thereto a solid delegation in the national convention for the Presidency if he so desires . . . . Senator Dick of course will remain at the head of the organization.[29]

To counteract the Foraker-Dick leadership, the Burton-Daugherty insurgents and those who desired the nomination of Taft for the presidency now worked more closely together. Several factors aided in knitting together a new faction that had as its aims the election of Burton as United States senator in 1908 and control of the Ohio delegation at the 1908 national convention. Much depended on George B. Cox. In 1905–1906, Cox was having trouble maintaining his strength because of the major reversals his organization had suffered in the 1905 election. Cox's troubles were compounded, moreover, by an investigation by the Drake committee, which had been established by the Ohio Legislature to investigate reports that various banks in Cincinnati had been paying interest for years on vast sums in the city's treasury but that the interest had gone to the Cox machine rather than into the city treasury. Other revelations regarding graft and improper influence forced Cox to announce that he was "retiring" from politics.[30] In reality, Cox merely stepped into the background and turned over the administration of the organization to Rudyard K. Hynicka and August Herrmann, his most trusted lieutenants. It was at this point that Charles P. Taft saw an opportunity to destroy the strength of the Cox machine entirely and to undermine the control of Foraker and Dick over the Ohio Republican party. While Burton was striking at Dick's center of monopoly in northeastern Ohio, Charles P. Taft began a campaign against both Foraker and Dick in southwestern Ohio.

Theodore Roosevelt played a prominent but indirect role in smashing the strength of the Foraker-Dick alliance. It was during the time in 1906 when Roosevelt was thinking of appointing Taft to the Supreme Court that his ideas about Taft and the presidency became firmer. He told Taft on March 15 that he believed "of all the men that have appeared so far you are the man who is most likely to receive the Republican Presidential nomination and who is, I think, the best man to receive it . . . and under whom we would have most chance to succeed." He warned Taft against thinking too lightly of the presidency. ". . . it is well to remember," he said, "that the shadow of the Presidency falls on no man twice, save in the most exceptional circumstances." "The good you could do in four or eight years as head of the Nation," Roosevelt observed, "would be incalculable."[31]

About all that Roosevelt had indicated thus far was both his admiration and respect for Taft. He believed Taft was the most prominent candidate for the nomination but there was no suggestion that he intended to throw his full political resources behind the Ohioan. In July, Roosevelt confessed to Benjamin I. Wheeler that he was getting anxious about the matter of a successor. He told Wheeler that Taft could take over the leadership of the movement Roosevelt had started. He revealed also that he saw no other person developing as a possible successor and he, Roosevelt, did not want renomination. The result, then, was that it would be necessary for Taft to step into the vacuum that Roosevelt was creating.[32]

During the fall of 1906, Roosevelt's time was taken up with the congressional election. He said very little about the distant presidential election and almost nothing about the nomination of Taft. He was aware, however, of the intraparty struggle in Ohio and of Taft's campaign work throughout the country. In mid-September Taft was forced to abandon his role in the campaign temporarily and go to Cuba with troops to quell a revolution. Roosevelt was deeply impressed by Taft's handling of the Cuban crisis. Taft returned to the United States in early October and resumed his participation in the campaign by speaking in Ohio, Illinois, and Idaho. Roosevelt was now even more impressed by his versatile and able Secretary of War.[33]

In late October, while her husband was campaigning in the West, Mrs. Taft approached Roosevelt on the question of his support of her husband for the presidency in 1908. She was surprised to learn that Roosevelt believed Governor Charles E. Hughes of

New York had special qualifications which might fit him for the presidency. Obviously shocked by the President's aloofness toward her husband, Mrs. Taft immediately protested to the campaigning Secretary of War. Taft himself evidently rejected his wife's protest and wrote to Roosevelt that the nomination of Hughes would be an excellent idea.[34] Roosevelt, however, believed that Mrs. Taft had misunderstood him. In a letter to Taft on November 5, Roosevelt protested that he had never said anything to Mrs. Taft about his supporting Hughes. He explained that

> what I said to her was that you must not be too entirely aloof because if you were it might dishearten your supporters and put us all in such shape that some man like Hughes, or more probably some man from the West, would turn up with so much popular sentiment behind him that there would be no course but to support him.[35]

Roosevelt's advice to Taft indicated that he was now ready to support his Secretary of War for the presidential nomination. The next move had to be taken by Taft. By December 29, Taft was prepared to make a statement about the presidential nomination. In a carefully worded statement issued in Washington, he said:

> For the purpose of relieving the burden imposed by recent publications upon some of my friends among the Washington newspaper correspondents of putting further inquiries to me, I wish to say that my ambition is not political; that I am not seeking the Presidential nomination; that I do not expect to be the Republican candidate, if for no other reason, because of what seems to me to be objections to my availability, which do not appear to lessen with the continued discussion of my duties, but that I am not foolish enough to say that in the improbable event that the opportunity to run for the great office of President were to come to me, I should decline it, for this would not be true.[36]

What did Taft's statement mean? Was he a candidate or was he not? Charles P. Taft threw his brother's hat into the presidential ring by stressing only the latter part of the statement. In an editorial, the Cincinnati *Times-Star* sought to clarify the statement with this explanation on behalf of Taft: "That although not a seeker after the nomination, a declination of same was entirely out of the question."[37] At the same time Charles P. Taft wrote to his brother in Washington. The statement, he said, "put the matter up to the Convention and opens up the contest in Ohio." Henry W. Taft told his brother that he liked the statement but that he did not think it would save him from "the importunities of the newspaper men." "My chief concern is that you don't let your feelings get so entangled that failure to receive the nomination will cause bitterness or pain." Theodore E. Burton told newspapermen that "Secretary Taft's statement no doubt expresses his feelings." "He would have very strong support in Ohio," Burton said, "if he is even only a receptive candidate." [38]

William H. Taft believed that he was misunderstood. Although he made no further public statement to clarify his views, he told Charles P. Taft on January 1: "You evidently think I am right in the fight for the nomination, whereas my statement was made for the purpose of showing that I was not." At the same time, he told his brother how he felt about running for the presidential nomination. "I suppose it is unreasonable, but I would be very glad to avoid the slightest appearance of getting into a political contest, for I have no spirit for it, and am sincere in saying that I do not wish to." Furthermore, Taft said, "the difficulty of being recognized as a candidate is, that it gives many people a motive for attacking you, and I have no doubt I shall have assaults all along the line now." In an afterthought, Taft advised his brother to "keep everything favorable to my candidacy or unfavorable to Foraker out of the Times Star. . . ." [39]

Even though Taft's announcement of December 29 seemed indecisive, several factors made him a more positive candidate. Charles P. Taft disregarded entirely his brother's wish to remain out of the political contest. On the very day the statement was released in Washington, Taft wrote his brother there a long letter detailing political conditions in Ohio. He noted specifically that all of the postmasters in Ohio were appointees of Foraker and Dick and therefore supporters of the two senators. Such a condition, Taft warned, was a serious handicap to his presidential candidacy. The solution to the problem was holding the postmasters aloof from the intraparty struggle. A further condition that necessitated watching, according to Charles P. Taft, was the political situation in Cincinnati. "In this last election, I received special assurances from the organization here in Hamilton County, that so far as the next National Convention was concerned, it would be either for President Roosevelt or the one he wishes nominated." Taft seemed to think that he could win over Cox on this basis and then control the local delegation to the national convention. "Of course I may be mistaken," he advised, "but I believe I have the key to the situation." Finally, Charles P. Taft recognized the danger of Foraker in Secretary of War Taft's move to win the nomination. Foraker was dangerous because he controlled the postmasters and allied himself with Cox. On the national scene, he was dangerous because his attack on Roosevelt and Taft over the Brownsville affair attracted Negroes and veterans to him. "Personally," the editor of the *Times-Star* observed, "I believe that outside of the President, you are the one man who can be elected on the republican ticket as against Bryan; certainly Foraker cannot be. . . ." [40]

Indirectly, Senator Foraker forced William H. Taft into becoming a more positive candidate for the presidential nomination. By antagonizing President Roosevelt over the discharge from the Army without honor of three companies of Negro troops in November, 1906, Foraker forced Roosevelt to take a more active role on behalf of Taft's candidacy.[41] On December 3, 1906, when Congress convened, Foraker introduced a resolution directing the Secretary of War to turn over to the Senate full information on the incident at Brownsville. Roosevelt, who had been requested to supply information of his own, replied shortly with a detailing of the facts surrounding the incident. On December 20, Foraker spoke at length in the Senate about the case and Roosevelt's message. The Ohio senator was sharply critical of the President's action, which he regarded as unconstitutional. In January, 1907, Foraker proposed an investigation by the Senate Committee on Military Affairs. After considerable discussion in the Senate and a further report by the President, a new resolution was agreed to on January 22.[42] By this time, however, Foraker had made political capital out of his championing the rights of the Negro soldiers. Taft feared the political results and the fact that Foraker was enjoying a great deal of popularity. Several days before he issued his statement of December 29, Taft observed that "Foraker is determined to make the President as uncomfortable as possible, and incidentally eliminate me from the Ohio situation." [43] Taft's statement of December 29, then, was designed to detract from Foraker's current popularity and return Taft to the good graces of Republicans.

The Brownsville affair proved to have more political dynamite than anyone suspected. It nearly destroyed Taft's chances for winning the presidential nomination, and it made Foraker a popular hero among Negroes, veterans, and anti-Roosevelt Republicans. The President himself proved to be the deciding factor. Roosevelt, who jealously guarded his presidential powers, refused to make any concessions to Congress over the discharge of the Negro troops. Instead, he believed that the attack upon him, especially that of Foraker, was motivated by political considerations.[44] This attitude on Roosevelt's part was emphasized by an impromptu debate between Foraker and Roosevelt at the annual Gridiron dinner in Washington. In his lengthy talk, Roosevelt criticized the Senate's debate over the Brownsville affair and observed that Foraker's motives were certainly political.

Foraker was called upon to speak informally in reply. He not only made a strong case against the President's position but also denied any political motivation on his part. When Foraker concluded, Roosevelt jumped up and demanded the right to reply to the Ohio senator. He contradicted the facts of the incident as cited by Foraker, pointed out that he, not Foraker, would pass judgment upon the case, and promised that he would absolutely disregard anything except his own convictions. After making his brief but pointed reply, Roosevelt departed abruptly. The Gridiron dinner incident served only to widen the breach between Roosevelt and Foraker and to push the President into a firmer position of supporting Taft for the presidential nomination in order to strike at Foraker.[45] While Taft may not have realized it, Roosevelt's activity on his behalf was partially designed to make the President more secure in his reputation.

By late March, 1907, the political struggle in Ohio between Foraker and Taft reached the organizational level. Charles P. Taft established a working staff headed by Arthur I. Vorys, a Columbus attorney, and took an active role in obtaining support from local political leaders for his brother's candidacy.[46] Editor Taft's major concern was the federal appointees in Ohio and he advised his brother on appointments of postmasters, federal judges, and collectors of internal revenue. The Secretary of War, who seemed reluctant yet to participate in a political contest, finally agreed with his brother's policies and, in most cases, his recommendations. In the matter of postal appointees and collectors of internal revenue, William H. Taft advised his brother to contact Secretary of Interior James R. Garfield, who would pass on Charles P. Taft's recommendations to the cabinet officers, Frank Hitchcock and George Cortelyou, in charge of those departments. In matters relating to federal judgeships, Taft took it upon himself to send brother Charles' recommendations directly to the President.[47]

Senator Foraker realized that the Taft campaign was designed to challenge his control of the Ohio Republican party. He recognized also that his position as senator was at stake in a contest between Taft-led Ohio Republicans and the Foraker-Dick machine.[48] Foraker, therefore, retaliated against the establishment of a Taft organization by issuing a statement on March 26. He did not wish, he said, "any political honors from the Republicans of Ohio without their hearty approval. . . ." He intended to request the Republican State Central Committee to issue a call for a state convention, the delegates to which would be elected at "duly authorized primary elections for the purpose not only of nominating candidates for state officers to be voted for at our next state elections, but also to determine the preference of the Republicans of Ohio as to candidates for United States Senator and for President." [49] The Taft organization took up the challenge immediately. Charles P. Taft wrote editorially in his own newspaper that the forthcoming contest between his brother and Senator Foraker was over both the senatorship and the presidential nomination. If in the primary election, Taft declared, one was selected for either of the posts the other would be automatically eliminated from "the political situation." To bolster his brother's candidacy even further, editor Taft stated frankly that "this is a direct contest between the friends of the administration of President Roosevelt and his opponents." [50] The idea of a primary election, then, was gladly endorsed by both groups of Ohio Republicans.

Of the two men, Foraker's task was more formidable than that of Taft. In order to win a victory in a primary, Foraker had several possible methods of attack. He had to reverse the sentiment of Ohio Republicans towards the popular President or convince the people anew that he was opposed to Taft but not to Roosevelt.

For victory, Foraker had to rely upon "himself and his power on the stump . . . the organization . . . [and] . . . the open and latent hostility to President Roosevelt among corporation men." [51] Foraker could use, also, the congressional investigation into the Brownsville affair as a means of attacking Taft. His control of the organization and his alliance with Senator Dick were advantageous factors as well. Undoubtedly, because of his many years of political service, Foraker had considerable personal popularity throughout the state. His experience as a political manipulator would serve him well.

Throughout the spring and summer of 1907, the battle within the ranks of Ohio Republicans raged furiously. Attempts to compromise the opposing viewpoints of Foraker and Taft were made, but in each case were rejected.[52] In early April, the President's son-in-law, Congressman Nicholas Longworth of Cincinnati, publicly endorsed Taft for the presidency and Roosevelt declared privately he thought "Nick's interview on behalf of Taft admirable from every standpoint." Meanwhile, Foraker was at work on his own behalf. On April 9 he spoke at Canton and defended his opposition to Roosevelt's policies. His speech was regarded as the opening of his campaign against Taft.[53]

Perhaps the most industrious person on the Ohio scene was Charles P. Taft. In late April and early May, he pressured politician after politician into the Taft camp. In Cincinnati he threatened to establish a Taft organization in competition with the Cox organization. While Cox favored Foraker for the senatorship, he remained noncommittal on a presidential endorsement. The Cincinnati editor found, however, that Cox did not have the same strength in his own organization that he had had previously. He found that Hynicka and Herrmann were more influential than Cox was willing to admit. Yet, Cox was the nominal leader of the regular party organization in Cincinnati and Hamilton County. Further investigation revealed that Hynicka and Herrmann were more friendly towards Taft than Cox; that many of the ward leaders of the Cox organization were anxious to come out into the open and endorse Taft; that Congressman Longworth was "a little backward" in the eyes of Charles P. Taft; and that the establishment of Taft clubs in Cincinnati would split the local Republican party, lose the November elections for the Republicans, but give control of the county executive committee to the Taft organization in early 1908. It was his purpose, Charles P. Taft said, to "clean the whole business up." After several interviews with Cox, Hynicka, and Herrmann, Taft was satisfied that conditions in Cincinnati and Ohio would be cleared up quickly. The threat of a competitive organization had its effect on the leaders of the regular organization. In early May, Cox met with Foraker and told the Senator that he was for Taft for the presidential nomination and Foraker for the senatorship. This news was passed on to Arthur Vorys, who transmitted it to Charles P. Taft, who in turn informed his brother of the events. By May 6, Charles P. Taft was satisfied that the local Republican organization would not hinder Taft's nomination.[54]

An equally important plan of Charles P. Taft's was to swing over the state Republican organization to the Taft side. He worked on the assumption that it would be necessary to eliminate Foraker not only from the senatorial contest but also from the presidential race. Furthermore, he believed that Foraker was not alone in his contest with William H. Taft. Foraker's objective, he said, was to delay the national campaign on Taft's behalf. "He is acting as a stalking horse for [Charles W.] Fairbanks or somebody outside of the state," editor Taft noted, "and for this reason we are bending every effort to make the situation in Ohio more pronounced and clear." [55]

By early May, 1907, Charles P. Taft was satisfied that the work done by Vorys throughout the state had had excellent results. Vorys had influenced a large number of local and county leaders in favor of Taft. His main prize was Walter F. Brown, a former Foraker supporter, who was chairman of the Republican State Central Committee. On May 6, Charles P. Taft informed his brother that Brown was ready to make a public statement endorsing Taft for the presidential nomination. Brown was prepared not only to make such a statement but also to call a meeting of the State Central Committee to obtain an official endorsement by that group. Taft concluded that the statement by Brown, when coupled with one by Cox, "would practically settle the matter in Ohio." William H. Taft was amazed to hear about Brown's switch from the Foraker-Dick camp to his own. He could not believe the news about Cox. "I can hardly believe that Cox and Brown will come out as you say," he told his brother Charles, "because neither has any particular reason to love me . . . ." The Secretary of War interpreted the news about Brown and Cox to mean that they really did not care for him but they wanted to see Foraker retained in the Senate. Evidently, Taft said, the two political leaders believed support of his candidacy was the price they must pay to retain their influential positions and keep Foraker in office. "Politicians are stupid and they don't always do shrewd things," he concluded.[56]

In the meanwhile, Brown called a meeting of both the state central and executive committees for May 15 in Columbus. The purpose was to confer about the political situation in Ohio. Secretary Taft prepared a statement on May 11 and sent it to Charles P. Taft "for publication if the occasion shall require it." "It expresses my exact sentiments," he noted. The statement was designed to prevent a bargain among the committeemen over the senatorship and the presidential nomination. He stated:

> I believe I have a right to ask those who honor me with good opinion, and to whom I very grateful, to exercise their independent judgment without respect to me, and not to do anything which shall, in its final analysis, be a bargain, for even the appearance of such a bargain would not make for the good of the Republican party of the state.[57]

Taft's statement proved unnecessary. On May 12, Foraker bitterly denounced the calling of the meeting and warned members of the committee not to attend. He charged that the purpose of the meeting was to endorse Taft for the presidential nomination. On May 13, Senator Dick, chairman of the State Executive Committee, cancelled the meeting scheduled by Brown. Brown, on the other hand, declared that both committees would meet as scheduled. On the following day, however, he cancelled the meeting of the committees without an explanation.[58] Foraker had won a temporary victory.

During May, June, and July, the Taft organization worked to line up a solid core of supporters within the State Central Committee and to commit the group to an endorsement of Taft for the presidential nomination. Foraker, however, with Dick's assistance, warded off the calling of the committee until a compromise among Ohio Republicans could be established. While he gave indications that he was interested in the presidential nomination himself, he wanted to compromise with Taft in such a manner that he would retain the senatorship. Both Tafts had rejected compromise before and they were still not interested in a compromise with Foraker.[59]

By late July, Brown was prepared to call another meeting of the State Central Committee for the purpose of endorsing Taft. The call of the committee for a meeting in Columbus on July 30 brought Foraker out into the open again. This time he was bolstered by an intercepted telegram from Herrmann to Charles P. Taft, who was vacationing in Point au Pic, Canada. The telegram revealed that the Hamilton County organization would agree to endorse Taft for the presidential nomination at the meeting of the committee but would not vote on an endorsement of Foraker.[60] What Foraker did not know was that Charles P. Taft had telegraphed previously to both Herrmann and Hynicka his objections to an alleged statement by Cox that the State Central Committee would not endorse Taft unless the committee also endorsed Foraker for the senatorship. Taft protested that Foraker's endorsement meant defeat in Cincinnati in the November elections and that it would damage the Secretary of War's reputation nationally because it would be evidence that a bargain had been made with Foraker on the senatorship. "The question of the senatorship at this time is premature at any rate and the necessity and advantage for an expression on the Presidential candidate are obvious." [61] The telegram intercepted by someone favorable to Foraker had been Herrmann's reply to Taft's telegram of July 24.

Bolstered by this additional information, Foraker published on July 29 a letter he had written to C. B. McCoy, a member of the State Central Committee and a Foraker supporter. In his letter, Foraker said he was opposed to the candidacy of William H. Taft, challenged the authority of the committee to make such an endorsement, and called attention to the fact that the delegates to the Republican State Convention of 1906 had desired to endorse him for the presidential nomination but had desisted because he believed the delegates had not been chosen for such a purpose. Even if the committee took the intended action, Foraker added, he would not announce at this time his own candidacy for the presidential nomination. Notwithstanding his latter statement,

Foraker's letter to McCoy was interpreted widely as a definite announcement of his candidacy.[62]

All efforts of Foraker to dissuade the State Central Committee from an endorsement of Taft failed. The committee gave an unqualified endorsement to the Secretary of War for the presidential nomination. It invited Republicans of other states to cooperate with Ohio Republicans in obtaining Taft's nomination. At the same time, the committee declared that it was opposed to the elimination from public life of Senators Foraker and Dick.[63] In spite of the latter statement, the committee remained divided over the resolution. The Foraker supporters wanted a full endorsement of the senior senator for renomination; the Taft supporters rejected such a commitment. The Foraker men rejected the unqualified endorsement of Taft; the Taft supporters wanted a unanimous vote for the endorsement. Both groups disagreed about the endorsements that were made. As a result, the resolution passed by a majority but not unanimously. The Cincinnati *Enquirer* concluded that "the fight ended just where it started." [64]

Perhaps to the surprise of the Taft organization, Foraker would not concede defeat. The Senator himself announced immediately after the meeting of the State Central Committee that "the action of the committee will not affect my course in any way." Recognizing that he had lost one battle, he now announced that "the next state convention will have authority to speak, and by the action of that convention it will be the duty of every good Republican to abide." [65] A rather weak defense was made by a spokesman for the Taft organization.[66] The committee's endorsement of Taft added a great deal to the national campaign on behalf of the Secretary of War. It touched off, also, a debate between Foraker and Taft during the summer of 1907. The debate revealed that Foraker was on the defensive.

During the summer of 1907, Foraker toured the state extensively. He usually found large audiences enthusiastically urging him on in his campaign against Taft. The theme of his talks was a defense of his attitudes toward the Hepburn Rate Act, joint statehood for New Mexico and Arizona, and the Brownsville incident. He criticized Taft for endorsing tariff revision in the Secretary of War's speech at Bath, Maine, in September, 1906. By fall, Foraker had completed his defense.[67] In late August, he wrote to a friend that "we are having a fierce battle, with many attending discouragements, but present indications point to a satisfactory result." At the same time, he and Dick hired John Malloy, secretary of the State Executive Committee, to "look after their interests" at a salary of $100 per week.[68]

The Taft-Foraker debate occurred in August. Taft spoke at Columbus on August 19, and Foraker replied in a talk at Georgetown on August 21. Taft's address was widely billed as the most important talk he would give in Ohio before the national convention of 1908. It was designed to make Taft's views on a number of issues known to the people. Taft consulted with Theodore E. Burton on the speech, and Burton observed that Taft was milder on the tariff question than he needed to be and was more apologetic. "I confess," Taft told his wife, "I don't like this for I thought I had spoken just as I did last year." It meant, he feared, that he would be criticized by both "wild protectionists" and "tariff reformers." Taft's speech had the approval of Roosevelt. Taft went to Oyster Bay and had a talk with the President. Roosevelt read Taft's speech while Taft glanced through a speech the President was to give on August 20. "There were parts of my speech he approved," Taft reported, "but I did not think he was as emphatic as he was about my Bath speech." [69]

In his speech, Taft covered nearly all of the topics discussed in public affairs at the time. Two topics caught the attention of most newspapers. He defended the Hepburn Rate Act but added that he thought it did not go far enough. Speaking about the tariff, Taft reiterated his belief in tariff revision but he believed now that it would have to wait until after the presidential election of 1908. Taft was pleased with the effects of the speech. His concern for public reaction took the form of noting what the newspapers said about his talk. He found that the papers in the East did not "gush over" the speech. "I am not troubled on that score," he said, "provided it meets the views of the Middle West." The Ohio papers, he noted, were very friendly in their comments.[70]

Foraker's talk at Georgetown was another defensive measure. He devoted much time to an analysis of the Elkins Act and the Hepburn Rate Act and he explained his opposition to giving the

Interstate Commerce Commission the right to fix rates. He called upon Taft to specify exactly what revision of the tariff he wanted, to give his views on the denial of voting privileges to Negroes in the South, and finally to state whether or not he would advise the Republicans of Cincinnati and Hamilton County to vote against the Republican ticket in 1907, as he had in 1905.[71] Taft did not intend to answer Foraker unless the need was obvious. Instead, he continued south and then went west after he left Columbus. He was beginning "a fateful political trip around the world." [72]

Taft's absence in late 1907 had many repercussions. On the national scene, the financial panic came, but Taft fortunately was not around to bear the brunt of the severe attacks on Roosevelt. It was during this period also that other candidates for the presidential nomination appeared. Roosevelt continued his support of Taft, however; but he gave Taft many moments of despair over the nomination.[73] Taft's absence and the financial panic brought a decline in the Taft campaign in Ohio. The decline was aided by the defeat of Theodore E. Burton by Tom L. Johnson for the post of mayor of Cleveland. Taft had endorsed Burton, and the election was viewed as a test of strength for the Taft organization.[74]

In late 1907, Senator Foraker made his most positive bid for the presidential nomination. On November 20, the advisory and executive committees of the Ohio Republican League, a state-wide organization, met. Many of Foraker's friends were on these committees, and it was not surprising when the two committees adopted a resolution endorsing Foraker for the senatorial and the presidential nominations in 1908.[75] Foraker responded to the League's resolution with a formal bow as a candidate for the presidential nomination. It was obvious that he intended to disregard the endorsement for the senatorship. In an acceptance letter, he defined his positions on government regulation of the railroads, Roosevelt's liberal interpretation of the Constitution, the tariff, and the power and independence of the Senate. Finally, he said that he would soon request the State Central Committee to "embody in its call for the next State Convention a requirement that all delegates to that convention shall be chosen by a direct vote of the

Republican electors of the State at duly authorized primary elections. . . ." [76]

The reaction to Foraker's announcement came swiftly. The Cincinnati *Times-Star* charged that Foraker was "the Wall Street candidate for the Presidential nomination." Identifying Taft with Roosevelt, the newspaper viewed Foraker's statement as "the formal declaration of war by those who are determined to turn back the hand of progress in the great work of national reform." The newspaper continued:

> To do that some one not in accord with the Roosevelt administration must be named as the Republican nominee and Secretary Taft being admittedly the one man it is necessary to defeat, Senator Foraker has started the fight by seeking to prevent Taft from getting a solid delegation from Ohio.[77]

Foraker himself realized that his chances for the nomination were slim but he hoped that at the national convention "we might be able to nominate Senator Fairbanks or some other Republican with whom we would be better satisfied." [78]

Following the endorsement by the League in November, Foraker spent the next four months preparing for the final contest with Taft. In reality, not much of a contest resulted. Foraker made several delaying actions but he never stopped the Taft organization from winning over the Republican county and district leaders.

In early December, Foraker requested that the State Central Committee "shall, in its call for the next Republican Convention, explicitly provide that all delegates to that convention shall be directly chosen at duly authorized primary elections, held in accordance with the statutes of the State applicable thereto." [79] On January 2, the committee met in Columbus and by a vote of fourteen to seven agreed that Ohio Republicans should vote directly for delegates to the state convention in a primary election scheduled for February 11. At the same time, the committee issued its call for the state convention to be held in Columbus on March 3–4. The purpose of the convention, the announcement stated, was to elect four delegates-at-large and four alternates-at-large to the national convention and to nominate candidates for state offices.

A provision in the procedure for electing delegates to the Republican State Convention brought an uproar from the Foraker organization. A provision of the call stated that before there could be a ticket for a candidate who wanted to run as a convention delegate there must be a petition signed by twenty times the number of the candidates for delegates and alternates in the county. Foraker protested immediately against the provision. He charged that the State Central Committee had no right to impose any conditions except that the delegates should be selected from the respective counties at primaries held in accordance with the Bronson Primary Law of 1904. The petitions, he argued, might require as many as four thousand signers in certain counties. Therefore, Foraker announced that he would not be bound by the "burdensome and unauthorized conditions" imposed by the State Central Committee.[80]

The Taft camp was jubilant over Foraker's reaction. Arthur I. Vorys said that he believed the call was fair and legal and that the Taft organization would comply with it and abide by the result.[81]

Foraker was not satisfied with a simple protest against the conditions imposed by the committee. One of his supporters filed a complaint with the Republican National Committee alleging that the selection of delegates by means of a direct primary was illegal because it was contrary to the Bronson Primary Law. The Republican National Committee's subcommittee on call agreed with the Foraker view but it could do nothing to forestall the action of the State Central Committee.[82] In an effort to overcome Foraker's objections, the Taft leaders took the issue through the courts until the Ohio Supreme Court ruled that the Bronson Primary Law was constitutional.[83]

Foraker disregarded entirely the Supreme Court's decision but recognized that the court's action had ended his hopes for success in the campaign against Taft. He stated privately that he did not "wish to make a vain contest" but "would be willing to act upon anything like a fair chance."[84] Foraker's hand may have been forced not only by the court's ruling but also by the fact that the Taft organization was winning over many of Foraker's loyal supporters.

By February 11, it was clear that Taft would have almost no opposition at the primary election. The results were overwhelmingly in his favor. The primary election provided Taft with the support of nearly 100 per cent of the delegates to the state convention. Foraker protested immediately that the primary election had not proved conclusively that Ohio Republicans supported Taft because only one-tenth of the state's registered Republicans had voted in the primary. He recognized, however, that the state convention would have a majority of Taft supporters.[85]

Foraker was accurate in his estimate of the work that would be done at the Republican State Convention. The temporary chairman of the convention was Secretary of Interior James R. Garfield, one of Taft's most active supporters. In his talk to the delegates, Garfield created an overwhelming outburst in Taft's favor when he mentioned the candidate's name. On the second day of the convention the delegates placed control of the state organization securely into the hands of the Taft group. The new State Central Committee, composed of twenty-one members, was entirely pro-Taft. Walter F. Brown was re-elected chairman. Attorney General Wade H. Ellis, who later assisted in the writing of the national Republican platform, was permanent chairman of the convention. It was Ellis who presided on the second day. Theodore E. Burton presented the state platform, which had been written by Ellis. Harry M. Daugherty reported for the committee on rules. Both men were greeted with ovations by the delegates. Besides the selection of state candidates, only two tasks faced the convention delegates. One was the selection of the delegates-at-large to the national convention and the other was the adoption of the state platform. The delegates-at-large were Governor Andrew L. Harris, Myron T. Herrick, Charles P. Taft, and Arthur I. Vorys.[86]

The planks presented by Burton represented the diverse interests of the modern Republican party. One called for revision of the tariff and another for a sound financial system. Others demanded civil and political rights for Negroes, completion of the Panama Canal, enactment of new employers' liability legislation, "a limitation in the exercise of the power of injunction, in order to prevent its abuse," a greater merchant marine and an adequate navy, generous pensions for veterans, liberal appropriations for improvement of the inland waterways, and the organization of all existing national public health agencies into a single national health department. The platform included a full endorsement of Theodore Roosevelt and his policies. It included the traditional plank congratulating the people of Ohio "that our representation in the Senate and House of Representatives of the United States maintains the State's high rank in the National Legislature." Finally, the platform gave full endorsement to Taft in a statement designed to appeal to Republicans elsewhere in the nation.[87]

With the adoption of the platform, Taft's major worry came to an end. While Foraker continued his efforts to get delegates to support him at the Republican National Convention, he found that his role in Ohio politics had diminished.[88] Taft no longer feared the competition Foraker might give him at the national convention.

The work begun by Charles P. Taft in late December, 1906, bore fruit as a result of the Republican State Convention of March 3–4, 1908. The time had been spent in planning, organizing, influencing, and in direct conflict with the opposition. The campaign not only had been well organized and carried out effectively but also well correlated with local and national conditions. William H. Taft had become the symbol of reform in local politics and the symbol of Roosevelt's policies in national politics. It was Roosevelt who had sought to steer national thinking along liberal lines and to destroy the predominance of the older conservative philosophy. By 1908, his campaign to establish a center between progressives and reactionaries was having some success. Taft was the symbol of Roosevelt's liberalism. Foraker posed as the symbol of reaction. Local leaders in Ohio were caught in the usual dilemma. Loyalty for past favors demanded their support of Foraker. It was to their long-run self-interest, however, to move over to the Taft camp. They looked to the future and forgot the past.

As a result of the contest in Ohio, Taft now had other advantages in his campaign for the presidential nomination. He had come out of the conflict with clean hands. He made no compromise with Foraker and he could now carry on his national campaign without fear of being charged with hypocrisy in his endorsement of Roosevelt's policies. Taft's independence in politics had been tested and he was not found wanting. He benefited also from the fact that the cycle of Ohio Republican politics had made another sharp swing. A new organization had taken over leadership from Foraker and Dick. Nearly twenty years of active leadership in Ohio politics were drawing to a close for Senator Foraker. Dick's strength declined also as Theodore E. Burton gathered his forces together in northern Ohio. Taft was able to benefit also from the general belief that a new era of democratic control in party affairs was opening for Ohio Republicans. His use of the direct primary and his willingness to support the direct election of United States senators indicated that his era of leadership for Ohio Republicans would be one in which the rank and file of the party shared in making important decisions.

A final advantage gained by Taft was perhaps the most important one. Taft now had the full support of the most potent factor in his national campaign, Theodore Roosevelt. Roosevelt's search for a leader of the liberal group was over. He had found not only a person who shared his own philosophy but also one who was a leader of his own state party. Taft had won the leadership in a manner which made Roosevelt respect him more than ever. The President now viewed Taft not only as a man who could be nominated by the Republican National Convention but also as one who would be a good president.

Secure in his hold on the Ohio Republican party, Taft faced his opponents elsewhere in the nation. His campaign became a zealous one because he was far more confident than he had been in 1906 or 1907. Mrs. Helen Taft and Charles P. Taft urged him to undertake a more strenuous campaign. He did not need to worry about money because Charles P. Taft and later Myron T. Herrick would supply the necessary financial backing.[89] The Taft "bandwagon" was rolling. Ohio Republicans were certain that Republicans throughout the country would join the movement to support Ohio's favorite son.

George W. Goethals and the Problem of Military Supply

Daniel R. Beaver
UNIVERSITY OF CINCINNATI

In mid-December, 1917, Secretary of War Newton D. Baker, in an effort to rebuild the shattered public image of the American War Department, named George W. Goethals to the dual post of Acting Quartermaster General and Director of Storage and Traffic in the War Department General Staff.[1] The appointment to the War Department was in part to associate the General's reputation with the war government, in part to use his genuine ability, and in part to take advantage of his well-known connections with the Republican party to meet charges that the war was a Democratic monopoly. From the moment of his appointment, Goethals struggled to bring about ordered change in the logistical support of the war. He sought information to make possible rational planning for the future and tried to standardize as many items of military equipment as possible. He fought changes and modifications in existing supplies, preferring second-class material in sufficient quantity to inadequate supplies of potentially superior hardware. He helped plan the 1919 military program, striving to bring the various supply and troop shipment programs proposed by General John J. Pershing and the American Expeditionary Force into line with existing ship tonnage. Indeed, in July, 1918, when his work brought him into conflict with the AEF, he was considered for the command of all military supply organizations, including those under Pershing's control in France. Working outward from his posts of Quartermaster General and Director of Storage and Traffic, he strove to bring all the army purchasing, storage, and transport under his direction. With virtual carte blanche from Secretary of War Baker's office and support from Chief of Staff Peyton C. March, he had by the end of hostilities concentrated power, contrary to tradition, in a newly created General Staff post, the Division of Purchase, Storage, and Traffic.

Goethals' innovations flew in the face of General Staff theory which dictated that the role of the staff was planning and supervisory rather than operational, but the General was never one to be held back by precedent. He was responsible for planning the movement of supplies and the procurement of war material on a massive scale. Necessity dictated, or so it seemed to Goethals, that the vast army supply system be brought under a central direction. His decision to press for such a course brought about a fundamental change in the relationship between his department and the purchasing bureaus of the War Department. Human relations played a role as well, and the consolidation of direct control over military purchasing, storage, and transportation in the General Staff reflected the interaction of personalities and events characteristic of men in crisis as much as any theory of organization and administration.

Goethals was also in touch with the great civilian agencies—the War Industries Board, the War Shipping Board, and the Railroad Administration. But at war's end, Goethals had not yet drawn all the reins of command into his hands. Conditions were so grave he predicted that in a short time the Army in France would face substantial, if not overwhelming, problems of supply. Fortunately the fighting ended before it could be seen whether his predictions were correct. There is insufficient space here for an investigation of all Goethals' activities during the critical months from January, 1918, to the armistice, but an analysis of his work and of his colleagues in organizing military procurement in the General Staff and in developing certain fundamental relationships with the War

Industries Board gives important insights into the relative significance of men and organizational structures and reveals something of the impact of World War I on American society.

Goethals did not want the War Department appointment. He preferred to be in France with Pershing. Shortly after arriving in Washington in December, 1917, he wrote former President Theodore Roosevelt:

> I find myself in anything but a pleasant situation. When the order came I was in hopes that I was going to take hold of the communications in France and was hardly prepared for this. How long I am going to last here depends upon the support received and the lack of interference.[2]

Goethals knew supply had already proved a burying ground for military reputations, and the situation looked forbidding indeed. Military purchasing was carried on by five separate bureaus under a complicated procurement system which made it difficult to ascertain which department was responsible for certain purchases, much less to decide how much material should be purchased.[3] War Department bureaus were organized vertically. A bureau purchased certain goods, sometimes even manufactured it, and controlled it from its point of origin to its point of distribution. Such an organization established five parallel purchase, distribution, and issue agencies that were bound to compete if uncoordinated. When the war began, the bureaus went into the market, placing contracts wherever possible, competing with others for existing finished goods and raw materials. Eastern manufacturing areas of the country were congested with war work, and there seemed to be little hope of organizing military procurement under the existing system.

One of Goethals' great strengths as an administrator was his ability to judge men and his capacity to delegate authority. Within a month of his appointment, he empowered H. M. Adams and Colonel H. G. Wells to handle problems of transportation and storage respectively. At first both officials merely supervised and coordinated wherever possible the activities of the various autonomous and semi-autonomous agencies. But as Goethals asserted his own influence throughout the supply organization, their roles became increasingly directive and operational, until in October, 1918, they assumed full operational control of War Department inland transportation and storage.

Goethals moved simultaneously to reorganize the Quartermaster Corps. He persuaded Robert J. Thorne, former president of Montgomery Ward and Company of Chicago, one of the leading merchandisers in the country, to assist him. Goethals chose to keep Thorne in a civilian capacity rather than to give him military rank.[4] Thorne set to work, building on his own experience in merchandising. He established in the Quartermaster Corps a requirements division that began to grapple with possible future demands for raw and finished materials. He analyzed existing contracts and was able to report to Goethals by April, 1918, precisely what had been purchased and what was yet to be purchased to fulfill the 1918 program and prepare for the anticipated 1919 program. Most significantly, he set it as his personal objective to convert the Quartermaster General's office into a purchasing agency and to divest it as much as possible of any operational functions.[5] Thorne carried his plan forward under Major General Robert E. Wood, one of Goethals' associates from the "canal gang," who was called home from France in late April, after Goethals took control of Purchase, Storage, and Traffic, to assume control of quartermaster affairs. In October, 1918, the title of Quartermaster General was abolished and Wood became Director of Purchases with Thorne as his assistant charged with the procurement of all standard supplies.[6]

Had conditions in Europe not required a substantial increase in American forces, further drastic changes in the War Department might not have been necessary. The original plans for the AEF, initiated in July, 1917, and approved in October, 1917, called for the movement of thirty American divisions to France by the end of 1918. During February and March, 1918, Goethals, as Director of Storage and Traffic in the General Staff, cooperated with the Operations Division in planning what seemed at that time a realistic program, one which simply continued the shipment of troops abroad until forty-two American divisions had appeared on the Western front in June, 1919.[7] But massive shipment of American troops abroad during April, May, and June, 1918, and Pershing's one-hundred division plan which arrived in Washington in early July, 1918, forced a major planning review. The War Department rejected the one-hundred division plan—it was simply beyond the capacity of the country in the time specified. Further investigation proved that an effort could be made with a reasonable chance of success to have eighty divisions in France by June, 1919.[8] The eighty division plan was officially accepted by President Woodrow Wilson on July 14, 1918.

If the 1919 plans were to succeed, procurement agencies would have to be organized in such a way as to make possible really accurate forecasts of requirements and more efficient use of the national potential. Goethals took that opportunity to secure more effective command of army procurement. In early January, 1918, shortly after he had been appointed acting Quartermaster General and Director of Storage and Traffic, another General Staff post was created, Director of Purchases and Supply, to which Brigadier General Palmer M. Pierce, former War Department liaison man with the War Industries Board, was appointed. At the same time, Edward R. Stettinius, a Morgan partner, was made Survey General of Supply and a little later Second Assistant Secretary of War, giving the Secretary of War's office close supervision, in theory at least, over military procurement procedures.[9] Pierce was in difficulties from the start. Stettinius had little confidence in him. Goethals complained that division of control between his office and Pierce's interfered with the implementation of the supply program, while Chief of Staff Peyton C. March harbored many reservations about his ability. It was only a matter of time before Pierce would go.[10]

The question of Pierce's future brought another personality, Assistant Secretary of War Benedict Crowell, into the story. None of the men associated with the supply program was immune from empire building, but Crowell seems open to that charge even more than Goethals or March. A metallurgical engineer from Cleveland, Crowell had been for years interested in military affairs. In 1916, Secretary of War Baker appointed him a civilian member of the Kernan Board which investigated emergency munitions production for the army. When war began, Crowell accepted a commission in the Ordnance Bureau where he served until Baker brought him into his office in November, 1917. Crowell was committed from theory and ambition to the view that control of supply should be concentrated in his office rather than in the General Staff, and it was possibly in hopes of achieving this ambition that, as Acting Secretary of War in Baker's absence on an inspection tour in France, he called for a full-scale study of the question of supply.[11] The Committee of Three which he named included Brigadier General Hugh Johnson, representing the General Staff,[12] Clarence Day of the Secretary of War's office, and Thomas N. Perkins from the Council of National Defense. It was to recommend a proper organization for the army's supply services.

The report of the Committee of Three marked an important stage in the history of supply in the War Department. First, it drew attention to the "vicious results . . . of the bureau system of supply" and warned that "serious disaster" threatened the war program "if the evils of the system were not speedily remedied." [13] Second, it rejected Crowell's contention, despite its consistence with existing General Staff theory, that supply responsibility should be concentrated in the office of the Assistant Secretary of War. Third, it identified function control and centralized decision making as keys to successful operation of the supply program. Supply was divided into six significant functions: raw materials control, priority, requirements, purchasing, production control, and accounting. It recommended that the Purchases and Supply Division of the General Staff, then headed by Pierce, be combined with the Storage and Traffic Division, to create one General Staff procurement and supply agency, the Purchase, Storage, and Traffic Division. Thus one man should ultimately be responsible for purchasing, storing, and moving all military supplies from the point of production to the French ports where responsibility would be assumed by the AEF.

The report of the Committee of Three became official policy on April 16, 1918, and ended Palmer Pierce's War Department career.[14] Everyone took it for granted that Goethals would get the new job, and the General wasted no tears at Pierce's departure. Writing to his son, Goethals gave this account of Pierce's relief:

> The news since last writing: as gleaned from the papers, is that they have gotten on to Palmer Pierce and he is to be relieved from the War Department and devote his time, energies and such abilities as he may have to the War Industries Board. March told me . . . that he wasn't any good and was thinking of having me absorb his duties . . . . Stettinius has qualified as Second Assistant Secretary of War and as his knowledge of Pierce's ability wasn't high, I am under the impression that I am indebted to him for my new duties.[15]

According to Goethals, March had ruthlessly read Pierce off, stating, "I have cut off your head and ordered you out of the War Department," and Goethals wrote his friend, Seth W. Tillman, "Pierce received quite a jolt. I chuckle over it everytime I think about it." [16]

The creation of the Purchase, Storage, and Traffic Division under Goethals brought a new and important personality to join Thorne in the general's coterie. Hugh S. Johnson became Director of Purchase and Supply in the General Staff and served Goethals loyally and efficiently until released for duty in the field in October, 1918. It was as Goethals' associate that he undertook the vast procurement responsibilities and gained the experience with industry which served him later in the National Recovery Administration. Johnson was appointed in early May at approximately the same time Wood returned from France to relieve Goethals of his direct responsibility for Quartermaster affairs.

With his flanks secured by loyal men in key supply posts, Goethals threw himself into his new General Staff job. The Purchase, Storage, and Traffic Division was conceived as having its most important relationship with the Operations Division and, of course, the supply bureaus, which were continued for the time being in their traditional semi-independent roles. The Division of Operations was charged with the formulation of the military program in terms of men and time. The new Purchase and Supply branch of the Purchase, Storage, and Traffic Division under Johnson received the program from the Operations Division and transmitted it to the supply bureaus, the most important of which was the Quartermaster Corps under Wood, for calculation of requirements and procurement of equipment necessary to carry out the program. The bureau chiefs, it was hoped, would gain a common interpretation of the military program and move in a coordinated way toward the common objective. Purchasing, transportation, and storage could be brought under General Staff control without rousing the enmity of the bureau chiefs or destroying utterly the purchase practices of the United States Army.[17]

Goethals also linked the Army more effectively to the nation's productive capacity. Army programs and Army orders came increasingly to shape the business life of the country. Since the War Industries Board's organization during the summer of 1917, relationships of its members and those of the Army had been difficult to say the least. The Army did not deal with the board through one agency, rather it moved through the representatives of the respective bureaus. Thus at least five independent bureaus had to be heard before any major policy was decided. Duplication and inefficiency were of increasing concern. The modest thirty-division program could have been fulfilled with the existing administrative structure, but the 1919 program and the tremendous weight it would place on the economy made it imperative that more care than previously be exercised in letting contracts.[18] The Committee of Three had recommended that a single representative, the Director of Purchase and Supply, be the means through which the Army's needs were represented to the board. Goethals adopted the substance of its proposal. Ultimately, as Army programs came increasingly to shape the business life of the country, Goethals himself served as the military representative on the WIB's vital Priorities Board, while Hugh Johnson, as Director of Purchase and Supply, handled routine matters of requirements, clearance, and production.[19]

Johnson's most significant contribution was the War Department commodity committees which he ordered established during April and May, 1918, to parallel those already created in the War Industries Board. Each committee controlled a particular product, such as wool, rubber, steel, hardware, and, in most cases, the ranking officer of the War Department commodity committee sat as the Director of Purchase and Supply's representative on the War Industries Board commodity section. Thus it became possible to make an appraisal of the nation's productive capacity and to compare it effectively with the Army's supply requirements.

Peyton March later wrote of Johnson's efforts:

> A record of this work . . . is really the whole story of the economic mobilization of the nation's resources . . . . It was through the contacts of the chairmen of the Army commodity committees with the commodity sections of the War Industries Board that plans were worked out . . . in meeting the urgent and rapidly changing needs of the Army supply program. If the United States should ever again be involved in a war comparable in magnitude with the recent war, one of the first steps which would need to be taken would be the reconstitution of a set of commodity committees similar to those which served the army during the late emergency. This should be done in any event whether or not an organization similar to that of the War Industries Board is to be created.[20]

The April reorganization which established a supervisory function in the General Staff over supplies seems to have been simply a first step in Goethals' plan. In late May and June, he began on a massive scale to shift procurement of standard articles to the Quartermaster Department, while the purchase of technical items remained in the hands of the regular bureaus. In mid-June Goethals prevailed upon Gerard Swope, of the Western Electric Company, to assist him in carrying his plans to fruition.[21] With the help of Johnson and other officers from Goethals' staff, and in consultation with certain bureau representatives, especially Wood and Thorne, Swope developed a plan which would create a central agency to procure all standard articles of Army supply and exercise direct control over storage and embarkation. As Swope envisioned it, the Director of Purchasing, Storage, and Traffic would assume full responsibility for the supply program, thus incorporating in the General Staff the vital supply and procurement functions formerly exercised by the bureaus. The bureaus would be absorbed administratively into the General Staff, while their purchase and issue functions were to be distributed among branches of the Division of Purchase, Storage, and Traffic.[22]

Swope's plan encountered considerable opposition, not only from the bureau chiefs who considered the whole affair an insult to tradition and a blow at their not inconsiderable accomplishments thus far in the war, but also from Assistant Secretary Benedict Crowell who still hoped to bring all supply under the control of his own office.[23] March hesitated to accept so revolutionary a proposal, causing Goethals to fret and fume for over a month.

Goethals persuaded Crowell to hold up his own plans until Swope's project was given a fair trial. Daily Goethals opportuned March for a decision, but no judgment was made until late August.[24]

March's final decision was a unique one, understandable only within the critical circumstances in which it was made. March tried to keep some grip on staff tradition and theory. Civilian and military control of supply and production was thoroughly mixed, attention being given essentially to the personal qualities of the men charged with supply responsibilities. War material for the 1919 campaign had to be procured and transported on schedule and Goethals' method seemed to be the most promising scheme available. But General Order 80 which carried the military portions of the reorganization into effect could be interpreted to mean that the Director of the Purchase, Storage, and Traffic Division still exercised supervisory and planning functions only.

When Goethals read the order he went straight to March and stated that he could not assume responsibility for the 1919 program unless he was granted operational control as well as supervision of the supply program. He demanded that Crowell be ordered specifically to stay out of Purchase, Storage, and Traffic affairs. In other words, Goethals must be in a coordinate rather than subordinate position in the War Department, responsible directly to the Chief of Staff and ultimately to Secretary Baker rather than to Crowell.[25] March acceded, apparently in part because of his own distrust of Crowell, in part to retain Goethals' undisputed ability in the War Department. The transfer of operating functions began in late September, 1918, and the major part of the project was complete by the armistice. The traditional bureaus virtually disappeared. They were replaced by a highly centralized purchasing agency closely associated with the General Staff.

For purposes of planning, the Director of Purchase, Storage, and Traffic was in direct liaison with the Operations Division of the General Staff which set the future military program. The Director of Purchases translated those requirements into wool, cotton, steel, and the myriad other materials required by the war effort. Storage and transportation policies were centralized in the same division, and the War Department linked with the national economy through the commodity sections and priorities board of the WIB. All concerned were aware that the Purchase, Storage, and Traffic Division was outside the planning and coordinating role by tradition assigned to the General Staff. Writing after the war, one anonymous champion of General Goethals claimed:

> These principles were not in accordance with those fundamental principles upon which the General Staff was established . . . . Officers of the Army who knew the history of the origins and development of the General Staff and who understood its functions were of the opinion that the assigning of executive and administrative functions to a Division of the General Staff, even in time of war, was a mistake.[26]

Upon Goethals' retirement in March, 1919, Major General William Burr returned executive control over all operational functions to the bureaus, reserving to the Purchase, Storage, and Traffic Division only the legal General Staff functions of coordination, supervision, and carrying to the supply services the decisions and orders of the Secretary of War.[27] But even Burr's more modest program was not a success. As the same anonymous spokesman wrote:

> The capable energetic young businessmen who had been called to service by General Goethals for his organization had returned to civilian life and their places had been taken by officers of the Army, the most of whom had no knowledge of the new system, had never been connected with it, and many were not loyal to it . . . its failures were due not to a faulty system but to inability or unwillingness of new officials to apply the war-time methods to the . . . work to be done. New methods require new men, but under the circumstances officers tied by tradition and practice to prewar methods had to be used.

Admittedly, the memorandum concluded, there had been shortcomings in the effort. But Purchase, Storage, and Traffic was a pioneering attempt to organize the industrial might of the United States in support of a massive military program.[28]

The changes that occurred in the War Department and in the General Staff were only part and perhaps a less important part of the war's impact. It is possible in this essay only to make tentative judgments about the wider effects on the industrial life of the nation. Despite grave misgivings on the part of substantial portions of the business community, state governments and, indeed, many federal officials, events pushed the nation away from traditional lines of individual enterprise and toward a highly organized national endeavor. Incidents such as seizure of railroads, shipping, and manufacturing plants, and the national allocation of raw materials were not accepted without protest. When automobile manufacturing was curtailed in the summer of 1918, the industry objected vigorously, insisting that the military program was unrealistic and that such government regulation was a violation of traditional national policy.[29] Edward M. Hurley of the War Shipping Board wrote Charles Schwab of the Emergency Fleet Corporation in July, 1918:

> Businessmen are claiming that their industries are being shut down by the War Industries Board and that all branches of the Government have enormous stocks of materials on hand which cannot be used for several months and some branches of the government are manufacturing materials which cannot be shipped for a year or two.[30]

But as the war grew in intensity such protests became the exception rather than the rule.

The *Iron Age*, spokesman for the nation's more important steel producers, which had at the beginning of the war seen little need for massive national regulation or regimentation, commented in April, 1918:

> A nation in such a war as this goes through a certain series of psychological reactions. Eventually a stage is reached where there is a steady plodding, a serious grind, but that is after years. The nation is then as fully permeated with the spirit of war service as it can be. The adopted attitude is so complete, and the public regulations are so well formulated and far reaching, that there is practically no occasion left for individual initiative.

The editorial stated immediately that the United States had not yet reached such a stage, but it continued:

> It is no case of the individual or the nation doing a bit, but a case of doing the best, of omitting nothing that can be done. The United States entered this war with no pledge of a portion of national or individual effort but with a pledge of everything . . . . There is no outside standard. The standard to be obtained is the utmost that it is possible to attain.[31]

The massive procurement program superintended by Goethals and his colleagues required of the business community levels of organization and control previously considered unwise or unnecessary. As the Purchase, Storage, and Traffic Division through its commodity sections established effective liaison with the War Industries Board, the latter organization reached out into the country's grass roots to support the war. Requirements were assessed and priorities assigned. Unused plants were located and new facilities developed. A project begun in 1916 to make an industrial inventory of the United States was given added impetus and an economic census was undertaken to seek out available resources.[32]

During the summer of 1918, the WIB organized the country into twenty-one production zones. Key businessmen in each production zone were assigned to resource advisory committees to help locate unused plant capacity, while local chambers of commerce helped create subordinate committees in the manufacturing centers within each zone. The regional committees developed an internal dynamism of their own—advising Army supply agencies of available plants, providing the WIB with information about plant conversion and new construction, and acting in some cases as contract agents in their production zone in securing government work. Franklin D. Crabb, chairman of the Regional Advisory Committee in Kansas City, wrote his opposite number in Cincinnati, "We find from experience that it will be absolutely necessary for us [to have a regional representative in Washington, D.C.] in order for us to secure any business for our manufacturers." [33]

By war's end, the important manufacturing regions of the country had lobbyists with access to the Army supply agencies and WIB boards in Washington. The Army was king; its demands more significant than prewar ideologies or traditional politics. In July, 1918, Samuel Vauclain, president of the Baldwin Locomotive Works and chairman of the locomotive committee of the WIB, stated well the impact of the war on the businessmen of the nation:

> The Secretary of War says "we want those locomotives, now you get them," by George, we will have to get them whether the domestic business stops or not, because the first business today is to fight this war. It does not make any difference what else there is.[34]

The Army's supply experience during World War I reflects the old maxim so well stated by Harold Ickes, who wrote of his experience as petroleum administrator during World War II:

> Able people working in accordance with a sound, clear-cut plan of organization are prime requisites to successful administration. Having both you can't miss . . . . With only one you are seriously handicapped—without either—God help you! [35]

Goethals' experience reflected that of Ickes. The General had to build a new organization and at the same time avoid interfering with the production, allocation, and transportation of material to the American Expeditionary Force. The success—limited as it was—of the Army's supply program was due primarily to the driving spirit of a few key men who made the system work in spite of poor liaison and inadequate organization.

The charge is well founded that the administrative innovations, especially in functional purchasing, were carried out in most cases too late to influence the outcome of the war. The supplies that were delivered in France had been contracted for under the old bureau system, and Major General Henry Sharpe in particular deserves more credit than he has received for his work during the first hectic months of the war. But Goethals and his colleagues, especially through their attention to neglected questions of storage and transportation, did make possible during the summer of 1918 the movement of materials from factory to seaboard and avoided the congestion that had plagued the country during the previous fall and winter. Peyton C. March wrote later of Goethals' contribution:

> The work he did as the virtual chief of supply of the Army far transcended in magnitude and certainly equally in importance in its effect on world history, the construction of the Panama Canal. Yet, he is known only for the latter work, while his great work as chief of supply is completely unknown to the general public.[36]

In a broader way, few in the War Department, including Goethals, grasped the possible future significance of the war effort.[37] Possibly Gerald Swope and Hugh Johnson understood that localism and bureaucratic independence had been struck important blows. The systematic association of the Army, the War Industries Board, and representatives from every part of the American economy in a great national enterprise was a catalytic agent in preparing the country for national planning. But most Americans merely sensed that the war's dynamism carried further than the lives affected, the treasure expended, the temporary dislocation endured. *Everybody's Magazine* caught the popular mood in an introduction to a popular series of articles, "After the War." It stated:

> The key to the future is not a matter of prophecy, but one of close observation, and diagnosis. Nothing will come out of this war that was not in it. The changes to come are going on under our noses; they have been observable since the beginning of the century; the war has merely quickened a tendency long developing. They are so definite and fundamental that their larger effects can be completed and realized before the end of the century.[38]

But *Everybody's* never did define precisely the condition it described. Something important had happened, but it would be decades before the nation could be brought to see that the war and its demands, as much as any other force, had shaped the course of American society.

The British Labour Party and the Paris Settlement

Henry R. Winkler
RUTGERS UNIVERSITY

By the end of World War I the Labour party had become the leading British advocate of a generous peace of reconciliation. Although there were differences of emphasis within its ranks, the party was able to reach something like a consensus in its rejection of any programs of conquest and annexation and in its support for a permanent international organization to ensure the durability of the peace.

The consensus had come about slowly. At the beginning of the war the constituent Independent Labour party had remained consistent with Labour's prewar views, emphasizing the British government's share in the responsibility for the convulsion and demanding from the start the early negotiation of peace. The trade union majority of the Labour party, on the other hand, had joined with the Fabian Society in supporting the war and by implication at least the view that it must be fought to a finish. The fact that the Labour party had permitted its leader, Arthur Henderson, to join the Coalition government in 1915 meant almost inevitably that the I.L.P. would be the most active part of the Labour party in developing a conception of postwar international policy unshackled by the limitations of official collaboration with Liberals and Conservatives.

These sections of the labour movement, nevertheless, eventually reached sufficient agreement to support a *Memorandum on War Aims* which may, without serious exaggeration, be labeled the first major pronouncement on foreign policy in the history of the Labour party. By early 1918 both the Labour party and the Trades Union Congress had accepted the *Memorandum.* After it had been adopted with little change by an Inter-Allied Labour and Socialist Conference held in February, 1918, the Independent Labour party had endorsed it as a contribution to the discussion of the peace settlement, while reserving its approval of certain of the specific proposals. The coincidence of views was in part made possible by the resignation of Henderson from the War Cabinet after the debacle of the Stockholm Conference in the summer of 1917. The Labour party continued to be represented in the Coalition government, but Henderson's resignation gave it a freedom of action, one of the results of which was vigorous support of the policy outlined in the *Memorandum.*

In brief, the *Memorandum on War Aims*—and it should be clear that in the circumstances of the times "foreign policy" and "war aims" are almost synonymous terms—denounced secret diplomacy, imperialism, and conscription; demanded that foreign policy be placed under the control of popularly chosen legislatures; advocated the limitation of armaments and the abandonment of their private manufacture; and argued for the need to achieve complete democratization of all countries. It pleaded, most importantly, for the creation of a League of Nations, which not only all the belligerents but every other independent state should join. The Labour proposal for the League envisaged an international court for the settlement of disputes and an international legislature for the gradual development of a binding system of law.[1]

The *Memorandum,* which preceded both Prime Minister David Lloyd George's important statement on war aims of January 5, 1918, and President Woodrow Wilson's Fourteen Points, became the platform upon which the labour movement carried its case to the country in 1918. By that year the official leaders of the Labour party were unquestionably the foremost political force behind the drive for a moderate peace. In effect they pleaded for a generous reconciliation with the enemy, whether as a result of negotiation or after he had been defeated. Since they were convinced that a League of Nations was fundamental to such a reconciliation, many of them came to believe that President Wilson's views were close to their own. When the Armistice was finally achieved, therefore, they looked with some hope to the forthcoming conference called to discuss the "preliminaries" of peace.[2]

It is doubtful, however, that this official position faithfully reflected the attitudes of labour's rank and file. For the moment the Labour party's leaders were out of step with most of their followers. As the war drew to a close, majority sentiment was represented neither by the Arthur Hendersons nor the Ramsay MacDonalds, but rather by men such as Robert Blatchford, the Socialist pioneer whose anti-German strictures before the war had helped estrange him from the party. Unlike some of the spokesmen for labour's extreme right wing, Blatchford considered it desirable to establish a League of Nations. But he wished to see it made up of the Entente Powers reinforced by the inclusion of certain neutrals. He thought it right and necessary to exclude the Central Powers for a time. War, he wrote, came not so much from economic causes as from the dynastic ambitions of autocracies. Hence, since such dangerous ambitions were to be apprehended only from the Central Powers, the first and chief duty of a League of Nations must be to protect the world's peace against them.[3] Advocates of an all-inclusive international organization denounced Blatchford's support for the "old balance of power theory,"[4] but their criticisms hardly conceal that his comments rang the changes on a very popular tune.

If evidence is wanting to demonstrate these popular attitudes, it may be found in the results of the December, 1918, General Election. During the election campaign, labour candidates made their case largely on the basis of the party's foreign policy views. Leaflets poured from the press attacking the past conduct of foreign affairs, demanding the "democratization" of foreign policy,[5] hammering home the thesis that the only way to end war was through a League of Nations, and insisting that a League of the present allies would be no League at all, but a military and political alliance made against another such alliance and looking toward another war.[6]

The Prime Minister read the popular temper much more accurately than the authors of these manifestoes. The campaign waged by many Coalition candidates was in effect one loud cry for vengeance. The electorate, grateful to the men who had brought the war to a successful end, were more than willing to respond to sweeping accusations and extravagant promises. The Opposition was swept aside. Although the Labour party returned fifty-seven members to Parliament as compared with forty-two in 1910, most of its representatives came from the trade union groups whose views toward the war and the peace were relatively close to those of Lloyd George and his supporters. With the exception of J. R. Clynes and J. H. Thomas, virtually every political leader of labour was rejected. Ramsay MacDonald, Arthur Henderson, Philip Snowden, all were defeated. To a country flushed with victory, their warnings that peace must be built on more than punishment hardly seemed worthy of attention.[7] Distrusting Lloyd George, they learned that they could not yet look to the people to compel him to work for the kind of peace that they desired. Yet, for a time at least, they were optimistic, counting on the President of the United States to use his enormous prestige in behalf of a settlement that they could support.

This is not to say that Labour party strategists were content to accept whatever lead was furnished by Wilson. On May 30, 1918, the first meeting of the party's new Advisory Committee on International Questions had been held.[8] In the months that followed, the Advisory Committee had undertaken to analyze some of the generalizations embodied in the party's policy statements. The result was a series of confidential briefs, marshaling information and presenting recommendations to the Labour party Executive and the Parliamentary Labour party.

Most significant among these reports was one that discussed the party's support for a League of Nations. The report opened with some well-worn ideas about the organization of an international body. But in the light of the later history of Labour party attitudes, the next section, dealing with the sanctions of the proposed organization, is vitally important. The Advisory Committee raised the question of how the nations of the League might coerce an offender. The answer, they felt, depended upon whether or not the various states remained armed. If they were to disarm, retaining only police forces to keep internal order, then a refusal of all intercourse with the offending state would probably be enough to bring it to reason. If the nations remained armed, it was conceivable that one of them might make an armed attack on another. In that case all the other members must be prepared to employ their forces to protect the member attacked. Armed force, the memorandum admonished, must be met by armed force or it could not be met at all.

This early warning of the need for military sanctions was coupled with a cautious approach to the question of disarmament. Granting that the smooth working of a League would be facilitated if all states disarmed at once, the Advisory Committee acknowledged that an immediate and complete disarmament, however desirable, was hardly to be expected. Short of that, they thought it might fairly be anticipated that, as the years passed and the proposed League demonstrated its ability to maintain the peace, the gradual disappearance of mistrust would make possible a gradual reduction and final disappearance of national armaments.

But while recognizing the need for coercion, the Advisory Committee stressed that a genuine League would have to undertake positive tasks of international cooperation, for these would do more for peace than any threat of coercion. From the outset the League should coordinate such undertakings as the control of backward areas and of international communications, the development of labour legislation, and the continuation of the joint purchases and distribution of materials inaugurated by the Allied nations as a wartime necessity. In the long run, the memorandum concluded, the habit of cooperation might bring nations to regard international war as contrary to good morals and good policy just as they now considered civil war to be.[9]

The implementation of labour's demand for an idealistic peace posed serious problems. Aside from Wilson, the Allied leaders who would determine policy at Paris appeared to offer little hope. Georges Clemenceau was already making plain his certainty that France required a system of alliances and strategic frontiers. Lloyd George's intransigence during the election campaign convinced the Labour party leaders that he would demand a vengeful settlement at Paris, while his failure to appoint a labour representative to the British delegation merely added to the mistrust with which he was regarded.[10] Two lines of action, accordingly, were adopted in an effort to influence the postwar settlement: a campaign in the labour press and from the platform to work up support for the socialist peace program; and an attempt to mobilize international socialist and trade union opinion through conferences to be held while the Peace Conference at Paris was in session.[11]

Carl F. Brand has demonstrated how fully the British Labour party and its allies supported President Wilson in the months following the Armistice.[12] As early as November, 1918, the Union of Democratic Control, most of whose major figures were by now affiliated with the Labour party, addressed a long letter to the President urging him to insist on the implementation of his Fourteen Points. Hailing his declaration of January 8, 1918, as one marking a new departure in the course of human affairs, the U.D.C. warned that his purposes would be fatally subverted if the Peace Conference should prevent the Russian people from determining their own form of government or if it should seek to impose crushing indemnities upon defeated peoples now striving to establish new regimes under the most difficult conditions. In addition the U.D.C. cautioned against the seizure of territory by the victorious powers no less than against the placing of further restrictions on the international flow of goods. Finally, in a slashing reference to what they feared was official British policy, the U.D.C. protested against any refusal to include naval disarmament in a general program of disarmament.[13]

In much the same spirit, a series of popular demonstrations was inaugurated. On January 2, 1919, for example, at a mass meeting in Albert Hall, leaders of the Labour party and the Trades Union Congress demanded the conclusion of a "Wilson Peace" and sponsored resolutions assuring Wilson that British Labour stood behind him in his efforts to achieve it.[14] The tone of much of this agitation may be summarized in a few words that appeared in the labour press on January 18. "The world," wrote George Lansbury, "must have a peace based on the principles adopted by Dr. Wilson or civilization will perish. The imperialists are in their last ditch and will die fighting to the last. . . . The Americans are eager for

British help. They look across the channel for a sign that our people understand that their president is the apostle of humanity." [15]

Support for Wilson, however, did not mean that labour was certain that his views would prevail. Indeed, even as the Peace Conference assembled, there were voices cautioning that too much must not be expected of him. As the American President made his swing through England, France, and Italy, a few of labour's most important spokesmen began to point to the dichotomy between his principles and the plans of other allied leaders. When Clemenceau publicly avowed his adherence to the "old system" of alliances and the balance of power, both A. N. Brailsford and Philip Snowden drew pessimistic conclusions.

Brailsford was perhaps the outstanding labour journalist of the period and already an important member of the Advisory Committee on International Questions. He warned that the kind of League of Nations to which Wilson looked forward would be impossible if the world were first to be constituted on Clemenceau's system of alliances. Such a system meant perpetual feud and the studied, deliberate, official fomentation of nationalist passions. Yet "Mr. Wilson has been silent—silent through many speeches. . . . He has moved with smiles . . . among the men who are preparing a helot's future for the German nation and neither by appeal nor by argument has he said a word to cool the fever of vengeance or abate the demands of greed." [16]

Snowden, who in October, 1918, had cautioned a meeting in Glasgow against trusting in any "capitalist" League,[17] echoed Brailsford's words in only slightly more tentative language. Among those who knew President Wilson, he noted, there were differences of opinion as to whether he would be strong enough to give the world a peace in accordance with his declared aims. If he failed, America would probably withdraw from the Peace Conference, enter into competition with the other European powers, challenge the naval supremacy of Great Britain, and perhaps maintain some form of military service. In the light of recent declarations by Allied statesmen, Snowden's whole tone reflected serious skepticism about Wilson's ability to carry them along with him, whatever his own views.[18]

This skepticism was bolstered in some labour circles by the

conviction that the Allied governments were more concerned to crush the bolshevist regime in Russia than to bind up the wounds of war. George Lansbury's *Herald,* for example, professed to see a close connection between the "wanton delay" of the Peace Conference and plans to launch a "new and senseless and wicked war." [19] Snowden charged categorically that Allied policy in Russia was not directed against bolshevist excesses but rather toward the overthrow of a form of government objectionable to the capitalist class in other countries. Such a policy, he declared, was in reality a war upon a philosophy of social democracy. To him, it was clearly incompatible with a real European partnership based upon the recognition of equal rights and enforced by a common will.[20]

While British Labour, then, attempted to influence the pending peace settlement through its various organs of opinion, its program to mobilize international working-class pressure on the Paris proceedings culminated in the calling of the Berne socialist and trade union conference early in 1919. Despite the opposition of the Allied governments, delegates began to meet on January 26, and the official Labour and Socialist Conference was opened on February 3.[21]

Previously, when the project began to take shape for a labour conference to be held at the same time as the official Peace Conference, the Advisory Committee on International Questions had undertaken to prepare recommendations as to procedure. As early as November, 1918, the Committee circulated a memorandum, written in large part by G. D. H. Cole, outlining the elements that should appear in a proposed labour charter. Arguing that any international labour conventions must have more binding international sanctions than in the past, Cole insisted that such sanctions could materialize only if the labour charter were made part of the fabric of an effective League of Nations. It would be necessary as part of the League to provide for the creation of a permanent body to initiate fresh international labour agreements and to supervise the administration of existing ones. The memorandum also contained Leonard Woolf's plea for official representation of all working-class parties at the Peace Conference, and a series of recommendations by Sidney Webb, reiterating the economic demands of the *Memorandum on War Aims.*[22]

Along with proposals for international labour legislation, the Advisory Committee again tackled the problem of international organization. Brailsford drew up a report in which he rejected the concept of a League of Nations consisting solely of government representatives. He recommended that the British delegation at Bern propose the inclusion in the League's machinery of a "deliberative international parliament" composed of delegations chosen by proportional representation from each national parliament. Its functions should be to create an international public opinion, to influence the other organs of the League, and to prepare for the governing body of the League suggestions for international legislation. In an obvious effort to conciliate those to whom any League was likely to appear as a capitalist instrument, Brailsford predicted that in the future the Labour and Socialist International would remain a powerful instrument of organization and agitation. It could never control the League, however, "unless indeed we look forward to the revolutionary triumph of the Soviet idea."

Those who rejected that conception were bound to work for the democratic evolution of the international body on the basis of parliamentary forms. This scheme, which reiterated demands made by Brailsford himself and by the Independent Labour party during the war, was considered by the Advisory Committee on January 21 and the decision taken to forward it to the British delegation at the Berne Conference.[23] It is of considerable interest, for despite its radical divergence from most of the conventional "Wilsonian" versions of a League of Nations, this was the project that in substance was pressed upon the Bern delegates by their British colleagues.

At Bern the British delegation was a strong one. MacDonald, Henderson, Ethel Snowden, C. T. Cramp, and J. M. McGurk represented the Labour party, while J. H. Thomas, Margaret Bondfield, G. H. Stuart-Burning, T. Greenall, and R. Shirkie came from the Trades Union Congress. From the start they played a leading role. In the eyes of the British Labour movement, the purpose of the conference was threefold: it must suggest solutions for the nationalist problems brought to a head by the war; it had to propose an antimilitarist policy, including a scheme for a really democratic League of Nations; and it had to organize a permanent body to safeguard and develop international standards for labour legislation.[24] Behind all these purposes, of course, was the need to ascertain whether the Socialist International could be rebuilt upon the ruins of war and revolution.[25] While other national groups had somewhat different conceptions of the purpose of the conference, it was within this framework that the British delegates carried on their work at Bern.

In the reconstitution of the Second International, Bern was a failure. The conference was divided by the emotion-charged question of who was responsible for the war, although a superficial formula of agreement was patched up. More importantly, delegates found it impossible to agree on their attitude toward bolshevism. The simmering controversy over democracy and dictatorship in the Socialist movement, symbolized in the conflicting Branting and Adler-Longuet resolutions, erupted with a force soon to split the old International. But on most of the issues confronting the Peace Conference at Paris, the Bern delegates were able to achieve virtually unanimous recommendations. With the proposed labour charter we are not concerned here, except to point out that indirectly at least the demands of British Labour may have influenced the creation of the International Labour Organization.[26] What is germane to this study is the illumination Bern provides on the emerging shape of Labour's foreign policy. Here the questions of the League of Nations and of territorial adjustments are most revealing.

The conference report on the League of Nations was introduced by Thomas and supported by Henderson, MacDonald, and Ethel Snowden. It is worth noting that the trade unionist Thomas pressed upon his colleagues the version of a League outlined for the Advisory Committee on International Questions by the Marxist Brailsford and supported during the war by the Left of the British Labour movement. There was, in other words, substantial agreement among the wings of British Labour. One can discern no sharp break between a solid, middle-of-the-road trade union element and a doctrinaire and extremist group of intellectuals on the Left. Indeed, at this stage Henderson and Thomas, neither of whom, for example, had ever joined the Independent Labour party, expressed views on a League of Nations difficult to distinguish from those of their more radical comrades.

Thomas introduced the resolution that argued that the League should be formed by the parliaments of the various countries. Representation in its central organ should not be by delegates of the executive branches of the government, but by delegates representing all parties in the constituent parliaments, thus ensuring "not an alliance of Cabinets or Governments, but a union of peoples." All nations organized on the basis of national self-determination should be part of the League. Those peoples who had not yet obtained the right of self-determination should be placed under the protection of the League and be encouraged and assisted to fit themselves for membership. All standing armies must be abolished and eventually complete disarmament brought about. Until then, any required armed force should be under the control of the League, which must also have the means of economic pressure at its disposal in order to enforce its decisions when necessary.

Expanding the conventional idea of an international court to arbitrate and mediate disputes, Thomas proposed that the court also have the power, where necessary, to rectify frontiers after consultation with the peoples concerned. Next he insisted that a major task of the League should be to promote free trade, the open door in colonies, the international control of world trade routes, along with the supervision of customs and the development of its power to regulate the distribution of foodstuffs and materials throughout the world. And finally, as Thomas pointed out, the resolution called upon the future League to establish, develop, and enforce an international labour charter. MacDonald, too, in an impressive speech, emphasized that the League must rest on disarmament and spoke out for an international council of representatives elected by the parliament of each nation. The drive of the British delegation largely moved the Bern assembly to accept unanimously the comprehensive statement introduced by Thomas. The leaders of the British Labour movement set their sights high in aiming at a system of international organization. Whether the more powerful statesmen at Paris would aim at similar targets remained to be seen.[27]

In the debate on territorial questions MacDonald also

played a leading role, and the final general resolution adopted at Bern reflected the vision of the British delegation fairly accurately. The Labour and Socialist Conference charged that the arbitrary and enforced union of peoples of different nationalities within a single state had been and always would be a cause of international disputes and a menace to peace. Accordingly, it laid down certain principles which in essence demanded self-determination for all nationalities under the protection of the League of Nations, advocated that the League guarantee the rights of minorities, and urged that the international body undertake the protection of the populations of dependent areas while fostering their training toward self-government. Rejecting any territorial settlement based on the claims of victory, strategy, or economic necessity, the Conference called upon the working classes to exercise all possible pressure on their governments in order to compel them to recognize these principles as necessary for lasting peace.[28]

Meanwhile, as labour drew up its blueprint for the postwar world, the shape of things to come was beginning to emerge at Paris. As the Peace Conference entered upon its deliberations after convening on January 18, there was some bitter criticism of its secrecy,[29] but on the whole the leaders of the British Labour party marked time until they could better judge the direction in which the Paris proceedings were moving. A small spasm of protest greeted the first public announcement of plans to make the major Allied Powers mandatories for the former German colonies,[30] but many labour spokesmen still were willing to count on President Wilson to block what they looked upon as the dangerous schemes of the Allied leaders.[31]

The first shock of disillusionment came with the publication of the Draft Covenant of the League of Nations on February 14. A few labour commentators greeted the draft with some degree of enthusiasm,[32] but, as its implications began to sink in, most of the labour press expressed the conviction that fundamental revision was necessary. Criticism was widespread, particularly on the Left. Snowden, who had never hidden his suspicions, branded the Paris scheme a fraud and expressed amazement that President Wilson should have given his support to such a flagrant device for constituting five Great Powers the dictators of the universe. It was grotesque to exclude more than two-thirds of Europe from the League and then to insert a condition that left it to the one-third to refuse to admit the two-thirds. The result would be the establishment of a counter-League and the rise of the old politics of Entente and Alliance all over again. Such a League, he warned, could become the most despotic instrument ever devised for crushing democratic movements.[33]

Snowden's charge of fraud was paralleled by other epithets. The *Herald* saw a plan not for a League, but for a "clique" founded on the principle of domination of the weak by the strong.[34] *Forward* saw in the Draft Covenant a shameless conspiracy. The Allied Powers had now appointed themselves a "League of Nations" with some outsiders like Siam and Spain thrown in for the sake of appearances. But Socialist Germany, Bolshevist Russia, and Republican Austria were to be regarded as degenerate pariahs. Such a League could succeed in keeping the world at peace—on its own terms. "Just as the armed highwayman keeps the timid old gent at peace, while he takes a gold watch and some coins 'under his tutelage.'"[35] The Union of Democratic Control, while welcoming the adoption of the principle of a League, regarded the Draft Covenant as undemocratic and inequitable in almost all its terms.[36]

Most of this group was pacifist in outlook and particularly disturbed that the League Covenant was to make provision for forcible sanctions. One spokesman was discouraged to note that the League had not succeeded in overcoming the old-time reliance upon physical force to enforce its decrees. There was no awareness that only a society of nations based on mutual trust and moral force could be really effective for the preservation of peace and good will. Altogether, the proposals seemed to envisage Anglo-Saxon hegemony in world affairs. And since President Wilson must be credited with good intentions, the whole Covenant seemed to resolve itself into the triumph of "Britannia über Alles."[37]

Only in the right wing of the labour movement was the Draft Covenant really accepted, and even here with little enthusiasm. The old-time *Clarion* partnership of Robert Blatchford and Alexander M. Thompson, in announcing its support, warned respectively that any League to be effective must possess the power as well as the will to enforce peace and that in any circumstances no League could succeed unless the United States, where it was getting a cool reception, participated.[38] For its part, the bellicose and nationalist organ of the British Workers' National League, the *British Citizen and Empire Worker,* conceded that the League of Nations would probably stop war for the present, not because of its existence but because men were temporarily tired of war. It was well enough to accept the League, but it was far from being humanity's Magna Carta: "it is mainly a patchwork of aspirations and good intentions strung together in a hurry to meet the convenience of President Wilson's domestic engagements." Not the League, but a stiff and punitive peace represented the ideal settlement to this intransigent journal.[39]

While the labour press was airing its reactions, the machinery for official consideration of the Draft Treaty was set in motion. On March 4, 1919, Charles Roden Buxton and Leonard Woolf, sitting as the Advisory Committee on International Questions, resolved to draw the attention of the Labour party Executive to the fact that the Draft Covenant did not fulfill certain vital conditions laid down by labour in its earlier demands. The Advisory Committee suggested in brief that amendment was required in the following four points if the Covenant were to conform to the expressed aims of the Labour party: the right for all civilized states to enter the League on equal terms; the establishment of a deliberative democratic assembly, representing peoples instead of governments and elected directly either from parliaments or from other organized democratic bodies; universal abolition of conscription; the mandatory system to be applied to all colonial possessions and protectorates instead of being confined to enemy territory.[40] The fact that the warnings of the former Liberal Buxton and the Fabian Woolf paralleled those sounded earlier by the more radical Brailsford is some indication of the general disappointment with which the various elements of labour greeted the Draft Covenant. It is well to note, however, that even at this early stage these members of the Advisory Committee did not attack the coercive features of the Covenant which were anathema to the Labour Left.

Further discussion among leaders of the Labour party and Trades Union Congress led to the acceptance of a series of twenty-two resolutions which were presented to a Special Congress of Labour party and trade union representatives on April 3. With Stuart-Bunning of the T.U.C. as chairman the meeting welcomed the publication of the Paris proposals, but endorsed the twenty-two amendments. As the amendments demonstrated, the strategists of the labour movement were disturbed at the way in which the League was to be constituted. Still holding out for proportional representation from national parliaments, they also demanded that the "Executive Council" of the League be expanded to eleven members including Germany and Russia.

These resolutions of the Special Congress asked for clauses in the Covenant guaranteeing that no armies would be raised by conscription and providing that both the manufacture of armaments and the maintenance of forces necessary for international police purposes be under the League's direct control. Further proposed amendments spelled out the view that the identification of aggression, application of sanctions, and declaration of war all ought to be under the aegis of the "Body of Delegates"—the later Assembly—rather than under a Council dominated by the Great Powers. In other words, the Assembly, not the Council, should have final authority.

Other familiar pleas appeared among the amendments. One called for a declaration in the Covenant urging national disarmament; another demanded that all colonies and native territories be under League mandate; a third insisted on direct and more adequate representation for labour in the proposed new international bureau of labour (the future International Labour Organization). And finally, still suspecting that Allied leaders were not serious about advocating an international organization, this labour conference supported President Wilson in his conviction that the Covenant should form a part of the peace treaty.[41]

This official position, which found more to criticize than to praise in the League Covenant, was, if more circumspect in its choice of words, nevertheless almost identical with the more colorful reactions in the labour press. As time went on, even some of those who had originally treated the Draft Covenant generously began to pick away at its supposed flaws. Most striking, perhaps, was the *New Statesman,* which came to the belated conclusion that "the lines of an international authority have not been firmly or boldly drawn; the Assembly is an unsatisfactory compromise between an Executive and a Legislature; there is only a shadow of an International Court of Justice; the problem of disarmament is shirked; the crucial sanction of the League is shadowy." [42]

Altogether, virtually all elements of importance within the labour movement, whether official or not, regarded the League of Nations as a vital test of the future being prepared at Paris. Even the Allied intervention in Russia, which was to elicit a constantly growing protest during 1919 and 1920,[43] tended to take second place to the Draft Covenant. The labour press was filled with denunciations of intervention,[44] and the special conference on April 3 passed an angry resolution demanding withdrawal of Allied troops from Russia.[45] Yet though it seems unquestionable that British Labour was at this moment most concerned with constructive plans for international organization it hoped to see developed by the Peace Conference, almost unanimously its spokesmen found themselves seriously disappointed by the first public proposals.

In addition to its various pronouncements, British Labour continued to take a leading role in the attempt of the Labour and Socialist International to influence the makers of the Peace Treaty. Two days after the announcement of the Draft Covenant, for example, Henderson, MacDonald, and Stuart-Bunning were part of a delegation that waited upon Clemenceau, as president of the Peace Conference, to present the resolutions adopted at Bern. Clemenceau agreed to lay the documents on the Conference table and referred the group to the various commissions responsible for particular problems. The interview, while cordial, was noncommittal, as was a discussion that the British representatives held with Lloyd George and Lord Curzon on February 21.[46]

The delegation to Clemenceau had been dispatched by the Permanent Commission of the Second International, which had been set up at Bern. Henderson was named a member of the three-man executive, while MacDonald and Stuart-Bunning were the other British members of the Commission. When this Permanent Commission met at Amsterdam on April 26, it was faced with a difficult situation. The Bern Conference had never really tackled the complex territorial questions that were plaguing the Peace Conference. It had proposed that the various national groups in the International work out their positions in advance and then hammer out a series of demands at Amsterdam. But by the end of April much water had flowed under the Paris bridges. At Bern, despite fundamental cleavages on crucial issues, the over-all atmosphere had been one of hopefulness. Two months later the Amsterdam Socialists looked upon Paris as the graveyard of most of their hopes.

The new spirit was quickly apparent when Henderson introduced a general resolution expressing dissatisfaction with the Draft Covenant and urging disarmament. The Amsterdam delegates decided that the resolution was not strong enough and appointed a committee, of which Stuart-Bunning was a member, to study the question. The work of this committee merged with the broader consideration of territorial questions. In the final drafting, the Socialist peace program reflected the suspicion with which its authors viewed the work of the Paris Conference.[47]

The Amsterdam resolutions began by supporting the right of independence for Finland, Georgia, Estonia, and Armenia. They protested against intervention in the internal affairs of Hungary, demanding that the Peace Conference not cut the country up until the populations of the regions in question had the opportunity to express their desires in a plebiscite conducted by the League. The Socialists asked that the Ukrainian people be enabled as soon as possible to decide for independence or for federal union with Russia. Applying the same standard of self-determination to Austria, they declared that German Austria had the right either to preserve its independence or, as the majority of the population now demanded, to unite the whole of its Austro-German territories with Germany. The Austrians must be permitted to oppose every attempt at separating national homogeneous territories against the will of their populations. The Permanent Commission refused to recognize historic or any other claims of alien nations to sovereignty over homogeneous German areas that formed a geographical unity with other German-speaking districts. Thus, not only did this resolution approve *Anschluss* with Germany if the Austrians wished, but it took sharp exception to Czech claims that the Sudeten

German districts of the Dual Monarchy must become part of the new Czechoslovak state.

While supporting the creation of the Polish state, the Amsterdam delegates demanded plebiscites to establish its frontiers with Germany where nationalities were mixed. As to the growing pressure for the establishment of a corridor, they damned all proposals that aimed to take from Germany territory, forming part of the eastern and western provinces of Prussia and inhabited by Germans, in order to cede it to Poland as an avenue to the Baltic Sea. With Danzig as a free port under the League of Nations, the Vistula River was enough to afford Poland free and assured access to the sea.

Turning to Western Europe, the Commission opposed all attempts, open or veiled, to separate the Saar, the Palatinate, and the left bank of the Rhine from Germany. Such moves would do violence to the principle of self-determination and would lay the foundations of new wars. Agreeing that Germany must pay reparations, the International's Permanent Commission proposed a series of safeguards to ensure that "economic annexation" for reparations purposes should not be used to bring about political annexation. In addition to these proposals, the Commission insisted that the Irish people be permitted to determine their own destiny, even if this should mean the political independence that they had the right to demand.

Socialist dissatisfaction with the Paris version of the mandates system clearly showed in a resolution that again requested that all colonies and dependencies whose peoples were as yet unable to stand alone, not merely the German colonies, be placed as wards of the more advanced states capable of exercising the responsibility. Denouncing imperialist annexations, the resolution asked that mandates not be assigned until the League of Nations was fully representative of the democratic nations, in other words, until nations like Germany became members. Finally, it urged that each mandate should be definite in the specific responsibilities imposed on the mandatory power and in its safeguards for the native population. Among the other resolutions was one recognizing the right of the Jewish people to create a national center in Palestine under conditions to be determined by the League of Nations.

All these proposals, in a sense, depended upon the League, which the International, like the British Socialists, regarded as the linchpin of the future. Approving the presentation of the plans for a League and for an international labour charter, the Commission warned that the League could attain its object—the methodical organization of a continuing regime of peace—only if certain conditions were met. It must be composed from the beginning of *all* the independent nations of the world willing to accept its obligations, having equal rights and duties and represented by delegations elected by their parliaments.

A supranational authority must be empowered to secure the fulfillment of all obligations undertaken. Moreover, the supranational authority must establish regulations aimed at the gradual abolition of all legal hindrances to international commerce and the international organization of world production and distribution. The League of Nations must at once take measures to prohibit fresh armaments, bring about the progressive reduction of existing armaments, and control the manufacture of such weapons as might still be permitted. The ultimate goal should be total disarmament on land and sea.

In order to prevent any danger to democracy, such armed forces as might be required by the international situation should, until total disarmament was effected, be placed under the control of the League. Members must submit all disputes to decision by the League through its court, binding themselves to accept these decisions and excluding recourse to war under any circumstances whatever. Finally, the governments must adopt the method of open diplomacy as the only technique guaranteeing that the claims of the different nations would be settled strictly on the basis of justice. These conditions, the resolution concluded, had not yet been realized by the Paris Conference. The Amsterdam Commission appealed, therefore, for "effective action" by the workers of all countries to raise their protest and demand that the League of Nations be organized on the solid basis of a durable peace.[48]

These detailed resolutions, in the drafting of which the British delegates took a central part, were the most thoroughgoing expression made by labour of its demurrers while the Paris Conference was in session. There is little indication, however, that at this stage they had any appreciable impact on its deliberations. The Amsterdam Commission saw to it that a Committee of Action, which had been set up at Bern and included MacDonald, Henderson, and Stuart-Bunning among its seven members, should remain in Paris in the hope of influencing the settlement, but whatever lobbying was attempted [49] appears to have had little concrete result. In part, of course, this reflected the fact that even the Paris negotiators were already face to face with a series of *faits accomplis,* as in the establishment of Poland and Czechoslovakia or the seizure of large parts of the Turkish Empire or the German colonies. But whatever its reasons, the disregard of labour's position ground in a lesson of weakness and impotence which contributed to a growing tone of frustration and bitterness in labour's reactions to the emerging settlement.

That lesson was further emphasized little more than a week later. On May 8 a summary of the preliminaries of peace, which had been presented to the German plenipotentiaries the day before, was released. Immediately British Labour began to develop its case against the treaty. Almost before the proposed terms had been circulated to the press, the Independent Labour party issued a manifesto charging that the proposed treaty was a "capitalist, militarist and imperialist imposition. It aggravates every evil which existed in 1914. It does not give the world peace, but the certainty of other and more calamitous wars." [50] On the same day the Labour party Executive issued its first manifesto which, while not so unrestrained, clearly was designed to put its objections on record as quickly as possible. Recalling labour's wartime struggle for a just settlement and its support of President Wilson's program, the Executive claimed that the published terms departed in certain essential particulars from Wilson's declarations and its own aims. Organized labour, which was not represented at Paris, could accept no responsibility for the violations of principle in the settlement. It called upon the working class to work for the eradication of the imperfections of the treaty and for its adaptation by the League of Nations to the needs of a changing European order.

Concretely, the Labour party manifesto deplored the treaty's failure to provide equality of trade conditions for all its signatories, warned that any permanent denial of a League mandate to Germany must result in international strife, and predicted that the increase in colonial territories under Allied control would involve a corresponding increase in military and administrative burdens for the Allied peoples. Agreeing that Germany must make preparations for civilian damage, the Executive nevertheless demanded that it should have representation on the Reparation Commission and that its total payment should take into account its obligation to meet the needs of its own population.

The Treaty, moreover, which imposed drastic disarmament upon Germany, included no provision for the progressive limitation of armaments of other signatories, with the object of finally arriving at general total disarmament. Similarly, while admitting the temporary French claim upon Saar coal, the Labour party Executive criticized the form of political and economic control envisaged in the treaty and protested against the attempt to separate the Saar from Germany permanently. Without attacking the arguments of France, the manifesto held that the inhabitants of Alsace-Lorraine should be consulted about their future, so as to remove a long-standing dispute from the common life of Europe. Plebiscites must be held in Malmédy and other contested areas between Belgium and Germany if the creation of another Alsace-Lorraine were to be prevented. As for Germany's eastern territories, the labour statement welcomed the plebiscite promised for the southern and eastern districts of East Prussia, but deplored the treaty's failure to apply the principle in delimiting other boundaries on the Polish-German and Czechoslovak frontiers.

Similarly, the people of German Austria ought to have free and unrestricted right to decide whether to join a federal Germany or remain independent. Any other solution would not only be an act of injustice, but the repression of national impulses might well imperil the peace of Europe. Noting that the workers always suffered most in international conflicts, the manifesto concluded with the hope that the treaty might even now be brought more into harmony with President Wilson's declaration that "all well-defined national aspirations shall be accorded the utmost satisfaction that can be accorded them without introducing new or perpetuating old elements of discord and antagonism that would be likely in time to break the peace of Europe and consequently of the world." [51]

This manifesto, then, outlined the major areas in which British Labour found the peace proposals to be wanting. Even more detailed was the statement issued on May 12 by the International's Committee of Action. Since MacDonald and Stuart-Bunning had collaborated with Renaudel of France in its composition, it reflected the further thinking of the leaders of British Labour as they took the time to study the projected treaty. The Committee of Action recalled that at Bern and Amsterdam the International had laid down four great principles upon which a just and lasting peace could be built. Like the British Labour party, the International agreed that reparation must be made for the wanton destruction of Belgium, northern France, and other invaded countries by the Central Powers. Second, it concurred that in redefining the national boundaries of Europe certain oppressed nationalities should be gathered into independent states, but held that in accordance with the principle of self-determination peoples should not be transferred from one state to another until they had been consulted. Next, militarism should be ended and a League of Nations representative of democratic influences established. Finally, the exploitation of native races by colonial imperialism should end.

Considering the peace proposals in the light of these principles, the Committee found much to praise, for example, the establishment of a League of Nations and the liberation of some peoples long kept under subjection. But when the terms were judged in their full effect, they contained much that was menacing to the future peace of the world.

The League of Nations in the first place retained all the defects identified at Bern and Amsterdam. It remained a league of governments and executives, not of peoples and parliaments. It did not compel its members fully to renounce recourse to war. It failed to include Germany and Russia, but seemed rather to be an instrument of the victorious coalition dominated by five Great Powers instead of an organ of international justice where all nations ought to find a place.

The limitation of German arms was necessary, but the Committee called upon the Allies themselves to indicate their intention immediately to reduce their armaments on land and sea. It noted, parenthetically, that the settlement of frontiers for military reasons and the predominance of strategic considerations in certain provisions of the treaty would tend to perpetuate armaments.

Polish boundaries were drawn in violation of the right of people to choose their political allegiance, while the division of Germany into two separate parts split by Polish territory must remain a source of trouble and ill will. The Saar proposals were animated by a spirit of annexation and of capitalist exploitation. The creation of French economic interests in the district, the setting up of a special administrative authority, and the plebiscite in fifteen years justified suspicions that what was sought was not only coal but territory, not compensation but dismemberment.

Like the Labour party Executive in its manifesto, the Committee of Action protested against the disposal of the German colonies, interpreting the denial of a mandate to Germany as imperialism satisfying itself with the spoils of war. In similar vein, the transfer to Japan of economic control in the Shantung Peninsula could be considered as nothing less than a frank recognition of the right of conquest. The faults were serious, making it plain that "this peace is not our peace and that the nations are still menaced by the policy of victors sharing spoils without thought of inevitable consequences."[52]

Not until June 1 did the members of Parliament who made up the weak Parliamentary Labour party join officially in commenting on the peace proposals. On that date a second manifesto was issued by the Executive of the Labour party in conjunction with the Parliamentary party. This brief statement rehearsed some of the major concrete objections already well ventilated in May, but charged that the treaty was defective not so much because of "this or that detail of wrong done," but fundamentally because it accepted and indeed was based upon the very political principles that were the ultimate cause of war. In customary fashion, the manifesto called upon the organized workers of all countries to join in an effort to bring the treaty more into harmony with the working-class conception of an enduring and democratic settlement. It was, however, unable to offer any prescription as to how this might be done immediately.[53]

In sum, aside from the territorial objections raised in these manifestoes, labour was most unqualifiedly exercised about the League of Nations. It placed great emphasis upon the introduction of a genuinely representative element into the machinery of the League, particularly on the representation of minority parties, believing that this would result in a true reflection of the main lines of political opinion in each country. And second, labour insisted that the League must be something more than a machinery of conciliation to prevent war; it must be a genuinely international body, coping with political, economic, and industrial problems, not only to prevent war but to ensure progressive development by friendly cooperation among all nations.[54] In the circumstances of 1919 this was a millennial conception, but it must again be emphasized that it was a conception held by both extremist groups on the fringes of the movement and by virtually all elements including the dominant leadership of the political party and the major trade unions.

Further evidence of this point of view is to be found in an important memorandum drawn up for the Advisory Committee on International Questions by Norman Angell. As the postwar years passed, the former Liberal Angell was to exercise a moderating influence on labour extremism and to help teach the movement that international authority required some sanction beyond the good will of sincere pacifists. But here, in a dispassionate analysis not designed for public consumption, he is a witness to the unanimity with which labour's vision of international organization differed from the future outlined in the Peace Treaty. According to Angell, the treaty neither fulfilled the promises made by the Allied governments nor conformed to justice and right. It was imperative to create an international system under which security, fair treatment, and economic opportunity would be ensured to all peoples, yet neither the treaty nor the League took even the first indispensable step toward accomplishing this. While the repressive and prohibitive features of the treaty were exceedingly severe and while the League Covenant provided elaborately for plans of coercion if its authority should be challenged, neither the one nor the other made provision for assuring the economic future or the political rights of the countries against which they were in fact directed.

The first task on the international scene, Angell suggested, was to establish a general organic law that should afford to all nations a minimum of right in the matter of access to raw materials, to markets, and to the resources of undeveloped countries, even if this necessitated crossing neighboring states to the sea. It was obvious that such an organic law would involve a limitation of national sovereignty. A society of nations that had complete sovereignty and independence was a contradiction in terms. The League must do the unprecedented things that President Wilson had once called upon it to do, regardless of whether great interests were challenged, national pride sacrificed, or some political factions in some countries made hostile.

This first task, then, was legislative in its nature and for that reason emphasis must be placed on the legislative functions of the League. But world legislation should not be the work of cabinets and executives that denied legislative powers at home. Yet cabinets and executives alone were represented in the proposed constitution of the League. More than ever, urged Angell, it would be necessary to insist upon the form of representation demanded by the Bern Conference. Only by some such representation of peoples as distinct from states and governments could the League become an instrument for ensuring continual and constitutional change of conditions which, if unchanged, would lead to conflict and war.

Finally, turning again to the economic side of the League, the memorandum warned that it would not suffice to establish an international regime of "equality," based on *laissez faire* and individual scramble. Wartime experience had shown the way to equitable control and distribution of the economic resources of the world. If such controls were placed in the hands of a completely democratic body, the workers of all nations would have some assurances of equality of treatment and would be in a position to exercise some check on the forces that had hitherto made for international conflict.[55]

While Angell concentrated on the spirit and structure of the

League of Nations, another Advisory Committee memorandum argued against the injustice and inadvisability of the repressive policy toward Germany. To maintain such repression implied that Poland, Rumania, Czechoslovakia, Yugoslavia, Italy, Japan, America, and Russia would remain at one in political purpose with France and England. If in the future Germany should, for instance, be able to detach Poland and Russia from the anti-German coalition, the present disarmament of Germany would immediately become ineffective. Since Poland was now to be armed as a measure against Germany, the greater would be the military power accruing to Germany "if the political policy which determines the direction in which the guns shall shoot is changed." Only by assuming about three decades of political unity among the states of the alliance, a unity for which there was no precedent in history, did the German policy of the treaty make sense.[56]

These Advisory Committee analyses were incorporated into a propaganda pamphlet issued by the Labour party under the authorship of Henderson.[57] Henderson followed the main lines of the Advisory Committee arguments and appended to his discussion of the peace terms the texts of the labour manifestoes of May 8 and May 11. Summing up labour's general reaction to the treaty, he declared:

The Treaty is based upon utterly inconsistent principles. The principles of justice and the League of Nations and the 14 Points are, it is true, included in the document, but only in the form of generalizations, aspirations, and vague formulae. Most of the actualities created by the terms, down to the minutest details, are governed by the idea of punishment, of strategy, or the snatching of some economic or territorial advantage for one or another of the Allies. The result of such a settlement can be predicted with certainty . . . . No nation of 60 million can be expected to acquiesce in the violations of nationality and the economic servitude imposed by this Treaty. The Allied Governments and the new League of Nations will therefore have to devote all their energies to the task of "keeping Germany down," and the peoples of the world will live under the shadow of the renewal of the war at the first favorable opportunity. Even if Germany and Russia are not driven into an alliance, every international dispute among the Allied Powers—the question of Fiume already proves this—will attain a dangerous and exaggerated importance as opening an opportunity to upset the unjust terms of this peace. There can be no security, no guarantee of peace, in the shadow of this settlement.[58]

Even more than Angell, Henderson symbolized the moderate, middle-of-the-road element in the Labour party. Yet his strictures against the treaty were at this stage difficult to distinguish from those of more extreme groups connected with Labour in one way or another. A case in point is the Union of Democratic Control. As we have seen, the U.D.C. was bitterly dissatisfied with the Draft Covenant of the League of Nations. It remained for the proposed treaty with Germany, however, to bring it to the pitch of passionate denunciation.

On May 9 its Executive Committee issued a long statement charging, like the official labour manifestoes, that the treaty violated the terms on the faith of which the German nation had laid down its arms. It constituted an indefensible breach of the very international morality that the Allied and Associated Powers had claimed to be fighting to ensure. For long they had insisted that their quarrel was not with the German people but with the rulers of the German state. Now, in the form of the new German Republic, they were dealing with the people. Yet the territorial arrangements concluded without consulting the peoples affected, particularly in eastern Germany, the Saar Valley, and Alsace-Lorraine, and were marked by the same lack of vision and disregard for human rights that the German government showed in 1871 and at Brest Litovsk. Poland, for example, which included large districts of a purely German population, must surely prove a center of national and cultural conflict in Europe.

But particular instances merely typified the general purpose underlying every section of the treaty. That purpose was obvious: to reduce the new democratic Germany to the position of a vassal state; to make its commercial recovery impossible; to drive it out of international life; and to crush the spirit of its people. Exclusion from the League of Nations, unilateral disarmament, the imposition of enormous and indefinite financial burdens, and the seizure of German colonies opened up for the Germans the prospect of becoming a "people of serfs working for their conquerors in arms."

Perhaps the German people would have to accept the treaty rather than see their children starve under the blockade, but the terms would rouse every true democrat to work ceaselessly for their revision. For its part the U.D.C. did not recognize the treaty as having any moral validity, but instead pledged itself to work for a peace that would correspond with President Wilson's Fourteen Points and with the aspirations and ideals of the common people everywhere.[59]

Here were the major lines of attack that the Union of Democratic Control was to pursue during the coming years. Under the leadership of E. D. Morel, the group was to make its particular cause the revision of the German settlement and was to use every available technique to create sympathy for Germany and contempt and anger toward its conquerors, above all toward France. And yet, as the May 9 statement demonstrated, it was at this early stage, despite its almost hysterical tone, quite close to the mainstream of labour policy in its assessment of the postwar settlement.

Despair at the character of the proposed peace ran through almost every quarter of the labour movement. In the press *Forward* featured an analysis by MacDonald, which charged that the provisions outlined were an attempt literally to destroy Germany in the interests of capitalist imperialism.[60] The *Labour Leader,* another Independent Labour party organ, warned that it was a chimera to hope that the League of Nations might later alter the objectionable and impossible features of the treaty. The Covenant was an instrument for the execution of the treaty and had been framed in every detail with that object in view. There could be no hope of amending the treaty so long as those who were responsible for it remained in power.[61] Even the *New Statesman,* which had welcomed the League of Nations with some warmth, was convinced that no treaty that embodied such terms as those published could lead to a permanent settlement. If the Germans felt obliged to sign it as it stood, then it would be upset and revised and revised again in the course of the next generation.[62] And the *Herald* published a comment that was to become, in its way, almost as well known as John Maynard Keynes' later *Economic Consequences of the Peace.* This was the cartoon drawn by Will Dyson after he had heard that Clemenceau, leading his fellow delegates down the Hall of Mirrors at Versailles, had stopped and said, "Curious! I seem to hear a child weeping." Dyson sketched the picture in a powerful cartoon. The weeping child, with the Peace Treaty at its feet, wore a band above its head entitled "1940." [63]

Words like "mockery," "bare-faced swindle," and "sheer and

unadulterated brigandage" [64] were used almost constantly to characterize the treaty. Only on the right could a good word be found for it. Even here, as in the case of Robert Blatchford and Alexander M. Thompson of the *Clarion*, the implication generally seemed to be that the terms were about as good as one might have expected.[65] But this group on the right, though it may have reflected the sentiments of many more of labour's rank and file than party leaders would have cared to admit, nevertheless was clearly a minority opposed to the main currents of criticism that welled up increasingly in the labour movement as disillusionment with the results of war grew day by day.

Labour's rejection of the Paris proposals continued through the days of the German counterproposals, the slight modification of some terms, and the final capitulation of Germany.[66] Meanwhile, the Labour party was gathering at Southport for its Annual Conference. Here, for the moment at least, may be discerned some slight cracks in the monolith of denunciation that had developed since May 8. As the German delegates prepared to sign at Versailles, some of the labour chieftains were torn between making the best of a bad situation in the hope of gradual improvement and a policy of complete and unadulterated rejection.

This dilemma appears clearly in the major speeches on postwar economic policy delivered to the conference. In his chairman's address, for example, J. M. McGurk of the Darwen Trades Council, while attacking the treaty's unhappy compromises and violations of principle, tended to look upon the League of Nations, unsatisfactory and weak though it was in certain details, as a substantial beginning in the direction of methodical organization to maintain peace. MacDonald, in introducing the resolution of the Conference on the Peace Treaty and the League of Nations, similarly denounced the "peace of punishment," [67] but then turned to the League as the one hope of the future. It was bad as it stood, but labour must make it better. They must encourage public opinion to change it from a "League of National Executives" to a "League of Peoples" inspired by "the peoples' mind."

MacDonald's speech was largely inspirational rhetoric. He was followed by J. R. Clynes, who brought the question back to earth, as he was so often to do on the parliamentary scene during the next couple of years. Clynes, in outlining the flaws of the treaty, summarized his argument by asserting that wrongs flagrantly committed and imposed upon a beaten foe were the real beginnings of the wars of the future. The treaty must be repaired; this could be done only through the machinery of the League of Nations. He did not conceive lightly of the League. It now had its defects, but these too must be mended. The beaten nations must be admitted, work toward disarmament begun, and the economic tasks of the League developed. As a labour movement, its responsibility now was to enlighten the people and to teach them to make the League a great cooperative agency for the people of the world in order to right the wrongs of the peace that had just been made.

Once MacDonald and Clynes had spoken, the Conference proceeded to adopt "with enthusiasm" a resolution accepting the treaty but calling for a campaign to revise its worst features.[68] All the familiar elements of labour's assessment of the treaty were embodied in the resolution, yet the tone is curiously laconic. It is significant that, aside from the speeches by MacDonald and Clynes, there was no discussion of the resolution, although the question of Allied intervention in Russia touched off considerable controversy. The report of the Conference gives the impression that some of the party's leaders were marking time, hesitating until the treaty was a fact, and, in the light of what followed, developing their attack more thoroughly.

That attack was certainly not developed in the House of Commons. Until the treaty was signed, the Parliamentary Labour party had little to contribute to the analysis of the emerging peace. Inadequately led, with most of the important labour figures defeated in the Khaki Election, the Labour M.P.'s displayed little eagerness to cope with questions of international import. Most observers have emphasized this timidity of the Parliamentary party,[69] but it can be argued that in the matter of the Versailles Treaty the Labour M.P.'s—certainly such a one as J. R. Clynes—had begun to recognize that the treaty was an accomplished fact and that their most responsible attitude would be to accept it and work for its amendment rather than indulge in the luxurious propaganda of complete rejection. For despite the severe criticism to which the Parliamentary party was subjected in labour circles,[70] arguments such as those of Clynes were eventually to become the orthodox position of the majority of the Labour party.

Once the Versailles Treaty was presented to Parliament, the labour benches had the opportunity to ventilate the party's case against it. Instead, William Adamson, the nominal leader in the Commons, rather weakly expressed gratification at its signature, only mildly criticizing certain features.[71] When the debate was resumed on the second reading of the bill to approve the treaty, J. R. Clynes spoke for the labour group in pointing out its blemishes. But Clynes, as his words at the Annual Conference had demonstrated, still felt that the League might be used to remedy the defects of the treaty as a whole. And while he pleaded for the early admission of Germany, he demonstrated a substantially different point of view from most of the party leaders outside of Parliament when he told the House of Commons that the very acceptance of a League by the Allies was encouraging, however inadequate it might as yet be. This was hardly the usual diatribe against capitalist imperialism. Its author drew further from the views of labour stalwarts, many of whom regarded the League as a pacifist instrument, when he warned that even the League would require some strength and some form of physical force behind it so as to make its decrees effective.[72]

Actually, the most thoroughgoing argument against the peace settlement was made by a Liberal who was subsequently to join the Labour party. Lt. Com. Kenworthy (later Lord Strabolgi) condemned the treaty, minimized the value of the League of Nations, and damned the proposal for an Anglo-French alliance that was also before the House. Improvement, he insisted, could come only if the treaty were rejected. But when the Commons divided on the issue on July 21, he was followed into the No lobby by only one labour member.[73]

If the Parliamentary party felt compelled to be temperate in its reception of the terms of the Versailles Treaty, the labour press had no such inhibitions. Once the treaty was signed, a full-scale assault moved into high gear. The I.L.P.'s *Labour Leader,* for example, reacted violently to the caution of the Parliamentary party. Noting that the Labour party might embark on a campaign for revision, the *Labour Leader* caustically predicted that if some of the same men were involved,

> it will partake of the character of the debate in the House of Commons, and eulogies of Lloyd George and perfunctory references to Conscription and Armaments will be mixed up with energetic references to the admission of Germany to the League of Nations when she has cleansed herself sufficiently to be fit to associate with Mr. Lloyd George, Clemenceau, and Wilson.[74]

Even the *New Statesman,* which had consistently been moderate in its approach, noted that with every passing week it was becoming clearer that frontiers drawn on the principle of recompensing friends and punishing enemies had no prospect of permanence, unless, the *New Statesman* commented with uncharacteristic cynicism, the friends happened to be stronger than the enemies.[75]

The real press campaign, however, was the work of the leaders of the party, men like Lansbury, Brailsford, Morel, MacDonald, and Henderson. Lansbury's *Daily Herald,* in particular, kept up a running fire of vehement criticism. To Lansbury, the treaty was simply a "peace of hate" and June 28 a day of "militaristic attitudinising over the ruins of Europe." Lloyd George's parliamentary defense of the treaty was "one long scream of triumphant boasting over the fallen foe." Altogether, the *Herald* cried, what had happened was more than enough to make those who had hoped and worked for a clean peace despair of the future.[76]

In more concrete fashion, H. N. Brailsford spelled out the objections so emotionally defined by Lansbury. The historian of the future, he wrote, would see in Clemenceau the epic figure of the age. First he had reduced Germany to economic and military impotence from which it appeared it might never rise. Then he had created a network of satellites around it, each with its conscript army under French leaders—the Poles, Czechs, and Rumanians. This alliance would of course be "defensive," as are all alliances of modern history, and it would be operated in the old way, with all the old evils of secret "conversations" between military staffs. France was now the dominant power on the Continent, seeking safety by imposing its will.[77]

Much like Brailsford in his point of view, yet sharing Lansbury's fervor, was E. D. Morel, the guiding genius of the Union of Democratic Control. With the first issue of *Foreign Affairs,* which he edited, Morel opened an attack upon the treaty and most of its works, together with an unrelenting presentation of the case for Germany. His first editorial set the tone he was to follow consistently for the next five years, speaking as it did of "the rape of nations, the dismemberment of states, the disruption of communities." He had little patience with the view that the League might be used to modify the evils of the treaty. International machinery created to enforce such pacts of violence as the Versailles Treaty or its Austrian copy, he insisted, was machinery whose purpose it was to guarantee stability to the institution of war. The project of a League of Nations could only become realizable policy when present governments were swept from power.[78]

Morel, then, left little room for compromise or accommodation of Labour party policy to existing conditions in the world. And in their press comments more moderate men like Henderson and MacDonald, shocked by the reality of the treaty, rapidly dropped the temporary caution that had so recently colored the debate at the Southport Conference.

In Henderson's view the treaty was neither a Wilson peace nor a labour peace, but rather in certain respects unreal, undemocratic, and unjust. It did violence to the principle of self-determination. On territorial questions, on reparations, and on armaments, the provisions were more an emulation of the brutal demands made at Brest Litovsk than an application of the principles for which the Allies and America were said to be fighting. What, then, should be labour's attitude? Henderson argued that the people must realize that deliverance could only come through themselves strengthening the League of Nations by rendering it really democratic and properly representative.[79] Henderson appeared to imply that such a change was possible, but MacDonald, in one of his many published assessments, tried, as it were, to carry water on both shoulders. His comment is so typical that it merits quotation:

Let us put a reasonable amount of expectation upon the League of Nations. We have had Leagues of Nations before. In subject nations today we see the blasting effects of peace enforced upon weak peoples. The wrong kind of League is worse than no League at all. Of course there is the chance that if Democracy comes into power in a sufficient number of States, this Executive of Executives may become a league of peoples. But whilst we must not err on the side of being ungenerous, we ought not to fall into the equally mischievous error of being complacent and of accepting the League as something good in itself. It is not that. It may be the worst part of the Treaty; it may be a bulwark for all those interests and methods with which we are at war—if they are to dominate Europe I prefer that they should do so unallied in such a League —if democracy is to emerge it will be far easier for it to form its own League than to amend this. This is why Germany, Austria, Hungary, and Russia should be in from the very first. They ought to be brought in not merely for their own sakes, but because without them the League will be weak on its democratic side.[80]

Whatever may be the interpretation of this analysis, it is apparent that the bitter disappointment of the more extreme elements was shared by the two men who were looked upon by a majority in the labour movement as their leading official spokesmen.[81]

The official position of the Labour party was summed up in a major pamphlet that epitomized its final reaction to the peace settlement. *Labour and the Peace Treaty* was prepared as a handbook for labour speakers. Published shortly after the announcement of the peace terms, it contained the labour declarations that have already been examined and an analysis of the terms of the treaties, German and Austrian, and other decisions of the Paris Conference in relation to those declarations. An important section was devoted to the party's major objections to the settlement.

In the first place, the pamphlet complained, the condition of "open covenants openly arrived at" had not been observed. Not only had conference proceedings and decisions been marked by the suppression of all opportunity for public discussion, but the bargains of secret treaties had marked the peace terms themselves. In the decisions on the Russian Revolution and the Socialist movement in Russia and Hungary, the democracies had been committed without their people's knowledge to support counter-revolutionary forces. Organized labour, progressive, and socialist movements had been completely without representation in the making of decisions that deeply concerned the general struggle for industrial democracy.

Second, the permanent causes of war—whether regarded as mainly nationalist rivalries or economic conflict—had been rendered more acute and more numerous than ever. Nor did the constitution of the League afford adequate means for their removal. Entente statesmen had repeatedly pledged themselves to remove all cause for the enemy's militarism and to win Germany to a peaceful international cooperation by guaranteeing its political security and economic justice through an equal place in the League. These promises had been directly violated. Germany was not included in the League; it was not to enjoy the rights and privileges that it was compelled to extend to others; and there was no provision giving Germany opportunities to win these rights even by good behavior. The destruction of German militarism was offset by the intensified militarism imposed on those Allies whose duty it would be to hold Germany by the throat through a generation or more.

The labour pamphlet went on to object that the Versailles Treaty made no truly international arrangement for the equitable distribution of raw materials. Instead, Germany's economic life, both internally through the Reparations Commission and externally through the Allied control of raw materials, was placed in the power of its former enemies and future competitors. They would be in a position to deny the German people even the means of livelihood. Worse, the controls over Germany were given not to the League but to the Big Four, who were free to act on their private interest and discretion. It was to be placed for years under an economic government in which it had no part, clearly a denial of democracy and self-government.

Finally, the League of Nations as devised by the Paris Conference, far from being mainly a democratic organ for the legislative modification of bad international conditions likely to cause war, was a machine giving coercive power primarily to the executive branches of a few great governments. To make matters worse, the project for a Triple Alliance among France, America, and Britain was in violation of President Wilson's dictum that there could be no league or alliance or special covenants and undertakings within the general and common family of the League of Nations. "If," cautioned the pamphlet, "we expect others—Poles, Ukrainians, Czechs, to say nothing of Germans and Austrians—to trust to the League for defence as well as justice, we must show that we ourselves believe in it, and have no special obligations which conflict with impartial justice for all its members." [82]

The analysis then proceeded to put flesh on the bones of these general objections in a point-by-point consideration of the various parts of the treaty. The League Covenant, territorial provisions, colonies and mandates, and financial arrangements were all exposed to a detailed criticism. On the basis of these, the pamphlet drew up labour's summary of points upon which revisionist efforts must concentrate.

Aside from the territorial suggestions that followed lines already developed, the first and foremost was the immediate admission of Germany and Austria to the League of Nations. Along with this must go amendment of the peace treaties in various of their aspects.

On the economic side, arrangements for securing payment through the Reparations Commission should be made by the League of Nations, not merely by the Allies. German and Austrian access to raw materials and economic opportunities should be assured by definite provisions, guaranteed by the League, and not left to the discretionary power of Germany's late enemies and present economic rivals. The control of credit, shipping, food, and raw materials should be definitely entrusted to bodies in which the late enemy states had representation under the League, instead of being in fact in the hands of bodies dominated by two or three of the chief Allies. The consideration governing the apportioning of the necessities of life should be the degree of vital need, not the degree of capacity to pay.

The control of colonial areas was a second major problem to which considerable attention was given. The Labour party here demanded that equality of economic opportunity in all nonself-governing colonies be assured under the League of Nations. All such colonies, and not merely the conquered German ones, should be subjected to the mandate principle. In addition, all conquered colonies should be ceded to the League, and Germany should be given the opportunity to become a mandatory state.

The most exhaustive proposals for revision centered about the League of Nations. The Labour party proposed constitutional changes involving the creation of a body, separate from the Assembly, representing the people, as distinct from states, "in the same sense in which the American House of Representatives, composed of Delegates from the people, is distinct from the Senate, which is composed of Delegates from the States." Whatever may be thought of this interpretation of the American system of representation, the Labour party expressed conviction that such a revision would fulfill the demand of the Bern International for a central organ representative of the peoples of the world.

Next, the party wanted to see established under the League of Nations a permanent world economic council to investigate and supervise the distribution of foodstuffs and raw materials, with the object of preventing monopoly, unfair pressure upon the weak, and international profiteering. And finally, the pamphlet called upon the new League Assembly to discuss the solution of the more pressing of those problems which, apart from the changes made by war, might affect the peace of the world. Such problems included the position of subject nations like Egypt, India, and Ireland, and of old possessions like Cyprus, whose cession to Greece ought to be considered.[83]

By the time *Labour and the Peace Treaty* was published, then, the Labour party, still bitter in its reaction to the peace settlement, had begun to think in terms of how it might be modified. Labour's proposals at this time were so extreme that they leave the impression of being designed to build a propaganda case rather than of having hope for any real immediate success. Certainly there is little indication that many within the ranks of labour leadership had yet reconciled themselves to the major lineaments of the postwar settlement and settled down to work within the system devised at Paris for the achievement of their ultimate aims. What is striking about the labour response is not so much its dissatisfaction with many of the specific terms of the Versailles Treaty, but rather the air of hopelessness and rejection that permeated virtually all of the movement's pronouncements in the spring and summer of 1919. Even in the case of the League of Nations, which it did not repudiate entirely, labour insisted that until it was revised so as to be a different organization it could have no real value and merited little support. Whether or not the Labour party could shake off the impact of the failure of its wartime aims and its suspicions of the capitalist governments and their instruments in time to move toward a more realistic assessment of what was possible on the international scene was still unrevealed in the shadows of the future.[84]

Leopold Amery: Man against the Stars in Their Courses

C. William Vogel
UNIVERSITY OF CINCINNATI

"Depart, I say, and let us have done with you. In the name of God, go!" So did Leopold S. Amery on May 7, 1940 echo over a void of two and a half centuries the charge of Oliver Cromwell dismissing the Long Parliament—now demanding the departure of the impotent government of Neville Chamberlain. It is an appropriate association, for Amery in the twentieth century embodied not a few Cromwellian characteristics. Both were fighters; tough, courageous realists with an appreciation of the fact of power, both were fanatics in their devotion to an ideal; both were impatient with the frustrations imposed by the compromises and half measures inherent in the parliamentary system. Both were, supremely, patriots.

It is often asserted that the times produce their man, and certainly the career of Cromwell fits the formula. What makes Amery so interesting is the narrow margin by which he failed to emerge as the salient British political personality of the twenties. As the *Spectator* declared in its obituary notice, "Amery was one of the few individual forces in British politics during this century."[1] Yet he is not generally placed high among the ranks of his contemporaries, and "it seems to have been assumed that there was some failure in his career which needed explaining." If failure there were, it would appear to have been in the tantalizing refusal of circumstances to synchronize by the narrowest of margins with Amery's political initiatives. He sought to turn at a fateful moment in its history the course of British imperial development into a channel that he was convinced would enhance the Empire's power, prosperity, and durability and to avert the eclipse into the pale shadow of its former self that it has since become.[2]

Amery's intimate association with the British Empire dates from the cradle. He was born, November 22, 1873, at Gorakhpur in the United Provinces, India, where his father was employed in the government service. The Amerys stemmed from a line of Devon farmers, but his mother, Elizabeth Leitner, was of Hungarian parentage. Soon after his mother came back to England in 1877 with her children, she was deserted by her husband and forced to raise the family on scanty resources. Although Amery was thus deprived at the outset of one of the primary assets for a political career in the Britain of those days—means and family—he was imbued with his mother's ambition, with a determination to excel. She inspired him to make a career in public life, and from her he inherited a gift for languages that he was to develop to the fullest.[3] Moreover, his mother saw to it that he was educated at the right places, and he made the most of the opportunity. John Stogdon, his master at Harrow, testified that "the cleverest boy I ever had in my house was Leopold Amery."[4] And he climaxed his career at Oxford (Balliol) by winning an All Souls Fellowship in 1897. A bit later merely as a tour de force, with three weeks coaching by (Sir) John Simon, he passed the English bar examination. Thus it was as an intellectual that he was to knock at the door of the Establishment.

Reading James Anthony Froude's *Oceana* and John Robert Seeley's *Expansion of England* before he was fifteen made Amery a fanatical imperialist for life, while Edward Bellamy's *Looking Backward* initiated a correspondingly permanent concern in him for social justice. With a mind equally at home in economics and in law, Amery looked here for the clue to social betterment. He immediately rejected the currently popular doctrines of *laissez-faire* and flirted briefly with socialism, being among the founders of the Oxford branch of the Fabian Society. While the role the Fabians assigned the state as the guiding force in the community appealed to Amery, he was repelled by other aspects of the socialist creed and remained a lifelong supporter of the capitalist system.[5]

It was a chance meeting in 1897, with William Lavino, *The Times* correspondent in Vienna, that guided Amery into his first career, journalism. As a member of *The Times* staff he quickly attracted the attention of Moberley Bell who sent him out in 1899 at the age of twenty-six to report the South African crisis, then moving toward the Boer War. Never one to be deterred by false modesty, he paid his first call on Sir Alfred Milner, the British High Commissioner, and his second on Cecil Rhodes, "the Colossus," with whom he dined at Groote Schuur. A tour of the Boer states followed during which he met President Paul Kruger and persuaded General Piet Joubert to attach him as *The Times* correspondent to the Boer Army. This association proved short-lived, and he returned to the British lines where he narrowly missed being captured on the same occasion Winston Churchill was taken prisoner.[6] Amery's ability won quick recognition at *The Times*. In 1900, he took over Flora Shaw's place as colonial editor and Bell shortly designated him to edit *The Times History of the War in South Africa*. This he made a work of top-level scholarship, writing many of the chapters himself. Already he was being considered a prospect for editor of the paper, and Lord Northcliffe did, in fact, offer him the position in 1912. But Amery then was determined on a political career and pressed Northcliffe to take Geoffrey Dawson instead.[7]

The years with *The Times* were an important formative period for Amery, the future politician. On one hand, they established for him a close association with the staff of one of the most important journalistic forces in British politics; on the other, he seems to have imbibed something of *The Times*' spirit of anonymity—not an asset for an aspiring politician. As one commentator was to say in 1928: "His name is not yet a household word in Britain, for he is contemptuous of popularity and makes little or no effort to parade his name or his person upon the public stage."[8] It became characteristic of Amery the politician to prefer to work where possible through small groups of important men rather than through the channels of wider immediate publicity. His service with *The Times* also contributed to Amery's versatility. In reporting the Boer War and in dealing later with its history, he acquired more than an amateur's insight into military matters, and in 1903 he became the paper's military specialist.[9]

Most importantly, the years with *The Times* enhanced Amery's direct knowledge of the Empire, clarified his imperial thinking, and established him as one of the inner circle of enthusiastic neo-imperialists who took their inspiration from Milner, who had been created a viscount in 1902.[10] The solitary aim of these neo-imperialists was the development of a British imperial superstate for which the Roman Empire provided the initial inspiration. A second source of inspiration was the United States because it had succeeded in assimilating a mass of variegated peoples, had made a success of a federal system of government, and seemed to share with Britain a common culture and purpose.[11] The neo-imperialists, like Benjamin Disraeli in 1872, derived their sense of urgency from the rise of the new political-economic power complexes such as Germany, Russia, Japan, and the United States, against whose larger populations and resources Little England alone would be unable to hold her own. Britain must call in the Empire to redress the balance by reversing the neglect by which the Liberal party had allowed it to decline.[12] By 1914, there was in Britain "a fairly determined body of opinion . . . which was set on developing the Commonwealth into a quasi-federal organization with common economic, common defence, and common foreign policies." [13] But Amery himself was always a pragmatist where constitutional development was concerned, looking more to unity "through free co-operation than through some definite constitutional scheme." [14]

With his flair for economic thinking, however, Amery's enthusiasm was fired to the pitch of fanaticism for the remainder of his life by Joseph Chamberlain's crusade for tariff reform and imperial preference. Here was a method that would assure an immediate advance toward a united Empire. "Chamberlain's campaign consequently seemed to me only a belated recognition of a self-evident necessity," he wrote, "and the opposition to it kindled my passionate indignation on intellectual as well as political grounds." [15] It appealed to him for both imperial and domestic considerations. For only with a "growth economy" arising from the resources of the Empire could he see hope for the development of real opportunity and incentive for social progress in England and the escape from class warfare. He declared:

If my long political life has had any meaning, it has lain in my constant struggle to keep the Tory Party true to a policy of Imperial greatness and social progress, linked with a definite economic creed of its own, and to prevent it drifting into becoming a party of a mere negative *laissez-faire* anti-Socialism.[16]

Repeatedly he returned to the theme in his memoirs: imperial preference "provides the indispensable key for every approach towards the great goal of Imperial unity." [17]

But Chamberlain's concept contained a fatal flaw which Amery, for one, would never admit. Chamberlain sought to impose tariffs on English imports as the means by which preference could be extended to colonial goods; if home manufacturers secured protection, this was incidental. Since, however, the produce of the colonies was food and raw materials, these would have to be taxed if preferences were to have any meaning. The industrial masses, however, had been schooled to believe that their high standard of living arose from cheap food and to them "stomach taxes" were anathema. If the Unionist party sought to avoid this political pitfall by omitting food taxes, its policy not only lost its imperial content but could be assailed as narrow protectionism designed to favor the selfish interests of British manufacturers.[18] When Chamberlain's campaign, launched in 1903, went down to defeat in 1906, the tariff reformers argued that it was because the tariff had not been pushed hard enough.

Just turned thirty in 1903 and burning with zeal for a great cause, Amery looked forward to launching his personal political career. Short and stocky, peering out from behind pince-nez, he was a bundle of pugnacious energy that later won him the name of "pocket Hercules." His pleasant manner in the intimate relationship of small groups made friendships for him with important men in both parties at home and in the wider reaches of the Empire. But he suffered from a limitation which he never was to overcome: he could not generate an appeal to the wider public—he had nothing of the crowd magnetism of, say, a David Lloyd George. His public form tended to be "hard, arid, vitriolic." [19]

Perhaps this stemmed from his intelligence and intellectual honesty which denied him the resort to demagogic tricks. As the *Spectator* remarked in 1955, "He was one man, during the past thirty years, of whom it could be truly said that he was not in politics for what he could get out of it . . . . He was in politics to promote ideas and for nothing else." [20] A further limiting factor was his association with Lord Milner. Like the members of the Kindergarten, Amery had been enthralled by Milner's exciting vision of what the Empire might become. Now he looked to Milner as both his idol and his patron. But Milner, like Amery, was too intellectual to develop any wide popular appeal, and he reacted in turn by developing something of contempt for the system of popular parliamentary government that refused to endorse his ideas. Milner was a great administrator; he was never an appealing political figure.[21]

With the great tariff election of 1906, Amery launched his own campaign for a seat in the House of Commons. As a virtual unknown political quantity, he had to fight for a seemingly hopeless constituency, the consistently Liberal Wolverhampton East. With no Conservative organization there, he had to build from nothing, but he made a hard fight, concentrating on tariff reform. He went down to defeat, however, in the great Liberal landslide and again at a by-election in 1908. But he was gaining the attention of both major parties. Eventually the Chamberlains offered him an opportunity in South Birmingham where he was elected in a by-election, May 3, 1911. He was to hold this seat for the next thirty-four years. Meantime he had been maintaining and extending his imperial ties. In 1907, he revisited South Africa, returning by way of Kenya and Uganda where he derived firsthand knowledge of the problems of East Africa. In 1910 he married, appropriately for one of his imperialist proclivities, a Canadian, the sister of a fellow Conservative Hamar Greenwood.

Meanwhile the structure of Conservative politics was being reshaped, and not entirely to Amery's advantage. While the 1906 election had appeared as a disaster to the Conservatives, it had momentarily seemed to clear the path for the tariff reformers in the party. Of the 157 Unionists who were returned to Parliament, 109 were tariff reformers and only thirty-two were supporters of

Balfour, the titular leader. The way seemed clear for Chamberlain to assume the lead of a party now united for his program. But in the summer of 1906, Chamberlain was totally incapacitated by a stroke and there was no tariff man in the Commons of sufficient stature to challenge Balfour. Only Lord Milner appeared available, and Amery at once began to urge him to put himself forward. Milner was extremely reluctant, and while he did agree to make two speeches in December, which Amery helped him prepare, he seems never to have thought seriously of challenging Balfour. Nevertheless the addresses had the appearance of a bid for Chamberlain's inheritance and gave Balfour a period of "acute distress." Although Milner attempted to make his peace with Balfour, Balfour remained suspicious. His fears appeared to be confirmed when Amery persuaded Milner to head the Tariff Reform League, greatly strengthening the tariff reformers. Their plans were reported to Balfour with the comment, "the result of all this has been a general weakening of your authority throughout the country." Amery was specifically mentioned among those responsible.[22] Balfour did not forget Amery's role in the episode, and put him down, no doubt, as a troublemaker.

Tariff reformers could take cheer from Balfour's resignation of the party leadership in November, 1911, and his replacement by Bonar Law, the leading tariff reformer in the Commons. Momentarily the cause of Empire preference appeared to be prospering, for Bonar Law always considered the imperial aspect the real heart of the case for the tariff. In this he was strengthened by his own Canadian origins and a meeting with Prime Minister Robert Laird Borden of Canada in June, 1912. Borden, who won the 1912 election on a tide of imperial sentiment, made clear that preference was meaningless for Canada without food taxes. Unless Canada was so favored, it might find comparable arrangements with other countries a necessity. This impressed Bonar Law so strongly that he determined to defy the "free fooders" of the party, who were predominant in Lancashire and the north under the leadership of Lord Derby. However, he soon discovered that sentiment in the party was against him and he ruthlessly dropped tariff reform in the interests of party unity. "The Chamberlain plan, however valid for imperial purposes, was a fatal handicap at elections in Britain." Amery, as ever, was uncompromising and urged Bonar Law to fight it out, to no avail.[23]

Meanwhile Amery had made his debut in the House where his extreme pugnacity and uncompromising Toryism worked to make him further enemies in high places. It was, one should remember, a period of extreme political tension during the fight over Irish Home Rule, when tempers were on edge and parliamentary bad manners commonplace. Amery did not curb his tongue, bringing personalities into his speeches with reference to Prime Minister Herbert Asquith as "a worn out party hack" and Lloyd George as "a flashy Welsh cheapjack."[24] Asquith, for one, never forgave him, and paid him off by excluding him from important positions so far as he could when the war came.

For Amery the outbreak of the war in 1914 was the confirmation of his prevision. He had long pointed to Germany as the menace, and indeed this had been a primary consideration for his imperial enthusiasm. Enlightened as he was on military affairs, he had been advocating military reform and a larger army for years. In July, he went at once to Birmingham where he launched a characteristically energetic and efficient recruiting campaign. But when he sought an active place in the war government, he found himself excluded by Asquith. Undeterred, he used his influence with General Sir Henry Wilson to secure a post as an intelligence officer, first in France and later in the Balkans where his linguistic talents proved most useful. By the close of 1915, he had come to support Lloyd George for the war leadership. Returning home at Christmas, 1916, from a tour of duty in the Balkans, Amery found that Asquith had fallen and Lloyd George headed the government, with Milner included in the new War Cabinet.[25]

At long last the fates seemed to be smiling on Amery and the cause to which he was devoted. Milner at once secured a place for him on the staff of the War Cabinet Secretariat under Sir Maurice Hankey. This was a post of second class level, but one not devoid of influence. No one, least of all Amery, could be blind to the way in which the war was fostering the spirit of imperial unity within the British Commonwealth. "Imperial unity was being demonstrated on the battlefields; Milner, its apostle, was in the war cabinet; the McKenna duties had breached Free Trade." [26] From 1915, Milner had been seeking to associate the Dominions more closely with the London government through the establishment of an "Imperial Cabinet." Asquith would not hear of it, but Lloyd George was another matter. At an early meeting of the War Cabinet, he agreed that the Dominion Prime Ministers should be invited to London to work for a more efficient conduct of the war. When Amery learned of it, he at once suggested that they be admitted to the War Cabinet itself to demonstrate complete equality of the Dominions with the mother country and their right to be at the very center of things. Milner proposed it and the invitations were sent out accordingly. Amery's principal concern in early 1917 became the preparations for the Imperial War Cabinet to which Hankey attached him as a member of the joint secretariat, and he began to construct the agenda in association with Sir Robert Borden, Jan Christiaan Smuts of South Africa, and William F. Massey of New Zealand.[27]

When the Imperial War Cabinet met for the first time, March 20, 1917, Joseph Chamberlain's and Amery's dream for closer Empire integration seemed, if not fulfilled, at least on the verge of fulfillment. Composed of the five members of the British War Cabinet plus the Dominion Prime Ministers, an Indian representative, and the Colonial Secretary, it was "an entirely new body, unknown to the constitution of Great Britain or the Empire." [28] When the Imperial War Cabinet adopted a unanimous resolution in favor of imperial preference and Bonar Law subsequently announced it in Parliament, Amery felt sure that the battle had been won, "at least in principle." [29]

But there was another side to the matter which even Amery, sensitive as he believed he was to Dominion sentiment, did not perceive. The Dominions, while they did not begrudge their support to Britain in its hour of need, were beginning to feel—especially the Canadians—that they had been drawn into war by a foreign policy that was controlled exclusively by Britain, and they were determined that this should not be repeated.

The crux of the matter was embodied in Borden's Resolution IX which declared that "the readjustment of the constitutional relations of the component parts of the Empire is too important and intricate a subject to be dealt with during the war." But when any such readjustment should occur it must entail "the full recognition of the Dominions as autonomous nations of an Imperial Commonwealth, . . . should recognize the rights of the Dominions and India to an adequate voice in foreign policy and in foreign relations, and should provide effective arrangements for continuous consultation in all important matters of common Imperial concern." [30]

The ambiguity and incompleteness of this formula enabled both imperialists and nationalists to extend it their applause, but Borden had made his point. The Dominions should never again be subordinate in external affairs and the concept of formal federation was excluded. The great problem would be how to achieve a practical form of continuous consultation in foreign policy. And finally the hope that the Imperial War Cabinet might become the executive for the Empire was ruled out by the Dominion Prime Ministers' insistence that they were responsible solely to their own parliaments.[31]

At the time, Amery saw only the brighter side. He wrote Prime Minister William Hughes of Australia, May 9, 1917:

> The experiment of an Imperial Cabinet was felt to be so satisfactory by everyone that the question of its perpetuation was mooted privately. . . . There was a good deal said in favour of trying to preserve direct continuity for the rest of the war by letting each Dominion appoint a confidential Minister here in London with a view either to a meeting of the Imperial War Cabinet being summoned say once a week, or at any rate to their being invited to all meetings of the British War Cabinet where matters of general Imperial concern were discussed. Apparently, however, neither . . . Borden nor Smuts liked the idea, . . . and in the end the suggestion of making the Imperial Cabinet annual . . . prevailed.[32]

But Amery had let his enthusiasm carry him away, and although the Imperial Cabinet met once again in 1918, it did not become an annual event.

For his part, Milner strove to establish some form of Empire federalism, but to no avail. Both he and Amery were trapped by their British outlook which failed to appreciate how differently things looked from the Dominions' side. Nor did they seem to be aware of the colonials' suspicion that they might be taken in by the smooth Londoners.[33] As Amery came to appreciate the realities, he remained undismayed. To him the line to take henceforth was to forget formal constitutional machinery, to recognize the principle of "complete equality of the partner nations of the Commonwealth," and to strive to make Empire preference a reality. With his knowledge of both the German Zollverein and the formation of the United States, he was convinced that economic interests developing from expanded mutual trade must inevitably work the magic of imperial unity.

As the war came to a close in November, 1918, the tide of circumstance seemed to be running favorably for Amery's principal hope of Imperial unity—the bond of economic interest to be nurtured by Imperial preference. This was the one device that aroused enthusiasm in the Dominions; only the mother country had been reluctant to apply it. If that reluctance could be surmounted amid the changed postwar atmosphere, Amery could feel that the battle for his ideal was well on the way to victory. The Dominions had been calling for preference and granting it themselves since 1897 only to see the initial battle lost in the United Kingdom in 1906. But the war had wrought great changes in the British attitude. In 1916, as an emergency measure, Britain had adopted the McKenna duties which levied a duty of 33⅓ per cent on imported "luxuries." Although no preferences were provided, it marked the first departure from simon pure free trade in fifty years. In February, 1917, Lord Balfour chaired a committee appointed to look into British postwar commercial and industrial policy. It reported strongly in favor of preference. This was followed by the unanimous resolution of the Imperial War Conference of April recommending the same principle. A definite trend seemed to have been established.[34]

Then came the election of December, 1918, which produced the postwar coalition government. Lloyd George, always the opportunist, had no firm convictions on free trade and was ready personally to take any line on fiscal policy that promised to win votes. Bonar Law, his partner in directing the coalition forces, of course favored tariff reform out of conviction and would advance it if it appeared, as it then did, to be politically realistic. True, it was not likely to stand out as a major issue in this campaign, pitched as it was on the slogans "hang the Kaiser" and "make Germany pay for the war." But it might easily have been slipped in as a plank in the coalition platform and thus have committed the country when the smashing victory came at the polls.

What curbed Lloyd George now and later was his personal following of coalition Liberals, doctrinaire free traders, whom he could not jettison. He could not, therefore, go the whole way with Bonar Law when the two framed their joint election manifesto of November 22, 1918. The section on fiscal policy was drafted in very general terms, but did plump for imperial preference. It stirred the free traders in the country to immediate protest, as registered by *The Economist,* the Manchester *Guardian* and the *London Nation,* and both the free Liberals and the Labourites stood for free trade in the campaign. On the other hand, a number of coalition candidates advocated preference and protection against a prospective flood of German goods.[35] Here appeared the fatal flaw in the coalition as Amery viewed it—the veto of the Liberal element on tariff reform—that was eventually to make him a leader among those who pulled it down.

As the coalition began to wrestle with the complex problems of postwar reconstruction, it became apparent that there was a rising discontent in the country over its failure to come out with a clear line on a permanent trade policy. Manufacturers especially began an organized agitation for tariff protection, expressing fear of the impact of revived foreign competition. This impelled the coalition, late in 1919, to assay the situation by offering Parliament an anti-dumping bill. Conservatives hopefully viewed it as the next great step towards a protectionist fiscal policy. But the "storm of protest" that it evoked which threatened to split the coalition led the government to a hasty retreat, and the bill was dropped before it came up for second reading.[36]

Success, however, crowned the effort to introduce imperial preference, at least in principle, into the British fiscal system. In his budget of April, 1919, Austen Chamberlain, Chancellor of the Exchequer, redeemed the 1917 pledge by proposing a reduction of the rates levied on products of imperial origin under the McKenna duties by one-third and on items such as tea, coffee, and rum by one-sixth.[37] It was not much, but for Amery it was the principle that mattered. Once the bridgehead was established it could presumably be expanded. Amery led the advocates of the measure and held up glowing prospects of future affluence for Britain and the Empire, once the system was established.

> That principle, which caused bitter party conflict for many years before the war, has, I think, now reached a position where it stands above and to one side of party conflict. We are all agreed that in so far as the interests of the revenue . . . of this country necessitate any particular duty being imposed in any particular direction, that duty should be lowered as regards the produce of the empire. That imposes no obligation on the country to tax itself in any way for the benefit of anybody. It is only the assertion of the general principle that we regard our fellow countrymen of the Empire as on a different plane from that on which we regard others . . . . We want more wealth, and . . . we have boundless wealth in the British Empire. It is only a question of bringing the people of this country into direct and fruitful contact with the immense undeveloped resources which the Empire contains[38]

He went on, with special reference to the great example of economic growth afforded by the United States:

> We have come out of this war with heavy burdens . . . , but we start this period with opportunities such as no nation in the world's history has ever had . . . . Look back on the history of the United States during the past century . . . . The United States is the greatest economic phenomenon of the nineteenth century . . . . The twentieth century is to be the century of the British Empire. We start with regions three or four times as great as the territory of the United States, with a far greater nucleus of a capable industrial population. It will be our fault, and our fault alone if, in two or three generations, the progress of this Empire in well-being of every sort . . . will not be the outstanding factor in the world's history since the Great War.[39]

Strong support was forthcoming from *The Times* which carried reports from the colonial press showing keen interest and declared that the government was lagging behind the country in this matter. The budget passed July 23 and the principle of preference was at last a reality.[40]

Heartened, the protectionists continued their drive, probing cautiously for the most favorable areas for extensions. Agitation in the country from manufacturers, principally, and spearheaded by *The Times* concentrated mainly on the alleged menace of dumping.

Cautiously, with tenderness for the Liberal wing of the coalition, the government secured first a protectionist export credits scheme and then in 1920 an act to limit the import of dyestuffs. By 1921 it felt able to go much farther with the Safeguarding of Industries Act which offered protection to "key" industries threatened by foreign competition. Britain had indeed moved away from free trade into both preference and protection, but if the trend was to have imperial significance the great battle was still ahead involving both more extensive protection and taxes on food and raw materials, which alone could bring realistic gains to the Dominions.

Meanwhile, Amery's political career was advancing as he moved into the ranks of the junior ministers of the coalition. In 1919, at the urgent behest of Lloyd George, Lord Milner exchanged the War Office for the Colonial Office and stipulated that he must have as Undersecretary someone with whom he could work on terms of complete understanding, Amery. With Milner absent from London a good part of the time, Amery was left with major responsibility for the business of the office.[41] He was no prodigy like Churchill, for example, for he was now forty-six, but he was on the way up and happy to be working in his chosen sphere under his idol, Milner.

His central effort lay in advancing the cause of Empire settlement. What he sought was to direct British emigrants away from the traditional destination of the United States into the open spaces of the Empire. Thus he hoped to develop a vast market for British goods. "The Dominions," he declared, "are our best purchasers; every man who goes to the Dominions buys, on the average, twenty times as much from us as the man who goes to a friendly country like the United States." In no sense would these migrants be lost to the mother country. Think, he said, "of those hundreds of thousands [who] have come thousands of miles to fight on the fields of France." They compose part of the strength of the Empire.[42]

His principal accomplishment was the enactment of legislation offering free passage to the Dominions for ex-servicemen desiring to emigrate.[43] In 1921 Lord Milner resigned and Amery left the Colonial Office to become Financial Secretary of the Admiralty. With a peer as First Lord (Lord Lee of Farehaven), Amery again had considerable departmental responsibility, speaking for the Admiralty in Commons. It was at this time, also, that he established his friendship with Stanley Baldwin.

Milner's departure removed the major claim of the coalition to Amery's loyalty, and he came increasingly to view it with apprehension. Unlike Baldwin, it was not Lloyd George whom he feared but rather Winston Churchill, a doctrinaire free trader possessed of tremendous powers of persuasion who was, in Amery's eyes, the principal obstacle in the coalition to the realization of his ideal. Not only did he block tariff reform but, as Amery saw it, he also prevented the Conservative party from advancing on the road to social progress which alone could check the growth of socialism at home. It "meant the abandonment of a policy of Imperial expansion which could kindle the imagination of the working men, as well as help to solve their immediate problems, in favour of a narrow insular anti-socialism which was bound to be defeated in the end." [44] Amery was, therefore, active in organizing the junior ministers to support the Baldwin revolt that overthrew the coalition in October, 1921.[45]

Now indeed the political omens appeared to be more favorable than ever for Amery; he seemed on the threshold of the realization of all his ambitions; high office was within his grasp and the Chamberlain imperial program must surely follow. The formation of Bonar Law's cabinet provided a magnificent opportunity for the Conservative junior ministers whom Amery had led in rebellion against the coalition. For the bulk of the talent and experience of the party boycotted the new government, remaining loyal to Lloyd George. Bonar Law had no alternative but to fill his ministries with peers and junior ministers. Thus Amery stepped up to become First Lord of the Admiralty far sooner than he might have hoped in the normal course of events. Bonar Law told him, when he offered him the post, it had been his original intent to give him the Colonial Office, but with Lord Derby at the War Office this would have meant that both heads of the service ministries would be peers, and he felt compelled to keep one in the Commons.[46] Amery also persuaded Bonar Law to make Neville Chamberlain postmaster general, thus adding another sure tariff reformer to the ranks of the government.

When it came to shaping the government's policy line for the forthcoming election, Bonar Law showed himself a shrewd and realistic political professional who viewed victory at the polls as the first priority of his party. The election appeared a real gamble, a very near thing, that would take some doing to pull off. Not only had the Conservatives failed to win an election on their own since 1900 but they were split, with the Lloyd George fellow travelers full of fight. They did not bother to conceal their contempt for Bonar Law's scratch team, whom Lord Birkenhead sneeringly referred to as "second class intellects." [47]

Tariff reform, of course, was a major tactical problem. While Amery knew that his leader believed in the principle, he was also aware of his past record of dropping it when expediency dictated. Thus he was prepared to move with caution and had no intention "of pushing his party too hard at the outset." When, after the party meeting that elected Law as leader, the new team met to decide the policy line that they should take, it was agreed that Law should not "tie his hands in any way." But Amery was insistent that the door should be kept open for tariff reform in the future. Amery, prone to exaggerate his own importance on occasion, says that he then drafted what became Law's election manifesto. The theme was tranquility and the fiscal issue was covered up with the promise of an early Imperial Conference.[48]

Unknown to Amery, however, Bonar Law was already being subjected to free trade pressures to which he was shortly to succumb. On October 19, Lord Derby called to discuss cabinet making and received assurance of the War Office for himself. Then Law mentioned tariffs and Lord Derby reared like a skittish horse. He had had one traumatic experience with tariff reform in 1906 when, as Lord Stanley, he had gone down ignominiously to defeat in his native Lancashire at the hands of a carpenter from Bolton, and he was determined not to have that "millstone round our necks." "This looks as if he was still thinking of putting on a tariff," Lord Derby noted in his diary, "I told him perfectly frankly if he did he and I should part company." [49] This chilled Bonar Law, for with the dearth of material with which he had to work, Derby's control of the Lancashire vote made him worth more than the Duke of Devonshire and Lords Salisbury and Curzon put together.[50]

One great asset that Bonar Law could count upon, as could Amery by inference, was the support of *The Times*. The editor, Wickham Steed, disliked the coalition as much as anyone, and had pledged the support of the paper to Bonar Law. In the uncertainty of the prospects of the coming election he had bucked him up with the prediction of victory by seventy-five seats (the actual Conservative margin turned out to be seventy-eight). However, Northcliffe had died on August 14, 1922, and the ownership of the paper passed to other hands. The new regime dismissed Steed and appointed Geoffrey Dawson in his place on December 1. This proved to be no loss to Law and Amery, for Dawson was very close to Lord Milner. Through him Amery could maintain a connection with the paper. Moreover, Dawson was both a strong supporter of the Conservatives and a convinced imperialist. His orientation was all toward the Commonwealth and away from continental commitments.[51] This more than balanced the opposition of such free trade papers as *The Economist* which hounded Bonar Law on the tariff issue throughout the campaign.[52]

Then came for Amery the first rude shock—subsequently he was to rate it a "major disaster"—but its full significance was not apparent until a year later. As the campaign warmed up, Bonar Law declared that he would allow no "fundamental change in fiscal policy" during the life of the new Parliament. It was, Amery wrote later, "destined to exercise a fatal influence on the whole subsequent course of politics." [53] When the vote was in, *The Economist* could crow that the electorate "has shown itself overwhelmingly in favour of Free Trade. The fact that Mr. Bonar Law has succeeded in keeping tariffs well in the background has been an immense asset to the Conservative Party, and the large Conservative successes in Lancashire . . . would have been impossible on any other condition." [54] Lord Derby had outweighed Amery in the careful calculations of the Prime Minister and the pledge not to close the door on fiscal change had been jettisoned. But Amery was resilient and he squared away to make the best of things. He could not read the future and he could still hope for the best. He was not disheartened; for example, one of the first acts of the new government was to dispatch Stanley Baldwin to Washington, D.C. to arrange a settlement of the war debt owed the United

States. Amery, unlike Bonar Law, refused to be shocked by the terms Baldwin brought back, but entertained "the hope that the problem of payment would compel us to face the need for a national and Imperial economic policy which would increase our productive power by many times the amount of the American debt." [55]

Meanwhile Amery set to work with his accustomed energy at the Admiralty to advance another of his pet schemes in behalf of the Empire: the Singapore naval base.[56] The end of the Anglo-Japanese Alliance and the Washington Naval Limitation Treaty of 1922 forced Britain to reexamine the entire subject of the security of the Empire east of Suez. Amery was not one to forget the complaints of the Australians and New Zealanders in 1917 that they had been left defenseless against the German China squadron in 1914, and he knew that he was soon to face them again at an Imperial Conference in 1923. Moreover, he was aware that the Washington Treaty had shackled the British Navy to a one power standard which denied its former capacity to be strong everywhere. Beyond that, battleships had grown so large that Britain possessed no docking facilities east of Suez capable of servicing capital ships. In short, what the Navy needed was mobility, which required the creation of a major base in the East, and every consideration pointed to Singapore as the ideal spot. With the main fleet in the Mediterranean, Britain would be able to meet any eventuality then contemplated: either a war in Europe or a conflict with Japan. Amery set about at once to marshal Tory support and secured a Cabinet decision to proceed with the Singapore base, after clearance by the Committee on Imperial Defence.

Well supplied with an armory of technical data in support of his project, Amery drove into the teeth of a determined Liberal and Labor opposition in the Commons. The opposition took the line that the base would be in fact a tricky evasion of the spirit of the Washington Treaty, that the League of Nations was ample insurance against wanton aggression anywhere, that the war just ended had been a war to end war and therefore no other need be anticipated, and that the base would be a sheer waste of money. One critic, indeed, with remarkable foresight, did prophesy that, as proposed, the base would be defenseless from the landward side.[57]

Amery met all the charges with skill and vigor. Everyone at Washington knew, he explained, that the Washington treaties had been drawn specifically to allow for the fortification of Singapore. Nor should Japan be offended, for the base was not "aimed at anyone." As to the League, of which the realistic Amery ever took a dim view, "it has laid down as one of its chief objects to prevent war by co-operation against wanton aggression. You cannot co-operate against wanton aggression unless you have some force co-operating with you. It was never the idea of the League of Nations that it should be the League of the Helpless." Singapore, far from being a jumping off place for aggression, was suitable only for defense. He carefully explained why the fleet required fueling and docking facilities in the Far East and made a good case for the base on grounds of economy. But for Amery the real crux of the matter was the issue of imperial security and the potential prosperity Britain might derive therefrom.

> You have got to think of this matter from the point of view of the British Empire. This is a question, not of the local defence of this country, but of the defence of the British Empire. The function of the Navy is today, as it has always been, not the function of the local defence of the narrow seas, but the function of defending the world-wide trade of Britain and its world-wide territories . . . . We must make it clear to all the partner States in the British Empire that we stand behind them to the last man and the last ship . . . . By making it clear to the Great Dominions that we are in a position in which we can, if need should arise, come to their assistance, we are doing the best thing we can for the unity of the Empire and for the peace of the world.[58]

The Tories rallied, as might be expected, to the cause of the Empire, and Amery got his base—for the moment. But his championing of naval might did not improve his popular image. Pacifism was becoming the fashionable pose in war-weary Britain, and power politics and militarism were nasty words. The intellectuals, bellwethers of the movement in the easy twenties, were quick to nip out at Amery. Herbert G. Wells had so admired him before 1914 that he portrayed Amery under the name of Crupp in his novel, *The New Machiavelli,* as one of the bright young leaders of the day. Now he sarcastically characterized him as "a perennial juvenile . . . still longing to play with battleships and soldiers, the kind of game that the civilized adult world had finally abandoned." And another commentator sneered that "wherever the spirit of force, untaught by war, is in the ascendant in the affairs of Government, it is Mr. Amery who is the driving force." [59]

Events crowded into 1923. France invaded the Ruhr, galloping inflation destroyed the German mark, Hitler made his Beer Hall *putsch,* King Tut's tomb was opened, and in Britain Bonar Law resigned and died. Stanley Baldwin, the dark horse, slipped past Lord Curzon to become Prime Minister. The course of British politics was making an abrupt turn. Momentarily it seemed to favor Amery, but the fates were only tantalizing him. By the close of the year, it was apparent that the stars were against him and that he had suffered a disaster; both his personal career and his ideal were shattered. How complete was the devastation was not immediately apparent, but the following decade made the reality all too clear.

The prospect looked fair enough for Amery in the early months of the year. Bonar Law was scheduled to preside over an Imperial Conference in August, and such an event always kindled Amery's optimism for Empire progress. "It would have been a symbolic occasion," Bonar Law's biographer writes, "the first Prime Minister in English history to be born in the overseas Empire would have directed the deliberations of the Dominion Prime Ministers. The statesman who had always put the greatness of the British Empire foremost among his aims might have had a chance of realizing some of the ideals for which he had entered political life twenty years before." [60] And Amery's hopes rode with Bonar Law. But in May, Bonar Law was taken fatally ill, resigned, and died shortly after. It was the first great blow.

In the maneuvering for Bonar Law's succession, Amery backed Baldwin and liked to believe that he had influenced the King's decision by cornering Lord Stamfordham on his way to the palace and making the case for Baldwin. In any event he won the enmity of Curzon.[61] On the other hand, Baldwin, looking for someone to fill his place at the Exchequer, offered it to Amery who declined, preferring to get on with the work he was doing at the

Admiralty (the Singapore base was up before the House in May and July). Years later he was to deplore this as one of his most serious errors of judgment. Had he taken the Exchequer then he might have returned to it when Baldwin formed his second government in 1924. He could not foresee that Baldwin would then install the immovable free trader, Winston Churchill, thus slamming the door on any remaining hopes for imperial preference in that decade.[62]

The major concern of the new government was the Imperial Conference which convened in London October 1 and met on alternate days with an Imperial Economic Conference. Amery looked forward to the meetings with anticipation, for they appeared to be the critical opportunity for advancing the cause of imperial unity and for consolidating the spirit of wartime before it flickered out.

This had been the purpose of an Imperial Conference in 1921. Here an attempt had been made to keep up the wartime concept of an Imperial Cabinet, which failed, but the principle had been adopted that there should be but one foreign policy for the Empire arrived at by frequent consultation with the Dominions. It had been anticipated that, with the Dominions and the United Kingdom united on a foreign policy, unity of Empire defense in support of that policy would follow. It had survived the first test, the issue of the renewal of the Japanese Alliance, when Canada got its way over the Australians and New Zealanders.

In 1922 the Chanak crisis, however, in which the Lloyd George coalition led the Empire to the verge of war without a semblance of prior consultation, had shown the hollowness of this device. Moreover, a political shift in Canada had replaced Prime Minister Borden, who had been an architect of consultation, by Mackenzie King, who mirrored the postwar Canadian isolationism more accurately than did his predecessor. Mackenzie King was also imbued with a deep suspicion of the insidious power of the English to charm colonials into doing what they wanted.[63] Canadians were determined that they should not be wheedled into another war for distant interests and King meant to make sure that they were not.

If Amery, attuned as he was to the Empire, did not appreciate King's nationalism, certainly Lord Curzon could hardly have been expected to. Since it was through unity of foreign policy that the British hoped to advance, it was left to Curzon to make the principal appeal. This he did in one of his masterful speeches wherein he declared:

> A common policy in international matters so that the Foreign Minister of this country, when he speaks, may speak, not for Great Britain alone, but for the whole British Empire . . . . Think of the addition to his power and his strength that will result if . . . he knows . . . that there lie behind him the sentiment and the might of the British Empire as a whole.

It left Mackenzie King cold. He could only remember how Britain had spoken first at Chanak and then come round asking the Empire for support. Stanley Bruce of Australia, ever concerned for security, came out for the British view. But King, supported by James B. M. Hertzog of South Africa, held out, and in the end the Canadian position that each Dominion might determine its own foreign policy was accepted.[64]

Now it was Amery's turn to exercise all his persuasive powers to win the Dominions to a common scheme of imperial defense. More alert now to the enhanced spirit of particularism, Amery reversed the previous Admiralty position that only a unitary navy could be efficient and came out in favor of autonomous Dominion navies. Here he hoped to concede the shadow while preserving the substance. Methods of indirect control might be devised that would suffice, and in an emergency the forces would be pooled in any case. Again King proved adamant for complete Dominion autonomy, repulsing all Amery's approaches. Britain might be building the Singapore base for the defense of the Empire, but Canada was not going to be committed to defend it.[65]

The final British effort was made in the economic field, by which Amery set great store, but in whose behalf he was not placed to play an open role. This was the province of the Imperial Economic Conference where Neville Chamberlain and Philip Lloyd Graeme were the advocates of the British position. Already on the eve of the conference *The Economist* had pessimistically predicted that an insoluble dilemma was in prospect. There could be no true control of trade without food taxes and these the British people would reject.[66]

Yet Amery's views, his inflexible single-mindedness, and his pervasive influence with Dominion delegates were so well known that it was widely suspected he was pressing the Dominions to make tariff demands on the British so as to force his more reluctant colleagues to come round to support for a British tariff with generous provision for Dominion preferences. At any rate this is what Bruce did, pointing to new concessions by Australia to Britain in its tariffs and asking that Britain assure it markets for its food and raw material exports. Again King applied the veto. When Canada granted Britain preferences it did so out of good will, not for bargaining. He simply refused to discuss the subject. In the end the British made as generous a gesture as they could, offering preferences on a few minor items such as dried fruits, wines, apples, honey, and fruit juices.

The British, Amery not least, had made a shrewd and determined effort to achieve a major advance toward imperial unity. But in the end it boiled down to a case of all take and no give from the Dominions. Something of a common defense policy did survive, but in reality it consisted of putting the British Navy at the service of the Dominions with Britain picking up the bill. In the area of preferences, while granting apparent concessions to British imports, the Dominions still retained a considerable measure of protection for their home industries. They were quite frank in their demands on the mother country: they wanted assured markets for wheat, wool, and meat. As *The Economist* pointed out, "That is what the Dominions produce, and that is what will bring about the development of the Dominions, and it is no good talking about better preference to the Dominions, and ever dodging what is the great issue."[67] In fact, this was the decisive moment in the history of the Empire, "the turning point where the Empire reversed its tendency of the war and postwar period and moved towards . . . the nationalism and independence of the Dominions."[68] Amery probably did not appreciate its full significance at the time and he continued to work with undimmed faith in the cause of Empire for the remainder of his life; subsequent developments show that from this time his career went downhill.

Yet one more major event of 1923 gave Amery's hopes reason to soar. This was Stanley Baldwin's decision to go to the country on the tariff reform issue. Throughout his life Amery never abandoned the conviction that this economic device would be the catalyst for a truly united British Empire. Bruce's appeal for a British tariff during the Imperial Economic Conference convinced him, in the light of the disappointments suffered in respect to a united foreign policy and imperial defense, this was the one path remaining open to the great end, a united Empire.[69] Yet once again his luck was out and he saw his hopes shattered.

As a matter of fact, Amery had been straining at the leash. From the time they took office in 1922, the Conservatives found that they had inherited from Lloyd George a plague of chronic unemployment. Amery could see no respite except through the adoption of a tariff, and he was seriously considering, in the autumn of 1923, resigning from the government in order to take the issue to the public.[70] From here on, however, we enter the terrain of mystery, the strange, mystical decision-making process of the Prime Minister, Stanley Baldwin. Exactly what impelled Baldwin to dissolve a Parliament that still had several years of prospective life ahead of it when he had a comfortable majority of seventy-eight and assume the risks of an election on so chancy an issue as protection remains a moot point with historians to this day. To what extent did Amery influence his leader's decision?

Certainly rumor named him the persuader. But as he tells the story, he was taken by surprise as much as anyone by Baldwin's unexpected decision. Suddenly, he remembers, the telephone rang on the evening of October 8. It was Baldwin to tell him that he was convinced that only a tariff could reduce unemployment.[71] Now, knowing how Amery was ever inclined to take credit for any memorable development with which he could claim association, it would appear logical to assume that he would come forward as the *deus ex machina.* On the contrary, he accepts the thesis that it was a tactical move by Baldwin to "dish the Goat" (Lloyd George). According to this story, Lloyd George, who had gone to America in September, had determined upon his return to make an issue of the tariff in 1923. He anticipated that this would rally the coalition Conservatives like Lord Birkenhead and Austen Chamberlain to his banner once more, the coalition could be reconstituted and Lloyd George would be swept back into power. Churchill seems to have had word of it, and Baldwin, who had remarkably sensitive political antennae, might well have picked it up, as indeed he later alleged that he did. In the event, when Lloyd George returned early in November, Baldwin had established his position as the proponent of protection and Lloyd George could only denounce it as "unutterable folly." [72]

Amery had his wish to carry the issue of protection to the country, but it was under circumstances that were far from what he would have chosen. Baldwin called Amery and Philip Lloyd Graeme to Chequers to consider policy. It was decided that Baldwin should seize the occasion of the annual Conservative party meeting at Plymouth on October 25 to announce a "wholehearted policy of protection and preference," but that the election should be timed for no sooner than mid-January to allow time to explain the issues to the country. Amery, however, soon found that he was dealing with a man who was as elusive as quicksilver. Baldwin's Plymouth speech went well enough and seemed to arouse enthusiasm in the party, but did not spell out what sort of tariff the Prime Minister contemplated. At once Baldwin began to feel the impact of opposing forces within the party that might presage a split. Lord Derby, uncrowned king of Lancashire, no sooner heard the news than he felt "in his bones that protection . . . would be disastrous for the party." He was impelled to write Baldwin October 22 anent protection, "Can it be done without putting a tax on foreign wheat, or other raw material?" [73] Baldwin responded with a speech at Manchester in the heart of Lord Derby's domain, tailoring his views to fit the Derby pattern. He proposed to tax manufactured imports, extend preference, but he would absolutely not tax wheat or meat.[74] This cut the heart out of Amery's position, but he still found cheer in the retention of the principle. Lord Derby and his "free fooders" once more had outweighed Amery and his theories.[75]

As Amery feared, the election, December 6, was not a happy one; in fact it was "one of the most unpopular ever held in Great Britain." Coming, as it did, a mere thirteen months after the previous one, it met apathy among the electorate. Moreover, it came too close to Christmas, inconveniencing both the trade and ceremonial of the season. Its incidence was so abrupt that it left no time, as Amery had predicted, for the party to educate its own speakers on an unfamiliar issue, let alone the electorate. As *The Economist* declared, "The suddenness of the change is bewildering . . . We cannot but deplore and set down as reckless statesmanship the imposition on an electorate . . . of the duty of deciding, in the space of three weeks of election turmoil, the most fundamental and intricate of national issues." [76] The press generally was unsympathetic and the Beaverbrook and Rothermere papers, traditionally strongly protectionist, created a sensation by throwing their support to Lloyd George.[77] For all Baldwin's concessions to Lord Derby, the party teetered on the verge of a split, while the Liberals were reunited, as in 1906, in support of free trade. Results of the polling were a defeat for the Conservatives, with Labour in line to form the next government. It was a bitter ending to a disastrous year for Amery.

All the Conservatives emerged from the ordeal smarting and snarling, while the Liberal press rubbed salt in their wounds. "Protection is dead," chortled *The Economist.* "Our great leader has led us to disaster," sneered Lord Derby, and Lord Curzon said the same thing with equal rancor. Baldwin seemed finished as the party leader, but survived through the absence of any more attractive rival.[78] Sir Archibald Salvidge, Tory boss of Liverpool, demanded that tariff reform be dropped from the party program lest the party disintegrate and socialism take over the country.[79] As if in response, the shadow cabinet met, February 7, 1924, and unanimously—Amery excepted—wiped the issue from its standard. But Amery refused to accept the verdict. He wrote Baldwin an open letter declaring that he would fight on for imperial preference regardless of the position of the party. Thus he became an odd phenomenon in the British politics of the day—a free agent.[80] At once he set busily to work to develop a new organization outside the purview of the party to carry on the work and soon had the Empire Industries Association going with ample funds.[81]

No sooner had the new Labour government assumed office than it set about to wipe out all vestiges of Amery's work. Amery awaited in extreme suspense to learn the fate of the Singapore naval base, and heard the worst when the government announced, March 18, that it was suspending work on the base. Snowden's budget did the rest, abolishing all such vestiges of protection as the

McKenna, and safeguarding duties and jettisoning all the commitments of the Baldwin government to imperial preference. The return of the Conservatives to power in November, 1924, resulted in prompt resumption of the work on the base, but its suspension during the previous year was just one more factor in destroying the momentum of the imperial movement on which Amery set such store.

Amery returned to office when Baldwin formed his second government in November, 1924, this time as master of the Colonial Office. But this was not 1895 and Amery was not Joe Chamberlain. True, his energy and spirit of enterprise spread throughout the office and he began as had Chamberlain by updating the maps, and moved on through a whole series of admirable measures benefitting the Empire. With Churchill, whom he never in his wildest nightmares could have expected to be at the Exchequer, he battled futilely for some expansion of imperial preference. But it was all to no avail, for his great moment had come and gone in the disastrous year, 1923.

For all his single-minded optimism, even Amery was disabused when he returned from a world-wide tour of the Empire that occupied him for most of 1927. He had gone out to preach his gospel that "a united British Empire could lead the world and need fear no power." While he was convinced that he had done some good abroad, he also felt upon his return much as had Joseph Chamberlain on his arrival from South Africa in 1903. His colleagues in the government avoided the controversial issues of Empire—"I had . . . lost ground, and found myself in a sense somewhat of a stranger, an intruder tiresomely anxious to stir up issues which well might be allowed to sleep a little longer." [82]

Already the forces of the world depression were brewing and shortly were to produce a level of economic nationalism everywhere that was to make the Ottawa Imperial tariff agreements of 1932 a travesty of the system of economic unity which Amery had hoped to achieve at such a meeting. He himself was to take no official part in the Ottawa conference, for he had been excluded from the National Government.

Amery's failure was partly attributable to his personality, especially to his inability to build a great popular following and a national reputation. He never reached the top ministerial level and was condemned to work for his goal through others. But as this essay, it is hoped, has shown, his failure lay more in the failure of circumstances to fit, often by the narrowest of margins, with Amery's initiatives for Empire unity. If only cancer had not struck down Bonar Law in May, 1923, or Borden had remained Prime Minister of Canada a bit longer, if only Baldwin had but timed the 1923 election a bit more judiciously, then the wartime spirit of Empire partnership might have been revived before Dominion nationalism could have grown too strong. If it had, the British Empire and the world might be quite different today and Amery's name would rank among the foremost of British statesmen. He suffered from the same deficiency as his idol, Joseph Chamberlain: he was unlucky—a fatal bar to greatness.

An Illusion That Shaped History: New Light on the History and Historiography of American Peace Efforts before Munich

Francis L. Loewenheim
RICE UNIVERSITY

Every era of war or great upheaval seems invariably to produce its share of tantalizing imponderables. One such imponderable episode concerns President Franklin D. Roosevelt's efforts, made in the years immediately preceding the Munich crisis, to head off another world war by convening one or perhaps a series of international conferences to discuss and, if possible, to resolve the outstanding and increasingly dangerous issues confronting the great powers in Europe and the Far East. It has long been believed that Undersecretary of State Sumner Welles first suggested such a plan to the President; that Roosevelt had then taken up the proposal with Neville Chamberlain hoping to enlist his support before proceeding any further, that the Prime Minister's reaction had been negative so that Roosevelt had, in the end, decided against going ahead with the plan altogether.

This at any rate is the conventional version of the story, first told by Welles himself, strongly seconded by Winston Churchill, and subsequently reaffirmed by Anthony Eden and Harold Macmillan.[1] Indeed, Churchill went so far as to say, in the first volume of his memoirs of World War II, that Roosevelt's plan was "the last frail chance to save the world from tyranny save by war."[2]

But was it really? In fact, was it Welles who first suggested the idea of a great international peace conference to the President, or had Roosevelt already decided to launch an initiative on his own? It is not too much to say that infrequently in the history of modern diplomacy, and rarely in the history of American foreign policy, has an important incident been for so long shrouded in so much mystery, and subjected to as many far-fetched and misleading interpretations. Now, more than thirty years since this episode took place, we can at last begin to discern the broad outlines of President Roosevelt's undertaking, and to observe, more clearly than has hitherto been possible, something of the ideas, political pressures, and international circumstances that led the President to act as he did.

The history of American peace efforts before the Munich crisis is an instructive story for a number of reasons. First, it serves to clarify the principal problems and prospects of a lasting settlement between the democratic and totalitarian powers in the 1930's, as well as the growing difficulty of trying to bring about a substantial and meaningful settlement at the very moment Germany, Italy, and Japan were, by their every action, bringing another great war closer with every passing day. Second, it sheds new light on the inner history of Roosevelt's diplomacy before Munich, a subject on which all too little has thus far been said. And finally, the gradual unfolding of the whole story over the last thirty years or more is a reminder of the cumulative nature of historical knowledge and study—that, as Herbert Butterfield once aptly put it, history is (or ought to be) "a process of unlearning." [3]

I

The first point to be made about the history of American peace efforts before Munich is that the first intimation that such efforts were being made came more than eight years before the appearance of Welles's *The Time for Decision* which was published in October, 1944. This was a story on the front page of the *Times*, August 26, 1936, by Arthur Krock, that newspaper's highly informed chief Washington correspondent, who wrote:

The President is considering a plan—his own—in the event of his re-election to propose a joint conference soon thereafter with the heads of the most important nations in an effort to assure the peace of the world . . . . The conference . . . would include the President, King Edward VIII, Joseph Stalin, Benito Mussolini, Adolf Hitler, President [Albert] LeBrun of France, effective representatives of Japan and China and a few others. . . . The conference would generally discuss the prospects and hopes of disarmament and peace, consider the seeds of war, and unite in a proclamation of personal purpose to use all their influence to prevent war in any part of the world.[4]

While international response to this sensational story was rather mixed—the Germans, for instance, were at once distinctly critical—the Administration moved quickly to cast doubt on the accuracy of the whole report. Secretary of State Cordell Hull told newspapermen the following day that he had never heard of such a plan until he read about it in the press, and Secretary of Agriculture Henry A. Wallace, after a meeting with Roosevelt, then on a campaign swing through the Middle West, quoted the President as saying, "there had been nothing in any shape, manner or form looking toward any meeting of the kind described." [5]

These emphatic denials soon diminished public interest. Nothing further was heard of the subject until the publication, in March, 1941, of the journal kept by Professor William E. Dodd of the University of Chicago while serving as American ambassador to Germany from mid-1933 to the end of 1937.[6] Dodd's diary revealed that he had several times in 1936–37 discussed with leading German officials the possibility of the United States convening some kind of international conference, but that the German response had been anything but promising.[7] Since it was unthinkable that Dodd should have undertaken such soundings without specific instructions from the President or the Secretary of State, here was the first indication that there was more than a little substance to Krock's report.

Dodd revealed that Joseph E. Davies, the American ambassador to the Soviet Union, had also discussed the possibility of an international conference with German officials, and indeed Davies, in his widely read memoir, *Mission to Moscow*, published at the end of 1941, confirmed that he had held talks in Berlin in January and again in June, 1937. Davies disclosed that the President had personally instructed him to take soundings, that he had reported directly to Roosevelt on his conversations, and that the President, in early 1937, had approached Hans Luther, the German ambassador in Washington, with a plan calling for the abolition of all weapons heavier than those carried by the individual soldier. All these efforts, however, had come to nothing, and Davies quoted the President as telling him at the White House in December, 1937, that "it was perfectly clear that there was no possibility of doing anything to divert the forces in Germany which, under Hitler's concept of world domination and conquest, were driving inevitably to war." [8]

It should be added at once that these reports of Ambassadors Dodd and Davies received very little attention, and it remained for Welles in *The Time for Decision* to set forth what became the basis of the most generally accepted version of American peace efforts before Munich.

According to Welles's account—somewhat elaborated in his later *Seven Decisions That Shaped History* [9]—the President had planned to call a meeting of the diplomatic corps at the White House on Armistice Day, 1937, to lay before the assembled diplomats a comprehensive program for international peace, calling first of all for the establishment of a detailed code of international conduct, to be agreed to by all the powers, to be followed by the appointment of a small committee to work out the detailed application of the code. Welles did not say who had first suggested the idea to the President, but noted that the plan was "almost hysterically opposed by certain of [the President's] closest advisers," that the President thereupon delayed taking up the plan with the British government until January, 1938, and that when he did so, Chamberlain's response to it was "in the nature of a douche of cold water." [10]

This was not, however, the end of the story. As Welles told it, when Chamberlain sent his reply to the President, Foreign Secretary Eden was away on a brief vacation in the south of France. Chamberlain had not consulted him, and when Eden returned to London soon after, his strong protests forced Chamberlain to send a second and rather different message, declaring that he "had reached the conclusion that he should welcome the President's initiative and that the British government would do its utmost to contribute to the success of the scheme whenever Mr. Roosevelt decided to launch it." By this time, however, according to Welles, too much invaluable time had been lost, and the President finally decided against proceeding further with his plan.[11]

Though rather sketchy and vague in a number of important respects, Welles's account had the expected effect, and when Winston Churchill in *The Gathering Storm,* the first volume of his memoirs of World War II, published in April, 1948, not only revealed that Eden's resignation as Foreign Secretary had been largely the result of his bitter disagreement with Chamberlain over the Prime Minister's handling of the President's plan, but went on to herald Roosevelt's proposal as signifying "the arrival of the United States in the circle of European hopes and fears,"[12] Welles's version acquired a kind of copperplated reputation.

While what might be called the Welles-Churchill version (for the two accounts were hereafter frequently cited together)[13] rapidly won general acceptance, it is important to note that even before the appearance of Churchill's memoirs, Keith Feiling's authorized biography of Neville Chamberlain, published in 1946, and Secretary of State Hull's memoirs, published in March, 1948, had begun to put a rather different face on the whole story.

Feiling, for instance, revealed that Chamberlain had been highly distrustful of American policies and pronouncements ever since the disastrous London Economic Conference of 1933 (with which, as Chancellor of the Exchequer at the time, he had been closely connected).[14] "The Americans," Chamberlain had written in his diary at the end of that eventful year, "are chiefly anxious to convince their people that they are not going to be drawn into doing anything helpful to the rest of the world."[15] American policies after 1933 had done nothing to change his mind. "I read Roosevelt's speech," he wrote after the Quarantine Address in October, 1937, "with rather mixed feelings . . . . When I asked U.S.A. to make joint *démarche* at the very beginning of the [Sino-Japanese] dispute, they refused."[16] This was hardly the sort of foundation on which effective Anglo-American peace efforts could be developed.

While Feiling stressed some of the reasons for British lack of confidence in American diplomacy, Secretary Hull, in his memoirs, revealed not only that Welles himself had first proposed to the President the idea of trying to achieve some sort of code of international conduct, but that the President himself had been considering some kind of peace initiative for more than a year, and had gone so far as to discuss his ideas with various friends and advisers, as well as with the Italian ambassador to the United States.[17] Hull made no effort to disguise his strong opposition to schemes of this sort, and set forth his position in vigorous terms:

At this late stage in 1937 . . . it would be fatal to lull the democracies into a feeling of tranquillity through a peace congress, at the very moment when their utmost efforts should actually be directed toward rearming themselves for self-defense. . . . Any half-informed person knew that every effort for five years had been made to prevail upon the Axis nations to join in a disarmament agreement, and that they deliberately refused and proceeded with rearmament on a colossal scale.[18]

Though the general public and most historians paid little attention to Hull's account, it was confirmed by the publication, in October, 1950, of the President's *Personal Letters 1928–1945*. These letters left no doubt that Roosevelt had been increasingly concerned about the world situation since he took office, that he had on a number of occasions expressed this concern to friends and associates, asking them what he might do to check its deterioration.[19] Most important, perhaps, they revealed that the President had in August, 1936, instructed Ambassador Dodd to approach the German government about the possibility of some kind of international conference:

I should like to have your slant, in the utmost confidence, as to what would happen if Hitler were personally and secretly asked by me to outline the limit of German foreign policy objectives during, let us say a ten year period, and to state whether or not he would have any sympathy with a general limitation of armaments' proposal. You cannot, of course, ask any questions regarding this in such a way as to let any inference be drawn that we were even thinking of such a thing.[20]

This letter, it should be noted, was written three weeks before the appearance of Arthur Krock's story in the New York *Times*, and if that letter was insufficient to confirm the essential accuracy of that article, the last remaining doubt was removed by the President's letter to Dodd of January 9, 1937:

> That story by Arthur Krock was not wholly crazy. If five or six heads of the most important governments could meet together for a week with complete inaccessibility to press or cables or radio, a definite, useful agreement might result or else one or two of them would be murdered by the others! In any case it would be worthwhile from the point of view of civilization.[21]

Six months later, in July, 1937, the President invited Chamberlain to visit the United States, though agreeing with Hull and the Prime Minister that "however desirable a meeting between us may be, it is necessary that it should be properly prepared and timed if it is to have fruitful results." [22] Chamberlain did not think the time propitious, and the meeting was never held. Finally, the *Letters* revealed that Roosevelt had also discussed the world situation and what to do about it with Canadian Prime Minister Mackenzie King during his visit to Washington in March, 1937, and that King had subsequently sent the President a detailed memorandum setting forth his own ideas on the subject—emphasizing, for instance, that "collective security should not be identified with reliance upon force . . . but with reliance upon reason—public opinion." [23]

It seems clear that the publication of the President's *Personal Letters* drew rather sharply the lines between the Welles-Churchill and what might be called the Krock-Dodd-Davies-Hull version, and though Welles, in his *Seven Decisions That Shaped History*, published in March, 1951, restated his case with great passion and pride—citing as his star witness none other than Winston Churchill himself [24]—it remained for William L. Langer and S. Everett Gleason in *The Challenge to Isolation 1937–1940* to reexamine the course of American foreign policy before the outbreak of World War II, and to lend their superbly informed judgment to those doubting the practical significance of the President's highly publicized peace efforts:

> Since the publication of the Axis records captured during the war, it has become perfectly patent that the ambitions of the Nazi leaders went far beyond what reasonable statesmen in other countries would have thought possible at the time, and that therefore the move contemplated

by Mr. Roosevelt, like the appeasement efforts of Mr. Chamberlain, would probably have been doomed to failure. Conceivably, a really strong stand by the United States Government in support of the British might have changed the course of events, but nothing of the kind was even remotely envisaged . . . . Under the circumstances Hitler was perfectly safe in discounting the influence of the United States.[25]

This was the authoritative verdict of masterful scholarship, and Langer and Gleason were further supported by the revealing memoirs of Sir Samuel Hoare, who served as British Home Secretary at that time. Hoare, an intimate friend of Neville Chamberlain, reemphasized the prevailing great strength of American isolationism as well as the continuing lack of confidence and trust between London and Washington, which explained Chamberlain's unsurprising reluctance to delay his own diplomatic efforts in favor of what he considered a rather woolly and hopeless scheme.[26] As Sir Samuel put it:

All the available evidence . . . pointed to the fact that, whilst Roosevelt sympathized with the democracies, he neither would nor could risk a conflict with his own isolationists . . . . In January 1938, Chamberlain was convinced that American isolationism made effective American action impossible. It was this conviction more than any other reason that not only made him impatient of American lectures on international conduct, and American reiteration of moral principles, but more than ever forced his mind in the only direction that then seemed likely to avert war, the negotiation of specific, and probably limited agreements, first with Mussolini, and secondly with Hitler.[27]

There may be some who would dismiss Hoare's remarks as little more than the unrepentant rationalizations of an inveterate appeaser. But the full account of American peace efforts before Munich remained even then far from fully told, and as the story began to unfold after the middle 1950's, it became increasingly clear that the generally accepted Welles-Churchill version was in fact inaccurate and could no longer be maintained.

II

Of all the new evidence on the subject appearing over the last twenty years none is more important than the official American documents on European political developments in 1937, included in the first of the State Department's *Foreign Relations* volumes for that year, published in June, 1954. First of all, the documents printed in that volume reveal that the idea of convening another international conference, whether devoted to all outstanding international issues or limited only to economic questions, had been discussed in Washington for more than six months before Welles first submitted his own proposals to the President. Second, it was generally agreed, both in Washington and in Europe, that a conference not only stood little or no chance of success but might well do considerable harm to the Western democracies. This was the position taken, for instance, by Herbert Feis, the distinguished economic adviser to the Secretary of State, by James C. Dunn, the veteran head of the Department's Western European Division, and by Ambassador Dodd, who set forth his own position in a number of urgent telegrams and personal letters to the President and the Secretary of State.[28] Moreover, the documents now published in *Foreign Relations* leave no doubt that the British and French governments, and some of their leading officials and diplomats, had the most serious reservations about the results of such a conference. Thus as early as March 11, 1937, Foreign Secretary Eden told Robert Bingham, the American ambassador in London, that

> so far as Great Britain is concerned the rearmament program has not advanced far [enough?] for the British to risk participation in a disarmament conference because he felt the dictators would look upon it as indicating weakness on the part of the British and inability to carry through their program; and . . . he felt that the time had not yet arrived when his country could contemplate any steps in [the direction of disarmament].[29]

On April 9, 1937, Eden told Norman H. Davis, a close friend of the President and Welles, that he, Eden, "hoped that [the United States] agree with [Britain] that it was not yet the time to make an effective move towards international agreement particularly with respect to armaments. . . . Any initiative which the British might take for a European settlement would now be construed as weakness."[30]

Much the same word came from Paris. For instance, on April 30, 1937, Ambassador William C. Bullitt reported to Secretary Hull that Sir Eric Phipps, recently transferred from Berlin to be British ambassador to France,

considered Hitler a fanatic who would be satisfied with nothing less than the domination of Europe. [Phipps] did not see the faintest possibility of coming to any agreement with Hitler. He was certain from his experience in Berlin that the only thing which could impress the Germans today was military force. He believed that any negotiations which might be begun today with Germany by England and France would end in failure unless France and England should be prepared to accord Germany absolute domination of the international situation.[31]

On May 11, 1937, Ambassador Bullitt informed Secretary Hull that André François-Poncet, the French ambassador in Berlin, had told him

the Germans would continue to talk about their desire to enter into economic collaboration with the rest of the world; but would ask a price . . . the world could not accept . . . . He believed that [Hjalmar] Schacht's conversations would be in reality a smoke screen behind which Hitler would await the propitious moment to lay hands on Austria and Czechoslovakia.[32]

These were compelling arguments from moderate and well-informed men, and it is only fair to add that Chamberlain, at this time, strongly agreed with these views. It would be difficult to find even a trace of appeasement in the important memorandum Chamberlain, then still Chancellor of the Exchequer, addressed to Treasury Secretary Henry Morgenthau, Jr., in March, 1937, shortly before becoming Prime Minister:

The main source of the fears of war in Europe is to be found in Germany . . . . The motive for this aggressiveness on the part of Germany appears to arise from her desire to make herself so strong that no one will venture to withstand whatever demands she may make whether for European or colonial territory . . . . With this intention in her heart she is not likely to agree to any disarmament which would defeat her purpose. The only consideration which would influence her to a contrary decision would be the conviction that her efforts . . . were doomed to failure by reason of the superior force which would meet her if she attempted aggression.[33]

It was rather obvious then that Chamberlain believed this was not an appropriate time to begin serious negotiations with the Germans, indeed that he saw little point even in discussing how such conversations should be approached. On September 28, 1937, therefore, Chamberlain replied to a letter dated July 28 in which the President had agreed that conversations between them needed to be most carefully prepared:

I am afraid that I cannot suggest any way in which the meeting between us could be expedited, though I greatly regret this both on personal and official grounds. Perhaps the community of sentiment between our two countries as to the events in the Far East and the developments of the European situation may be doing something to create a favorable atmosphere.[34]

Chamberlain's memorandum to Morgenthau and his personal letter to Roosevelt strongly suggest that at this point at least the new policy of appeasement—the mindless and immoral course of seeking to dissuade and distract the aggressor states from their chosen path by making substantial concessions often at the expense of third parties—was still a thing of the future. On the contrary, it appears that throughout most of 1937 both the British and French governments still believed they could meet the aggressor states on reasonably equal terms. They therefore sought to gain time to rearm and desired to avoid further premature concessions. They feared that the Axis powers would utilize any international conferences to make additional demands on them. It was doubtless this last concern that moved Chamberlain to write in his much criticized message to the President, of January 14, 1938, that

Germany and Italy may feel constrained to take advantage of the President's suggestion both to delay considerations of specific points which must be settled if appeasement is to be achieved, and to put forward demands over and above what they would put forward if we were in direct negotiation with them.[35]

Moreover, Chamberlain's repeated reference to the growing Far Eastern crisis serves further to support the contention of Langer and Gleason that there was indeed a direct connection between events in China and British reaction to an American-sponsored peace initiative. It is interesting to note that, as early as June, 1937, the United States began to make it clear to Great Britain that it was not prepared to consider joint action against Japan in the Far East. A memorandum from the State Department to the British Embassy in Washington expressed this policy as follows:

In the event of . . . aggression in the Far East . . . we are not, as we assume the British Government would not be, in position to state in advance what methods . . . this country would employ. It is the traditional policy of this country not to enter into those types of agreement which constitute or suggest alliance.[36]

Nor were the British alone at this time in appreciating the fact that, in the end, the only language the aggressor states understood was that of superior force. Thus in May, 1937, Ambassador Bullitt, who was rapidly becoming something of a father-confessor to French statesmen, reported to Washington that Camille Chautemps, a former Premier and one of the ablest political leaders in Paris, believed that

unless the President could back his words by pledging the support of the armed forces and the economic and financial strength of the United States against an aggressor words would be without effect. He added that of course he knew that any such intervention by the United States was impossible.[37]

In May, 1955, eleven months after the publication of these documents, appeared the *Foreign Relations* volume covering European political developments in 1938. At first glance, it might seem that the documents contained in this volume were less revealing and significant than those included in its predecessor, but this was far from being the case. On the contrary, the 1938 documents covered the last and in some ways most highly publicized phase of the President's peace initiative. They contributed substantially toward correcting the picture of that episode and, in the process, illuminated anew the position of the American and British governments and of some of their leading spokesmen.

On the surface, the documents published in the 1938 *Foreign Relations* volume would appear to bear out Welles's account of this last phase: how Roosevelt's first message to the Prime Minister had met with a distinctly doubtful response; how the President had reluctantly agreed to delay his initiative for a short time; how a second message had then arrived from Chamberlain agreeing to the President's proposal; and how Roosevelt, largely because of the uncertain situation in Germany, had finally decided to postpone his move until a more suitable time.[38] But Welles, in his two books, had told considerably less than he knew about the Eden-Chamberlain relationship. He had strongly suggested that it was Chamberlain who had favored delay of the President's proposal so the Prime Minister could proceed with his efforts to appease Mussolini, while Eden, having no faith in these efforts, held the view that Great Britain should lend strong and full support to the President's plan. Throughout his accounts of this period, Welles was careful to portray himself as a staunch opponent of all forms of appeasement,[39] while appearing to castigate all those who supported such compromising agreements as the Anglo-Italian accord of April, 1938, by which Great Britain, among other things, extended *de jure* recognition to the Italian conquest of Abyssinia.

This seemed to be a plausible interpretation of events, and considering the respective reputations of Welles, Chamberlain, and Eden, it is not surprising that it was generally accepted. But, as the 1938 *Foreign Relations* documents reveal, the actual story was rather different. For instance, on February 4, 1938, in the course of a conversation with Herschel V. Johnson, the American chargé d'affaires in London, and Hugh R. Wilson, Jr., the recently appointed American ambassador to Germany, Eden gave every indication that he supported Chamberlain's efforts to reach a general agreement with the Axis powers, stating that he expected Germany's contribution to the agreement to include "effective guarantees from Hitler that the peace of Central Europe would not be disturbed." There was no suggestion that Eden had any doubts about the value of guarantees of this sort; indeed he went on to remark that there was no "good ground for belief in the practical possibility of peaceful settlement of German-Czechoslovak difficulties."

For his part, Welles told Sir Ronald Lindsay, the British ambassador in Washington, on February 25, 1938, five days after Eden's sensational resignation from the Foreign Office, that he "trusted that the really energetic efforts which the British Prime Minister was making toward reaching a peaceful solution to the various adjustments in Europe might meet with success and that there might result therefrom the opportunity for a general world appeasement." Sir Ronald, whose credentials as an opponent of appeasement seem unquestioned, responded that he "was really at a loss to understand the position which had been assumed by Mr. Eden inasmuch as he could not see that any question of principle was involved." From his "official mail . . . from London, including memoranda of the conversations which Mr. Eden himself had had in London only the week before with Count [Dino] Grandi, the Italian ambassador," Lindsay judged that "in these conversations Mr. Eden had evidenced his own desire to reach an agreement through the negotiations now proposed by Mr. Chamberlain . . . and that Mr. Eden himself was morally and officially obligated to exactly the same course as that which Mr. Chamberlain had now announced." [40]

Although Welles in *Time for Decision* had suggested that Chamberlain, following his initial message asking the President to delay his initiative for a brief period, had expressed only routine support for the President's plan in later messages, the *Foreign Relations* documents strongly support Sir Samuel Hoare's account that the British expressed considerable interest in the American proposal. Thus on February 1, 1938, Ambassador Lindsay called Welles, in response to a telephonic inquiry from Eden in London, to ask the Undersecretary whether the President planned to go ahead, but Welles replied that he could give him no indication until he had spoken with Roosevelt, and when Welles and Lindsay met the following day, Welles could say only that he hoped to have some information "within the next few days . . . and that for the moment the President had nothing more to say." [41]

When Welles and Lindsay met again on February 9, Welles told the British ambassador that the President had asked him to say that he

> had further delayed taking the action envisaged . . . because of the recent acute situation . . . in Germany and that until that situation should appear a little clearer . . . the President felt it would be unwise to go ahead. He desired the British Government to know, however, that he intended proceeding with his plan in the relatively near future and would send further word on this matter later to the British Government.[42]

Lindsay told Welles that he wanted

to reassure [him] in the most positive manner . . . that the British Government was committed with every means within their power [to support] the successful realization of the President's objectives . . . . [The United States] could count upon his Government's carrying out this commitment with the utmost loyalty and energy.[43]

Within a fortnight the Austrian crisis broke, but instead of seeking to lend some sort of assistance to Britain in the hope that this would serve to strengthen Chamberlain's determination to make no concessions to Germany, American policy seemed concerned to leave Britain in no doubt that no such support was to be expected. Thus in the course of another long meeting at the State Department on March 7—less than a week before the *Anschluss*—Welles reiterated to Lindsay that

the President frankly recognized that certain political appeasements in Europe with which this Government had no direct concern and in which this Government could not participate were evidently an indispensable factor in the finding of bases of world peace . . . that this Government trusted the negotiations for these political appeasements would prove completely successful, but that . . . this Government had not attempted to pass upon the methods of approach determined upon by Mr. Chamberlain.[44]

Moreover, said Welles

the President had made it emphatically clear that this Government did not intend to participate in any way in the questions of European political appeasement and that the only initiative which the President had contemplated was that concerning which the British Government had been fully informed . . . the President had determined to hold that initiative in abeyance [but] . . . the British Government would be informed should the President at some subsequent date determine that it was desirable to take any action of the kind which he had previously contemplated.[45]

"It seemed to me exceptionally important," Welles said at the close of the conversation, "for there to be not the shadow of misapprehension on the part of the British Foreign Office of the attitude of this Government nor as to the limits of activity beyond which this Government could not and would not go." [46]

Since Welles in *Time for Decision* placed such great emphasis on the aggressive stance Hitler had taken in his interview with the British ambassador in Berlin on March 3, 1938,[47] it seems only fair to note that the 1938 *Foreign Relations* documents include the text of a telegram dated March 11 from Lord Halifax, Eden's successor at the Foreign Office, transmitted to the State Department by the British Embassy, describing an interview Halifax had had the previous day in London with Joachim von Ribbentrop, the German ambassador. The general tenor of the telegram was by far the strongest that had come from London in a very long time, and for a brief moment it appeared that the British seemed determined to warn the Germans against engaging in precipitous action the ultimate results of which could not easily be foreseen. Halifax had said to Ribbentrop:

> The last thing we wanted to see was a war in Europe. But once war should start in Central Europe it was quite impossible to say where it might not end or who might not become involved in it and it was clear that the language used in Germany of late might, contrary to the intention of the German Government, precipitate a general conflict . . . . In these circumstances I am bound to confess that one of the twin efforts which His Majesty's Government was anxious to make to prepare the way for an appeasement, and on account of which we ask the President to postpone his initiative, has failed.[48]

But if the British policy of seeking to reach some general accommodation with Germany seemed to have met with disaster, one is bound to ask if Washington had some understanding of why the British Government had acted so falteringly at the time. And the fact of the matter is that the 1938 *Foreign Relations* documents do contain an important explanation of British policy clearly supporting the view that the British Government was increasingly concerned by the large gap between its commitments in Europe and the Far East and its distinctly limited political and military resources. Since the British believed it impossible to establish a working relationship with the United States in the Far East, and since the United States had repeatedly indicated that she would have nothing whatsoever to do with European affairs, the British government had good reason to think it had no choice but in some way to reduce its obligations. As Herschel V. Johnson, the American chargé d'affaires in London, put it in a report to Washington on February 15, 1938:

> The view of the service departments . . . is that it is essential for Great Britain at once to detach at least one member of the German, Italian, Japanese anti-Comintern combination. Their view apparently is based on reasons of national safety as they believe if a war should break out Great Britain cannot cope with a combination of all those powers; it becomes virtually necessary for her to settle her differences with at least one of them.[49]

In the light of such authoritative advice, it was hardly surprising that Chamberlain should have continued to press ahead, whatever the obstacles, in order to achieve some kind of agreement with Italy. This he finally succeeded in doing two months later. To be sure, the Anglo-Italian agreement of April, 1938, fell considerably short of what both Chamberlain and Eden had originally hoped to obtain. But under the circumstances the British government appeared to believe that it had little choice in the matter, especially since the German annexation of Austria in the middle of March had dramatically confirmed Eden's remark, a month earlier, that "although Mussolini was by far a greater immediate difficulty than Hitler there was no question that, as far as a general European settlement was concerned, Germany presented the real problem." [50]

It cannot be said that either Welles, speaking for the State Department, or President Roosevelt himself fully appreciated the British dilemma in the face of the rapidly deteriorating world situation or the urgent necessity for a general review and rethinking of long standing American policies toward European and Far Eastern affairs. Indeed, there was no little irony in the fact that, having attempted to warn Great Britain against extending *de jure* recognition of the Italian conquest of Abyssinia [51]—"a surrender by His Majesty's Government of the principle of non-recognition at this time would have a serious effect upon public opinion in this country," the President had advised Chamberlain in his message of January 17, 1938"—the United States took a rather different attitude once the British government had in fact accorded such recognition.

Speaking to the Chinese ambassador who had learned of

the Department's official position concerning the Anglo-Italian agreement, Welles said on April 18, 1938 that

> since among [the principles of international relations] in which [the United States] believed was the solution through pacific negotiation of controversies and difficulties which arose between governments as opposed to the solution of controversies through the use of force . . . [and] in as much as the British-Italian agreement was obviously the result of . . . pacific negotiation, the result was viewed with sympathy by the United States and with the very earnest hope that the accord . . . might prove to be a factor in the furtherance of world peace.[52]

And at a press conference the following afternoon, President Roosevelt put the American position on the record even more unequivocally:

> As this Government has on frequent occasions made it clear, the United States . . . believes in the promotion of world peace through the friendly solution by peaceful negotiation between nations of controversies that may arise between them. It has also urged the promotion of peace through the finding of means for economic appeasement. It does not attempt to pass upon the political features of accords such as that recently reached between Great Britain and Italy, but this government has seen the conclusion with sympathetic interest because it is proof of the value of peaceful negotiations.[53]

It is not difficult to imagine Chamberlain's reaction when word of this presidential statement reached him in London. After the President's Quarantine Speech, in October, 1937, Chamberlain had written in his diary: "It is always best and safest to count on nothing from the Americans but words."[54] Now it appeared from official American pronouncements on the German annexation of Austria—which the United States did not even formally protest—as well as on the Anglo-Italian agreement,[55] that not much was henceforth to be expected from the United States even along that line. And although Welles preferred to ignore this aspect of American diplomacy, both he and the President seemed to accept the widely held opinion, fashioned in clever intellectual circles, that the overriding problem of contemporary international affairs was something called "peaceful change," a doctrine suggesting that the actual provisions and consequences of international agreements were not nearly as important as the fact that they were not brought about by the use or threat of military force.[56] Indeed, it was this intoxicating doctrine that provided the basis for American acceptance of the Munich agreement six months later.[57]

In 1957, two years after the publication of these *Foreign Relations* documents on European political developments in 1938, there appeared in Lord Halifax's memoirs, *Fullness of Days,* a brief postscript to the eventful days of early 1938. Lord Halifax was an old and weary man when he wrote his memoirs. He had witnessed in his time, and on several occasions had played a vital part in, the long retreat of the imperial way of life. He had seen the old order pass first in India, then in Europe, and finally after 1945 in Britain itself. It was not his desire, in this autumnal account, to reopen old wounds, and he passed rather lightly over the dramatic events surrounding Eden's resignation from the Foreign Office and his own appointment as Foreign Secretary, in February, 1938.

But he told one story that sheds some further light on how Roosevelt himself seems to have felt about the fate of his peace initiative. Halifax recalled that once during World War II, when he was serving as British ambassador to the United States, he called on the President to prepare for Anthony Eden's forthcoming visit to this country. He started, he reported, to tell the President something of the circumstances leading up to Eden's resignation in 1938 and the role the President's peace proposal may inadvertently have played in that decision. But the President, Halifax recalled, was plainly not interested in hearing any more about the matter, and cut him short by inquiring whether he had ever seen the telegram he, the President, had sent to Chamberlain after hearing he was going to Munich. "The shortest telegram I ever sent," the President said, "two words, 'Good Man.' "[58]

III

The revelations of the 1937 and 1938 *Foreign Relations* volumes marked a watershed in the historiography of American peace efforts before Munich. When discussion of that subject resumed in the early 1960's, the intellectual climate in this country and in Europe was quite different. Given that change, it was hardly surprising that the subject should then have evoked so little interest and response, and much of that was clearly uninformed.

In the 1940's and 1950's there had been a deep revulsion in the Western democracies against everything connected with Munich and the age of appeasement, but by the early 1960's the Suez disaster had destroyed what remained of Britain and France as world powers—together with most interest in the history and significance and reasons for that decline—while in the United States the advent of the Kennedy administration symbolized the ascendency of a new ambiguity about the meaning and relevance of the Munich era and everything connected with it.[59]

The most recent phase in the discussion of appeasement and American peace efforts before World War II began with the publication of Iain Macleod's biography of Neville Chamberlain in 1961. Though based on extensive use of Chamberlain's private diary and personal correspondence, Macleod's work achieved no great success on either side of the Atlantic. This was hardly surprising, for (in addition to a rather one-sided defense of Chamberlain's policy during the Munich crisis) his book recalled too many unfashionable facts, among them that Chamberlain had long detested everything Hitler and the Nazi regime stood for, that appeasement was a policy of necessity not a policy of hope,[60] and that the schizophrenic attitude of the Labour Party—"sanctions but no rearmament"—had made it enormously more difficult to achieve effective national unity on foreign policy and the kind of defense policy desperately needed to meet the rising threat of aggression in Europe and elsewhere.[61]

Anglo-American relations, unfortunately, were not one of Macleod's main themes, and his work does not add greatly to the background and history of them before World War II. He quotes Chamberlain's bitter reaction to Roosevelt's blowup of the London Economic Conference in July, 1933: "The whole situation was changed," Chamberlain wrote in his diary, "by the issue of the President's most offensive message to his Secretary of State. This effusion so completely declared his intent to go his own way." [62] It seems obvious that Chamberlain remembered and bitterly resented this incident much longer than is generally realized.

When Macleod came to the President's initial message to the Prime Minister in January, 1938, he once more let Chamberlain's diary speak for itself:

Roosevelt sprang a surprise by informing us that he proposed to issue a sort of world appeal to end international tension . . . . If this proposal had a favorable reception he would summon to Washington representatives of various small nations . . . to formulate a plan for submission to a subsequent conference. He said he would not publish unless by the 17th Jan. (I got this on the 13th) I could assure him of whole-hearted support and co-operation. I was in a dilemma. The plan appeared to me fantastic and likely to excite the derision of Germany and Italy. They might even use it to postpone conversations with us . . . . There was no time to consult Anthony, for in view of secrecy on which Roosevelt insisted . . . I did not dare to telephone . . . . Therefore, after consultation with [Sir Horace] Wilson and [Sir Alexander] Cadogan, I sent a reply depreciating immediate publication . . . . This produced a somewhat sulky acquiescence . . . and some strong worded warnings against shocking public opinion by giving *de jure* recognition to Italy.[63]

On January 16 Eden returned from France and complications began:

[Eden] did not like my reply [Chamberlain went on] and without consulting me sent a fresh note to . . . Lindsay . . . saying I had not exactly meant what I said . . . . [Finally after a meeting of the Foreign Affairs Committee of the Cabinet that supported the Prime Minister] we agreed on a compromise reply . . . . Subsequent despatches from Lindsay showed that this had the effect desired by me. The course proposed "entirely met the President's views" and there was no reason why we should not proceed [with our conversations with Italy].[64]

Eden's own account of British foreign policy before Munich and of the role he had played in the development of that policy appeared less than a year after Macleod's biography of Chamberlain. By the time *Facing the Dictators* was published in 1962, Eden's political career had been shattered by the Suez crisis, and nothing that he had written in his account of that great turning point of modern British history[65] had done much to rehabilitate either his judgment or his political reputation. Nevertheless, Eden's memoirs of the 1930's were awaited with great anticipation, for that was the period in which he had first made his mark and achieved considerable stature as a supposed enemy of appeasement.

Facing the Dictators did contain a wealth of new details, based on Eden's own papers and on still unpublished documents of the British Foreign Office. And though his extended, dramatic, and polished account of his growing differences with Chamberlain and Sir Horace Wilson, the Prime Minister's Advisor on Industrial Relations specializing in international problems—one of the high points of the whole volume—largely confirmed the essential facts of the situation as known from earlier accounts, *Facing the Dictators* nevertheless added considerably to our knowledge and understanding of Anglo-American relations and American peace efforts before Munich.

Eden began by revealing that he first learned about American plans for some kind of international peace conference from Sir Eric Phipps, the British ambassador in Berlin, in November, 1936. Phipps quoted his source, Ambassador Dodd, as saying that "the President had in mind summoning a world peace conference the following spring. If the 'gangster powers' declined to attend, or to give satisfactory undertakings at the conference, the peace-loving states should come to a close agreement." Eden had some doubts whether such a plan could succeed but, even if it failed, it would, he thought, serve to educate world (and especially American) opinion. "In any event," he wrote, "it would be clearly a great error to discourage the President in his idea, if it is his idea." Eden noted however that some of his advisers at the Foreign Office were even then "skeptical about the prospects of this project for peace," and he instructed Sir Robert Vansittart, the permanent under-secretary, to inform Sir Ronald Lindsay in Washington of "the importance we attach to thorough preparation for world conference . . . [and] to try to arrange that invitations should not be sent out until there had been time for confidential discussions between our two countries," an idea Welles, as will be recalled, strongly disparaged.[66]

Unfortunately Eden took no note of the important documentary evidence contained in the 1937 and 1938 *Foreign Relations* volumes. But his own account of a conversation with Ambassador Bingham in London, on March 20, 1937, serves both to confirm some of Bingham's reports, previously published, and to cast further doubt on Welles's version of events.

The Ambassador said [according to Eden] it was quite true that President Roosevelt had been contemplating some initiative to attempt to better the present international situation. He was, however, determined to take no initiative except in close consultation with us . . . . President Roosevelt was not only ready but eager to help, . . . he would be ready to take an initiative if and when we thought the moment right, and . . . he would take none unless we were in accord as to its appropriateness. This message, the Ambassador said, he had been specifically instructed by the President to deliver personally to me. The Ambassador continued that it was his own impression that the time for any initiative by President Roosevelt was not yet. He had given the United States Government a full record of our last conversation, and made it clear that this was my view also. He further explained the apprehension I felt lest any premature move might create an impression that our armaments programme was bluff. At the same time, if he understood our position aright, we thought careful watch should be kept so that the appropriate moment was not missed. I replied that His Excellency had correctly defined our position.[67]

Nothing further seems to have come of these conversations between Eden and Bingham. Though Eden, unlike Hoare, was disinclined to dwell at length on the unsatisfactory state of Anglo-American relations, he too could hardly overlook the ominous fact that even the renewal of Japanese aggression in the Far East in the summer of 1937 had failed to move Washington toward joint Anglo-American action in that part of the world.[68]

Events in the latter part of 1937 were hardly more promising. To be sure, Eden rather overestimated the adverse response to the President's Quarantine Speech, but his account of the abortive Brussels Conference and its aftermath did nothing to suggest that the future of Anglo-American cooperation was at all promising. For instance, at the beginning of the Brussels Conference Norman H. Davis, the head of the American delegation, had told Eden that the President "was deeply concerned at the world outlook and sincerely anxious to co-operate in an attempt to stop the rot." If the conference failed, "further action by the United States could not be excluded," but three weeks later Davis reported receiving a telegram from Secretary Hull explaining that the President had not wished to use any words that "might seem to indicate hostile action was a possibility." [69]

After the attack on the *Panay* and a British warship in Chinese waters in December, 1937, Eden telegraphed Lindsay in Washington:

It seems clear that some action will have to be taken by both the United States Government and His Majesty's Government to curb this dangerous spirit before it goes to still more intolerable lengths. There is no doubt that this action should be taken jointly otherwise it will fail to end which will in any case be difficult to attain.[70]

When Ambassador Lindsay, the President, and Secretary Hull met in the strictest secrecy at the White House on December 16 to consider what action to take, the President, drawing on his World War experience in the Navy Department, agreed to send Captain Ingersoll to London for Anglo-American staff conferences, but beyond that he refused to go. "Mr. Hull in his only contribution to the conversation," Eden reported, "spoke of the inadvisability of any talk in London about joint action with the United States. The President endorsed this strongly." [71]

It should be noted that throughout his memoirs Eden rightly placed great emphasis on the necessity for the closest possible Anglo-American collaboration in world affairs. But whatever his own personal desires, there was no avoiding the harsh reality that in 1937 the United States was not prepared to enter into such collaboration. This fact doubtless weighed heavily upon Eden, who sought to put the best possible construction on the American position. "Suspicion was rife," he wrote, "that British diplomacy had as its aim to entangle the United States in problems which were not properly its concern and that we were trying to get that country to pull our chestnuts out of the fire." [72]

Chamberlain, it was clear, felt that such charitable interpretation made little or no difference. The cables from Washington spoke for themselves. He and most of his colleagues still had fresh and bitter memories of 1933. The Cabinet's overwhelming decision to press on for a settlement with Italy may have been, as Eden contended, highly unwise. But *Facing the Dictators* contains no new evidence to support Eden's eloquent argument that so much was to be expected from the latest American peace initiative.

If Eden's memoirs did nothing to dispel the impression that American diplomacy in 1937–38 was a policy of uneasy drift, this impression was further confirmed by Dorothy Borg's important work *The United States and the Far Eastern Crisis of 1933–1938,* published in 1964, which not only demonstrated again the relation of Pacific and European affairs in the 1930's but also shed new light on the history of American peace efforts during this period.[73]

Beginning with an account of Arthur Krock's original story in the New York *Times* (Borg seems to be one of the very few historians aware of its existence), of the Buenos Aires Conference on Inter-American Peace (which she had already discussed in an earlier study),[74] and the President's meeting with Prime Minister Mackenzie King in March, 1937, Borg, drawing on the Norman Davis papers, examined at greater length than she had previously done Davis's mission to Europe in the spring of 1938, and what it suggested about the state and prospective trend of American and West European foreign policy. She wrote:

> In speaking to Davis before his departure the President said that he might discreetly try to ascertain the reaction of European statesmen to the idea of possibly reorganizing the League of Nations so as to divest it of its political functions and transform it into a sort of Economic Council in which case "the United States ought to be able to go along" . . . . He also told Davis to sound out European statesmen on the subject of a general agreement to "neutralize" the Pacific . . . [and] to see if he could find a means of bringing the European governments together in a cooperative attempt to arrest the rapid deterioration of the international situation.[75]

But Davis's conversations were not encouraging; what he learned was hardly more encouraging than what he was able to state about American policy. Eden, for instance, told Davis that

> Great Britain could not propose any scheme for a general international agreement, as her doing so would be regarded as a sign of weakness and would thereby detract from the beneficial effect that her rearmament program was having upon Japan, Germany, and Italy . . . he thought the initiative would have to come from President Roosevelt, but he did not believe that the time was as yet quite ripe for action.[76]

To this Davis replied that he was

> absolutely certain that the President would not allow himself to become involved in the political controversies of the European powers, but that he would be willing to participate wholeheartedly in a concerted effort to find a solution to economic questions and to the problems posed by the competitive construction of more and more armaments.[77]

Chamberlain in a conversation with Davis, on the other hand, continued to stress that "political appeasement" must precede economic cooperation and efforts at arms reduction. The Prime Minister brought up the simmering Far Eastern crisis, and, as he had done in his letter to Secretary Morgenthau some months earlier, expressed the view that

> if England should get into trouble with Germany, Japan would take advantage of the situation to attack British interests in the Pacific . . . this could be avoided by a firm Anglo-American stand in the Far East which, in his [Chamberlain's] opinion, would cause the Japanese to abandon their hostile attitude in favor of co-operating with England and America to "promote peace and economic recovery in China and the Pacific." [78]

Davis parried this remark and brought up the possibility of "neutralizing the Pacific area," but Chamberlain doubted "the practicability of trying to do anything so important before there should be an improvement in the political situation in Japan." [79]

Borg also shed further light on the President's determination, in January, 1938, to proceed after all with his earlier plans for some sort of peace initiative. She revealed, for instance, that there had been a series of top-level meetings to review American policy at the State Department in early January, and that the President's decision was apparently the outgrowth—though certainly not the intended result—of these meetings.

According to Borg, Secretary Hull made it clear at these sessions that

> his own attitude toward the Axis countries was rapidly hardening as he felt Japan's policy was growing increasingly "desperate and dangerous and that the Japanese were working in close association with the Germans and Italians who were embarking upon a far-reaching program to impose their will upon the world." [80]

He proposed, therefore, that the United States and Great Britain give serious consideration to parallel naval measures in the Pacific and in other ways demonstrate their political and economic closeness.

Welles, according to Borg, countered that such measures were either likely to lead to war ("and that the American people would not support close cooperation with the British") or were so cumbersome that, in the meantime, the Axis powers would have had sufficient time to commit additional acts of aggression.[81] Welles urged the President, therefore, to revive his earlier plan for a special meeting of foreign diplomats at the White House, contending that his proposal would, in effect, not only lend added support to British and French efforts to reach a more general agreement with Germany and Italy but also would tend to reduce the prospects of effective cooperation between Germany, Italy, and Japan.[82] It is not clear if the President was in fact swayed by Welles's logic. It should be noted, however, as Langer and Gleason have done, that at the time Welles argued for his proposal as a measure favoring appeasement of the dictator-states.[83] In any case the President reversed himself and decided to go ahead with the plan, agreeing only to Hull's urgent stipulation that he first of all take up the matter with the British government.

Borg, like Eden, believed that Welles was the author of the President's January, 1938, peace initiative. Eden in *Facing the Dictators* even printed as an appendix the pertinent pages of *Time for Decision.*[84] But on its publication a suggestion appeared, for the first time, that possibly Welles was not the author of the President's peace initiative after all. Commenting on Eden's discussion of this episode, the reviewer of *Facing the Dictators* wrote in *The Times Literary Supplement:*

> What Lord Avon, like other commentators, does not seem to realize is that, as the files of the Franklin D. Roosevelt Library (President's Secretary's File: Canada Folder) reveal, the plan was the brain-child not of Roosevelt but of the Governor-General of Canada. When Lord Tweedsmuir put it up to Mr. Roosevelt in April 1937—also without consulting the Foreign Office—it was as a method of breaking "the vicious circle of fear among nations" and of avoiding the increasingly obvious danger of war. He hoped to achieve this by a congress which would discuss the fundamental questions behind the world's unrest, and by doing "something to save the face of Germany and Italy; and it is desirable to save their face, for the situation would be in no way bettered by an internal breakdown in either country." [85]

Nothing further was heard about Lord Tweedsmuir's possible role in the President's peace initiative until the appearance in 1965 of Janet Adam Smith's authorized biography of the late Governor General of Canada.[86] Tweedsmuir, probably better known as the writer John Buchan, first met the President when he came to New York to deliver the principal address at the opening of the new Columbia University Library. Appointed Governor General of Canada by King George V in early 1935, he lost no time in trying to bring about closer relations between the United States and Canada. In March, 1937, he and Prime Minister King had paid separate visits to President Roosevelt in Washington,[87] and Roosevelt had used the occasion to discuss with his Canadian guests the prospects for world peace and what might be done to head off another world war.[88]

Shortly afterward, Prime Minister King had sent the President a memorandum setting forth his own views, and three weeks later Tweedsmuir likewise sent the President a long and carefully prepared memorandum on the same subject. Tweedsmuir contended that no peace conference could hope to succeed except one under the President's personal direction. On the other hand, he recommended that "political and defense questions in the ordinary sense . . . be wholly excluded, and the aim would be to deal only with those fundamental economic difficulties which are the real cause of world disquiet," and concluded, "in any case, it seems to me essential that the President must be present himself at the Conference, both for the sake of his personal influence and as an advertisement that America means business." [89]

Though Tweedsmuir's memorandum did not in some important respects go as far as Prime Minister King's, the two were agreed on the necessity for avoiding all political and military issues, so as not to reopen all the old and fruitless arguments over disarmament. Tweedsmuir and King believed the root of international difficulties and disagreements was primarily economic, and that once existing economic and social grievances had been removed or significantly reduced, the way would be opened for a more harmonious and peaceful era in world affairs.

The President was most interested in the proposals King and Tweedsmuir submitted to him, although it is only fair to point out that these proposals were not the only significant recommendations on the subject reaching the President about that time. Moreover, both King's and Tweedsmuir's proposals failed to provide for the distinct possibility that the dictator states would, for one reason or another, refuse to cooperate with the kind of peace conference or peace plan they had in mind. Prime Minister King, additionally, placed great emphasis on the importance of avoiding the use of force in future international disputes.[90]

This rather idyllic view of international politics may have seemed realistic in Ottawa in 1937. But as Chamberlain viewed the situation from London, the time for hard decisions was close at hand. It was one of the merits of Ian Colvin's authorized biography of Lord Vansittart, published in the United States late in 1965,[91] that it should have brought us back from the make-believe world of elaborate peace plans and proposals to the harsh realities of international life as the British government was confronted with them in the middle and late 1930's.

Colvin showed, for instance, how Vansittart, in a comprehensive review of the international situation addressed to the Prime Minister, Stanley Baldwin, at Christmastime 1936, had pointed out that the signing of the German-Japanese Pact a month earlier clearly introduced Japan into European affairs at a delicate and dangerous moment, thus directly linking European and Far Eastern affairs.[92] Britain was indeed entering a period of great diplomatic and military insecurity:

> The year 1939 [Vansittart wrote to Baldwin] is the first in which we shall be able to breathe even with comparative relief . . . . But on any showing Germany will be ready for big mischief at least a year—and probably more—before we are ready to look after ourselves. To the Foreign Office therefore falls the task of holding the situation at least till 1939, and . . . there is no certainty of our being able to do so, though we are doing our utmost by negotiations with Germany.[93]

Vansittart strongly believed that Britain must "manufacture time" and do everything she could to retain American sympathies, going so far as to extend economic and colonial concessions to Germany—concessions which, Vansittart seems to have believed, the United States favored. Fortunately, he thought, the United States was "inclined toward our fellow democracy" and "they might be further so inclined," he wrote, "if Mr. Roosevelt carried out his vague idea of calling a 'World Peace Conference,' rendered abortive by the dictators. Such a step on his part might, indeed, help us in manufacturing time." [94]

Finally, Colvin sought to explain how it was that Chamberlain "the man of clear and cautious judgments in 1935 . . . became an addict of wishful solutions." Colvin believed that Chamberlain "made up his mind on high policy in the summer months of 1937, and nothing that happened between then and March, 1939, altered him in his obstinate course." If correct—and there was considerable evidence available to support Colvin's judgment—that would go a long way to explain his attitude toward the United States and the Axis powers in 1938.[95]

Chamberlain's changed attitude, Colvin believed, was the result of a number of related factors. One of these was that early in 1937 the British Chiefs of Staff had drawn up a comprehensive report on "Planning for War with Germany," which concluded that it would be unsafe to venture into war with Germany—even into a war of blockade—before 1939. The Chiefs of Staff repeated their warning even more emphatically in March, 1938.[96]

Another disturbing factor was the President's wavering course. Late in 1936 the British government had learned that Roosevelt hoped to convene some kind of international peace conference. A letter from Treasury Secretary Morgenthau to Chamberlain, then still Chancellor of the Exchequer, soon after confirmed the fact that the President still believed peace could be achieved through some form of disarmament—an approach Chamberlain felt he could hardly support in the light of existing international conditions.[97] Finally, there was congressional passage, ineffectively opposed by the President, of the Neutrality Act of May, 1937—called by Colvin a "grave setback to the Vansittart policy of strength in Europe."[98]

Under these circumstances, it was hardly surprising that the British government should have been unenthusiastic about the President's peace proposal of January, 1938. As Colvin puts it:

> It was plain that some of the Cabinet were for an alignment of Britain, France and President Roosevelt, even a Roosevelt encumbered with the Neutrality Act. Others thought of cultivating relations with Italy, or with Italy and Germany simultaneously, or with Germany to the exclusion of Italy. The unwritten rule that haunted these Cabinet discussions [of the President's peace proposal] was that Britain could not make war in 1938.[99]

The year 1966, finally, brought answers to several important, hitherto unanswered questions connected with the history of the President's peace efforts before Munich. The first of these questions concerned the source of Arthur Krock's original story in the New York *Times*, in August, 1936, that in the event of his reelection the President was seriously considering trying to arrange some great international peace conference. It was Krock himself who provided the answer to that question. Reprinting most of that dispatch in a volume of selected columns, *In the Nation 1923–1966,* he wrote in a prefatory note:

> The . . . dispatch . . . [was] an authorized report of a conversation with Roosevelt at Hyde Park. Since he was then a candidate for re-election, and some of the details of his plan (getting Stalin and Hitler to the same table—which they did, nonetheless, in 1939) exposed him at the time to Republican charges that he was encouraging hopes he knew were false, Roosevelt replied to all demands for verification of my dispatch with "no comment." I had conditioned use of the conversations on his promise not to deny the story, however it was publicly received. He kept the letter of the compact. But when some of his own associates joined the Republicans and press critics of his plan to prevent war, Roosevelt encouraged Henry A. Wallace, Secretary of Labor, to cast heavy doubt on my professional integrity and/or reportorial capacity.
>
> Emerging from the President's private railroad car, during a campaign tour, Wallace told reporters he had "discussed" the article with the President and "did not believe" it was "true." When I informed Wallace of the facts, he apologized—but only in private, to me.[100]

The second question concerned the attitude of the German government toward the President's peace plans. If the appearance of Krock's *In the Nation* was greeted with the respectful attention due one of the most experienced and best-known Washington correspondents of his time, the publication in December, 1966, of the *Documents on German Foreign Policy 1918–1945* for the period from March to December 1936—a volume of outstanding importance based on the records of the German Foreign Office captured at the end of World War II [101]—received practically no public attention. Yet the documents published in that volume, perhaps more than any other now available, serve to suggest the realistic prospects of the President's reported peace proposals.

Ambassador Dodd's journal, published in early 1941, revealed that he had discussed the President's plan with various leading German officials. Until its appearance, however, there had been no way of judging precisely what the Germans knew and thought of the President's initiative. It now seems clear from their tone that the Nazi regime had precious little interest in discussions of international peace save on its own particular terms.

The first document was a record of a conversation made by Dr. Hans Dieckhoff, Acting State Secretary in the Foreign Ministry, and later German ambassador to Washington:

> The German Ambassador called on me today [he wrote on September 17, 1936] and asked whether the German Government were still ready to collaborate in a general limitation of armaments and stated in confidence that it was possible that President Roosevelt, whose re-election was as good as certain, would approach the Powers in the course of November or December with a suggestion for a general disarmament conference. Mr. Dodd asked how such a suggestion from the American President might be expected to be received in Germany. In reply I told the Ambassador that it was naturally impossible to fix today the attitude of the German Government to a hypothetical case in the future, but that I took it that the principles laid down by the Führer in his speech of May 21, 1935, on the limitations of armaments, still applied. According to this, the plan for a limitation of armaments could only have prospects of success if it were really binding on all the States concerned and, furthermore, if it did not contain exaggerated demands but proceeded step by step, more or less on the lines the Führer had indicated in his aforementioned speech. After the unfortunate experiences the world had been through with the Geneva Disarmament Conference, which had dragged on for years with total lack of success, a new disarmament or armaments limitation plan would have to be drawn up with special care.[102]

A month later, on October 16, 1936, Ambassador Dodd had a conversation on much the same subject with Konstantin von Neurath, the German foreign minister, who recorded the following:

> The American Ambassador called on me this morning. The purpose of his call remained somewhat unclear to me. He muttered something about "Roosevelt's intention of calling a new Peace Conference" and then wanted to know what attitude we would adopt towards such a plan. I told him that I would first have to know what peace Mr. Roosevelt wished to conclude at the new conference, i.e., what was really to be discussed at this conference. Mr. Dodd could give no reply to this question.[103]

But if the German Foreign Office was at all disturbed by the thought that the German government might soon be confronted with a carefully planned American peace offensive, its fears were soon relieved by a report from the German ambassador in Washington in December, 1936:

Careful investigation amongst all circles concerned has shown [Ambassador Hans Luther wrote] that the President is not, in the foreseeable future, expected to take the initiative for a peace conference or in the sphere of disarmament . . . . A project of the nature indicated by Dodd has been described by Hull to a confidant as quite hopeless, since it was inconceivable that a compromise between European Governments who were diametrically opposed to each other in politics could be reached through an international conference . . . . Instructions to Dodd to take soundings in Berlin were not issued by the State Department. Dodd's *démarche,* which, incidentally according to information from the State Department, corresponds to Bullitt's similar unauthorized soundings in Paris, is presumably to be ascribed to the fact that when receiving American Ambassadors during their home leave the President is in the habit of informally discussing the international situation, with special regard to creating a lasting state of peace through the better distribution of raw materials and other economic methods. Circumstances permitting, a possible initiative by the American Government on this basis is more likely than that they should intervene in political conflicts in Europe which are regarded as hopeless here.[104]

There the German record ends, and no one who reflects upon it is likely to conclude that the Germans had good cause for concern that they would soon be confronted with another Grand Alliance, Model 1917. On the contrary, for the time being the German government had every reason to believe that it had nothing whatever to fear from the United States. From that certainty Hitler was soon to draw his own historic conclusions.

IV

From all the evidence published over the last three decades, what conclusions can be drawn concerning the origins, history, and significance of American peace initiatives before Munich?

Doubtless the first conclusion is that the conventional story of these peace efforts—that is, the story based essentially on the accounts of Welles and Churchill that these efforts began in the autumn of 1937 and reached a climax in January, 1938, that they were first delayed by Secretary Hull's myopic obstruction and finally wrecked by Chamberlain's naive faith in his ability to appease the dictators—this story can no longer be maintained and must, in the light of all the evidence now available, be abandoned as essentially inaccurate and misleading.

The story of American peace efforts as it begins to emerge from all the published evidence is somewhat as follows. Although Roosevelt had understandably given domestic problems the highest priority when he became President, he realized from his first days in the White House that the international situation was highly unstable and might easily deteriorate into another great war unless efforts were made to reduce existing political tensions and economic disorder. The President lost little time trying to ameliorate these conditions. He exchanged cordial letters with Hitler. He met in Washington with leading European statesmen, including Prime Minister Ramsay MacDonald of Great Britain, Premier Êdouard Herriot of France, and Dr. Hjalmar Schacht, the head of the Reichsbank. He proposed to the Geneva Disarmament Conference an even more sweeping program than President Hoover had done a year earlier.[105]

None of these efforts, however, proved successful, and for several years Roosevelt seemed undecided on what to do next. Though he had gradually moved away from supporting the League of Nations and other policies associated with President Wilson,[106] Roosevelt seemed increasingly to have come to the conviction that he must take a personal hand in the international situation. By the summer of 1936, at the latest, he seems to have concluded that the most promising approach to peace might be a meeting of the heads of state of all the great powers, perhaps somewhere at sea, to discuss outstanding international differences and ways and means of reducing them.

The President apparently discussed his idea with a number of close friends and associates in his administration, including some of his leading ambassadors, and also talked with a number of foreign diplomats, including Ambassador Rosso of Italy, whom he asked to sound out Mussolini on the matter. (Roosevelt seems long to have had a remarkable trust in Mussolini's peaceful intentions in international politics.)[107] The President asked Joseph E. Davies, American ambassador to Moscow, to discuss the matter with Dr. Schacht in Berlin, and he corresponded at length with Ambassador Dodd, hoping the German government might take an interest in the proposal. Ambassadors Bingham and Bullitt were asked to take up the subject informally with the British and French governments.

None of these efforts proved notably successful. Mussolini showed no great interest. Schacht blew hot and cold. Other German officials indicated any peace conference would have to follow Hitler's announced principles. In London there was considerable skepticism and a strong feeling that no such conference could succeed without considerable advance planning and consultation, the very thing the President sought to avoid. The French, perhaps most realistically of all, believed the only thing that mattered was a specific promise of American assistance—economic, political, military—but realized at once that such a promise was out of the question.

In July, 1937, the Japanese resumed their aggression against China, and the President's concern over the international situation rose once more. He gave expression to that concern in his famous Quarantine Speech in Chicago, on October 5, 1937, and the following day Welles submitted to him an outline of his own ideas on the world situation, a statement out of which grew Roosevelt's peace proposal of January, 1938.

It seems clear from this brief reconstruction of events that the background of the President's peace efforts before Munich was rather different from what Welles and those following his version of events have made it out to be. Perhaps the single most important fact is that, to be fully and properly understood, the President's peace efforts must be viewed in the broad framework of contemporary international politics, in the context of Anglo-American relations, and against the background of American politics and the American climate of opinion. It ought, for instance, not to be overlooked that only two days before Roosevelt sent his first message to Chamberlain, the House of Representatives in which the Democrats then had a majority of over 175 seats, on January 10, 1938, by a margin of only ten votes—209 to 188—refused to take up the so-called Ludlow Amendment to the United States Constitution, which save in case of invasion would have required a national referendum before the Congress could in the future declare war. This amendment, though strongly opposed by the President, was vigorously supported by all the peace, pacifist, and isolationist groups in the country,[108] and it is not difficult to imagine what impression this narrow victory of the President created abroad.

Second, there can be little doubt that since the early 1930's, the Far East and Europe had become part of one and the same international system, and that neither the United States nor Great Britain could henceforth ignore this inextricable relationship. Yet for years the United States and Great Britain sought to maintain the fiction that these two parts of the world could in fact be treated separately and differently. An incisive recent study of the subject observes:

> In one sense . . . it may be said that it was the failure to agree on collective security in the [Far] East, as in Europe, that stifled any effective action which might have prevented the intolerable from arising . . . . Yet Britain never quite understood why America was unwilling to join her [in the Far East], and while she realized the American desire to keep an independence of action, she never really grasped its depth, nor did she ever quite understand Hull's faith in the possibilities of educating public opinion. Hence the American rebuffs to British overtures, and the fact that the overtures themselves occasionally embittered relations between the two countries.[109]

There is considerable evidence to suggest that the unhappy course of Anglo-American relations in regard to the Far East cast a heavy pall over all other efforts at international cooperation between the two countries, including the President's peace proposal of January, 1938.[110] Moreover, contrary to Welles's assertion, there is no reason to believe that failure of the President's proposal would have led to a closer relationship between the United States, Great Britain, and the other democratic states.[111] There was nothing in the history of conference diplomacy going back to 1933 to suggest that such would be the case.

Third, given the rather vague nature of the President's proposal of January, 1938, as well as the circumstances under which it was made, it was hardly likely that the proposal would be greeted with much interest or enthusiasm either in Great Britain or in France (whom Hull had wished to consult before proceeding any further with the whole project).[112] Given the fact that the international balance of power was moving rapidly in favor of the Axis, it seems extremely doubtful that Germany, Italy, and Japan would have agreed to it when, so far as they could see, the effect of the proposal might well be to limit or slow down their rapid strides toward a reordering of the international power structure. Certainly the German documents now available suggest strongly that the Nazi regime had no interest whatever in a conference unless it was based on their own prohibitive terms.[113]

Fourth, far from bringing about a closer relationship between the English-speaking peoples, there is some reason to believe that the course of recent events in the Far East, including the abortive Brussels Conference and the conversations at the White House in December, 1937, between the President, Secretary Hull, and Ambassador Lindsay,[114] only further strengthened Chamberlain in his belief that little effective assistance was to be expected from the United States, and that under the circumstances, he must seek to achieve, if at all possible, an early and honorable settlement with at least one of the Axis powers. In this connection, it is not without interest that on the same day the President delivered his Quarantine Speech, October 5, 1937, the State Department, replying to a British suggestion about possible Anglo-American cooperation in the Far East, declared that although the United States would not lead, she would be willing to examine any plan "to cooperate by pacific methods . . . toward bringing an end to the present hostilities in the Far East."[115] Since the President strongly urged Chamberlain not to accord *de jure* recognition to the Italian conquest of Abyssinia, one wonders at the effect on the Prime Minister of the President's statement, after such recognition *was* accorded, that the United States "government has seen the conclusion [of that agreement] with sympathetic interest because it is proof of the value of peaceful negotiations."[116]

Finally the experience of World War I had conclusively demonstrated that the technological resources and military might of Germany were so enormous that, even with Russia, Italy, and Japan on their side, Great Britain and France could scarcely cope with Germany. By 1937 both Italy and Japan had joined the Axis, and the future policy of the Soviet Union was as enigmatic as the precise strength and probable effectiveness of its armed forces. Under these circumstances, it seemed increasingly clear that only the intervention of the United States could suffice, as it had done in 1917, to redress the uncertain balance of power. Nor, it should be added at once, was this only the wisdom of hindsight.

The fact of the matter is that Ambassadors Dodd, Messersmith, and Bullitt, for instance, had repeatedly stated, in letters and reports to the President and the State Department, that the position of the Western democracies was fast becoming increasingly precarious, though only Dodd suggested the President should consider direct intervention. (As late as 1940 Bullitt believed the United States should keep out of any future European war and told French political leaders that "the Yanks were not coming again.") [117] The President, in turn, had every reason to be aware of the realities of European and world politics, and it was his failure to act accordingly that constituted perhaps his single gravest error throughout his years in the White House.

If these, then, are the principal conclusions to be drawn from the history of the President's peace efforts before Munich, what can we conclude about the respective roles of the leading individuals in that episode?

From all the published evidence, both Anthony Eden and (much more so) Sumner Welles emerge diminished in stature. Indeed, it must be said that Welles, in his evident bitterness and determination to discredit Secretary Hull, vastly exaggerated the importance of his own proposals and, by seriously misstating the background against which they were set forth, attributed to them an originality they simply did not possess.

Eden's role, too, in this whole episode begins to appear in somewhat different perspective. Like Welles's accounts, *Facing the Dictators* was in a sense Eden's reckoning with *his* chief, but as in the case of Welles, it is by no means entirely clear that it was Eden who had the better of the argument; and, as he perhaps inadvertently discloses, Eden was by no means as staunch an opponent of appeasement and concessions to the Axis as is generally assumed.[118]

Concerning the role of Neville Chamberlain in all these events, the evidence contained in the *Foreign Relations* documents and in the authorized life of Lord Vansittart, serves to confirm the impression conveyed by Iain Macleod (and before him by Professor Feiling) that, far from being an avid or credulous appeaser of Nazi Germany, Chamberlain in fact despised everything Hitler and his regime stood for. The fact of the matter is that once he became Prime Minister in June, 1937, Chamberlain found himself confronted with a large and dangerous imbalance between Great Britain's worldwide commitments, on the one hand, and her severely limited political and military resources, on the other. Inasmuch as the isolationist mood in the United States—a mood confirmed by the passage of a second Neutrality Act in May, 1937—was almost certain to prevent its timely intervention on the side of the other Western democracies, Chamberlain concluded that he had little choice but to seek a rapid and reasonable settlement with the Axis powers or at least with one of them. The advice that Chamberlain received from his military chiefs doubtless further confirmed him in this judgment.[119] It should not be forgotten either that Chamberlain's naive belief that Mussolini might prove a moderating influence in international affairs, and on Hitler personally, was also shared by Roosevelt.[120]

But the central figure in the whole story, of course, is President Roosevelt, and what can we say now about his performance and the meaning of his peace efforts? Richard Hofstadter has noted, in discussing the origins of the President's foreign policy, that

> [Mr. Roosevelt] had no consistent history of either isolationism or internationalism. Having begun his career in national politics as a strong navalist, an admirer of Mahan . . . he had turned about in the 1920 campaign to defend the League of Nations . . . . As the tide of isolationism rolled higher in the 1920's and his party dropped the League, Roosevelt went along with the trend, refusing to expose himself by defending an unpopular cause in which he had no vital interest.[121]

On the other hand, as observed earlier, the President was not oblivious to foreign affairs, even during his first few years in office, and repeatedly expressed to friends and associates his growing concern about the world situation. "One cannot help feeling," he wrote in February, 1936, to Jesse I. Straus, the American ambassador in Paris, "that the whole European panorama is fundamentally blacker than at any time in your life time or mine." [122] But although the President was well aware of what was going on in Europe and the Far East, his response to these developments long remained both ambiguous and uncertain. As James MacGregor Burns has rightly said:

[The President] hoped that people would be educated by events; the error of this policy was that the dire events in Europe and Asia confirmed the American suspicion and fear of involvement rather than prodding them into awareness of the need for collective action by the democracies. In short, a decisive act of interpretation was required, but Roosevelt did not interpret.[123]

This was not surprising. Until the end of 1940 the President was largely a prisoner of the domestic climate of opinion. He was caught in a crossfire between the increasingly ominous reports reaching him from his extremely well informed diplomatic representatives abroad and the massive efforts of powerful and intransigent isolationist and pacifist forces at home. The fruits of this isolationist movement, including the various Neutrality Acts, the Nye Investigation, the Ludlow Resolution, are well known; it is tempting to attribute much of the isolationist sentiment in the country to the writings of a few revisionist or muckraking historians, such as Harry Elmer Barnes, Walter Millis, and Charles C. Tansill.[124]

But in fact the roots of the isolationist movement were much deeper and broader. As Manfred Jonas has pointed out:

Isolationism transcended socioeconomic divisions and was supported by Americans of widely divergent status. On the subject of America's relationship to the conflicts in Europe and Asia, Socialist intellectuals shared the views of the American Legion. The Chicago Federation of Labor agreed with Henry Ford . . . . Herbert Hoover's arguments were supported in the pages of the *New Republic*.[125]

It is only fair to recall that the great majority of American scholars, writers, and intellectuals supported the isolationist cause. From Charles A. Beard [126] and Edwin M. Borchard[127] to Robert Maynard Hutchings and Norman Thomas,[128] the academic and intellectual community, together with numerous church and women's groups and professional peace associations,[129] poured out a steady stream of literature designed to persuade the American people that the United States should never again become directly involved in affairs abroad.[130] Even Harry Hopkins, as Robert Sherwood has written, "would undoubtedly have been . . . in this category of liberal isolationists had it not been for his fervent conviction that Roosevelt could not possibly be wrong on any major issue." [131]

This isolationist tide reached its greatest heights in the years immediately preceding the Munich crisis, at precisely the moment when timely action by the United States might have averted the coming of World War II. During those years, the President and his administration were bombarded with a steady stream of organized petitions, pleas, and protests of one kind or another, all aimed at persuading the President to preserve the strictest kind of neutrality in the growing world crisis.[132] Indeed, not until the noisy and violent "peace protests" of the later 1960's were the passions of well-intentioned students, ministers, and academicians again so inflamed as they were at the high tide of the isolationist movement.

The President, who occasionally met with some peace delegations himself, seemed uncertain how to deal with the movement. On the one hand, the President had little or no personal sympathy with any pacifist or isolationist views. But he was well aware that many of these peace-minded elements were strong supporters of his other domestic programs. He knew, too, how once before in his life the Democratic party had been wracked by a bitter and futile quarrel over foreign policy, and given the multiplicity of domestic problems confronting him, he seemed reluctant to move toward a showdown with these isolationist or pacifist elements.

The fact of the matter is that the President seemed ambiguous in private as well as in public. Thus in January, 1936, he wrote to John Cudahy, the American minister to Poland: "Everywhere people ask me, 'If there is a European war can you keep us out of it,' and I tell them that I can and will when the people of the Nation back me up." But in October, 1937, he wrote Endicott Peabody, "As you know, I am fighting against a public psychology of long standing—a psychology which comes very close to saying 'Peace at any price.' " [133] Once in a while the President became thoroughly fed up with some of the isolationist charges and interpretations of recent American history. In September, 1935, for instance, he poured out his wrath to Colonel House:

> You may be interested to know that some of the Congressmen and Senators who are suggesting wild-eyed measures to keep us out of war are now declaring that you and [Robert] Lansing and [Walter Hines] Page forced Wilson into the war! I had a talk with them, explained that I was in Washington myself the whole of that period, that none of them was there and that their historical analysis was wholly inaccurate and that history yet to be written would prove my point. The trouble is that they belong to the very large and perhaps increasing school of thought which holds that we can and should withdraw wholly within ourselves and cut off all but the most perfunctory relationships with other nations. They imagine that if the civilization of Europe is about to destroy itself through internal strife, it might just as well go ahead and do it and that the United States can stand idly by.[134]

But such sentiments the President kept mostly to himself. In public he was not beyond seeking to conciliate the advocates of the fashionable "merchants of death" thesis of international war. Thus in his famous address at Chautauqua in August, 1936, he said:

> . . . if war should break out again in another continent, let us not blink the fact that we would find in this country thousands of Americans who, seeking immediate riches—fools' gold—would attempt to break down or evade our Neutrality.
>
> They would tell you—and, unfortunately, their views would get wide publicity—that if they could produce and ship this and that and the other article to belligerent Nations, the unemployed of America would all find work. They would tell you that if they could extend credit to warring Nations that credit would be used in the United States to build homes and factories and pay our debts. They would tell you that America once more would capture the trade of the world . . . .
>
> If we face the choice of profits or peace, the Nation will answer—must answer—"We choose peace." It is the duty of all of us to encourage such a body of public opinion in this country that the answer will be clear and for all practical purposes unanimous.[135]

This appeasement of popular prejudices was a dangerous mistake and the President gained nothing from it. While he was much concerned to preserve the political initiative in domestic affairs, the President seemed unable to achieve a similar initiative in the realm of foreign policy. It is tempting to believe that in those difficult years the President was seeking to steer a middle course between the vocal and influential isolationists and the ardent exponents of collective security. But collective security in the true sense of the word enjoyed almost no support at the time, and instead of using his unassailable political position to inform the American people of the facts of international life as he knew them to be, and instead of arguing on the basis of these incontrovertible realities that the United States must henceforth take a strong and unequivocal stand on the side of the Western democracies—the policy advocated by former Secretary of State Henry L. Stimson [136]—the President fell back on a diplomacy of ambiguous rhetoric.

It seems evident that the President's peace plans from 1936 on, including his proposal to Prime Minister Chamberlain in January, 1938, fall in that general category. Fine sounding and impressive on paper, they gave the appearance of action without intervention, the impression of a new departure without the assumption of greater responsibility. A dubious compromise between what Roosevelt had every reason to know was demanded by events abroad and what he thought feasible and desirable from the domestic standpoint suggests that his various peace plans never had any real prospect of success.

Did the President himself believe that something might come of the heads-of-state conference he discussed with Arthur Krock and others in the summer of 1936? Did he think something was likely to come of his January, 1938, peace initiative? Why, after Chamberlain agreed to support his efforts, did Roosevelt himself repeatedly postpone further action, and ultimately abandon his initiative altogether? Was he aware that unless the spread of aggression was speedily checked it would assume such momentum and proportions that efforts to halt its further advance were almost certain to bring on another great war? It is difficult to say, but it is interesting to note what Ambassador Bingham wrote the President from London in July, 1937:

> Once the Germans realize that they have invoked a race in arms which they must lose, and that they have a chance to obtain more by conciliation and concession than they can hope to obtain through making war, then indeed the moment will arrive when, at their request, a conference

may be called, which you alone could call, with the prospect of incalculable benefit of mankind. In my opinion, until and unless this idea penetrates the German psychology, any move on our part or on the part of the British, would simply be construed by the Nazis as evidence of weakness.[137]

Perhaps the most that we can say, then, is that Roosevelt was fully informed about the tide of world affairs, and that he was never unmindful of the possible effects of these developments on the United States. Yet he long believed—even after Munich—that it was somehow possible to bring about a lasting and honorable settlement between the democracies and the aggressor states. In that illusion, to be sure, he had much distinguished company on both sides of the Atlantic. But it was, all the same, an illusion that shaped history.[138]

The American Arsenal Policy in World War II: A Retrospective View*

Richard M. Leighton
INDUSTRIAL COLLEGE OF THE ARMED FORCES

I

The role of the United States as the "arsenal" of the Western Alliance in World War II is a commonplace in historical accounts of that conflict. American material aid, as Winston Churchill gratefully recorded, enabled Great Britain to wage war as though she had been a nation of fifty-eight million instead of only forty-eight million people.[1] Soviet officials have been less gracious in acknowledging the contribution of American aid, but the statistics speak for themselves. In the European war, where the Soviet Union concentrated virtually its entire military effort and the other European allies most of theirs, the United States, despite its heavy involvement in the war against Japan, produced an estimated 35 per cent of all the munitions brought to bear against Germany and her satellites. For the war against Japan, the proportions of the American contribution are more difficult to appraise, largely because of

* This is a greatly expanded and revised version of my article published in the *Revue d'histoire de la deuxième guerre mondiale*, XVII, No. 65 (Jan. 1967), under the title "Les Armes ou les armées? Origines de la politique d'Arsenal de la Démocratie."

the uncertainty of available figures on Chinese and Indian munitions production, but the overwhelming preponderance of American material in this theater is beyond question; an estimate of 85 per cent is not unreasonable. In the war as a whole, the United States accounted for more than half of all the combat munitions produced by the anti-Axis coalition.[2]

This role was a logical use of America's great industrial superiority in the coalition. It was not, however, the only logical use of that superiority, and post-war interpretations have tended to obscure both the consideration of alternative policies and the degree to which the policy itself represented a blend of alternatives. The nature of the problem of choice that the United States faced can be seen most clearly, perhaps, by noting the contrasting case of Germany, also a highly industrialized power, in the same conflict. Germany chose, or was obliged by circumstances, to expand its armed forces well beyond the size which, with the labor force remaining, the nation's economy was able to equip and support. The deficiency was made up by importing slave labor from satellite and occupied countries to man German factories and farms, and by exploiting their economies through forced exports to Germany and support of occupying armies.[3]

The United States equally waged war as though it were a more populous nation than it was. But in this case foreign manpower served, not as a supplementary labor force, but as a supplementary "market," in the form of allied armies, for an expanded American war industry employing American manpower at the expense of American armed forces. The policy of arming allies through lend-lease made it necessary to allot a larger labor force to industry than would have been required to supply American armed forces alone, even if the latter had been able to draw on a larger manpower pool. Had American manpower been allocated to industry and the armed forces purely on a "go it alone" basis, the armed forces would have leveled off at a ceiling somewhat higher than that in fact attained. Conversely, Germany's armed forces, without the manpower of allies, satellites, and occupied territories to supplement the German economy, would have been substantially smaller than they actually were. In neither case, of course, were the alternatives clear-cut or the choices uncompromising. Germany, like the United States, equipped and supplied large satellite forces; the United States, while not the colossus of the Western coalition that Germany was in the European Axis, fielded larger forces than most of her allies and mobilized as large a proportion of her population as most of the major belligerents on both sides—largely in consequence of the extraordinary productivity of American industry and labor.

II

The choice of the "arsenal" alternative by the United States, and the particular form of the policy that emerged, owed much to the circumstance that she sat on the sidelines for the first two years of the European war. During that time, especially after the fall of France in June, 1940, the policies and mechanisms of support for Germany's adversaries developed within the framework of formal neutrality and rearmament for defense of the Western Hemisphere. For the United States was caught in the classic dilemma of a neutral in a war in which its clients are on the losing side. Unlike the situation in 1914–16, the American public this time was neither indifferent nor sharply divided in its sympathies. Popular support for the Axis powers was negligible, sympathy for the British almost universal. And yet, until the very eve of the Japanese attack on December 7, 1941, public opinion was overwhelmingly opposed to outright intervention to save Great Britain and her surviving allies from defeat.[4] President Franklin D. Roosevelt, who like Woodrow Wilson in 1916, had campaigned on the promise not to send American boys overseas to die on foreign soil, accurately sensed these two contrary but deep-seated popular desires: to help the "opponents of force," as he styled them, but also to stay out of war.[5] His policy, until the Japanese struck, hewed consistently to that line.

To give all possible aid to Great Britain and her allies, short of war, was thus a cardinal objective of United States policy almost from the moment, in spring of 1940, when the Wehrmacht burst through the Allied defenses in Western Europe. What stood in the way of its execution was the conflict between this aim and another which seemed even more urgent: to build up America's own defenses against a German assault on the Western Hemisphere. From mid-1940 on public opinion oscillated erratically between these two competing goals, as the latest news from Europe made the threat of a German invasion of Britain, capture of the French fleet, or a southwestward sweep through Spain into the western bulge of Africa appear alternately more or less imminent. From the continuing tension emerged two radically opposed concepts of neutrality, competing for mastery in high councils. One was essentially isolationist, narrowly concentrated on preparations for a purely American defense of the hemisphere. The other, candidly straining both the spirit and the legalities of neutrality, aimed at a *de facto* partnership with the anti-Axis powers through large-scale supply of war material and services.

Each conception contained its own projection of the role the United States might eventually play as a full belligerent—on one hand, full-scale participation with forces of all arms, mainly in theaters of primary American interest; on the other, continuation of the supply of war material and services on an expanded scale, with only limited participation by American forces. In the former role, the United States would throw its own armed manpower into the struggle in the classic manner, leaving its allies to wage war similarly with their own resources. In the other, the United States would serve as the "arsenal of democracy"—another phrase popularized by the President—mobilizing its industrial might primarily to arm the manpower of its allies.[6]

The United States reacted to the German victories in the spring of 1940 by launching a massive program of rearmament and mobilization. The Army's munitions program of June 30, 1940, aimed at producing equipment and reserve materiel for a hemisphere defense force of two million men by the end of 1941. Aircraft production was to be expanded to a capacity of eighteen thousand planes a year, aiming at an air force of twelve thousand planes and fifty-four combat groups by the spring of 1942. Eventually a munitions production sufficient to equip and sustain an army of four million men was envisaged. At the same time, Congress on July 19 approved a two-ocean Navy, doubling the strength of the existing fleet. During the summer of 1940, legislation was enacted to provide military manpower for this mobilization, through induction of the National Guard, calling up the organized reserve, and selective service. These measures envisaged expansion of the Army to an actual strength of 1.4 million by the middle of 1941.[7]

The sense of urgency behind these measures can be better appreciated in the light of the frail state of existing United States defenses. The peace time strength of the United States Army on the outbreak of European hostilities in September, 1939, was less than two hundred thousand, backed up by the same number of partially trained National Guardsmen and an officers' reserve corps of about 110,000. For all practical purposes, it was an infantry-artillery army: the tiny air corps had only 1,800 planes of all types, almost all obsolescent, and the minuscule armored forces had only 329 tanks, mostly light. The basic weapons were of World War I vintage, such as the Springfield rifle, the 75-mm gun, and the 3-inch antiaircraft; provision of more modern equipment awaited production. Less than fifty thousand troops were deployed outside the continental limits, largely in five outpost garrisons—Hawaii, the Canal Zone, the Philippines, Puerto Rico, and Alaska. The remainder were scattered among training camps in the continental United States, organized in four field armies which actually had no staffs and contained only four organized and seven partially organized divisions, all far below war strength. Little was done during the winter and spring following the war's outbreak to strengthen these meager forces, as the United States with the rest of the world anxiously awaited the outcome of what appeared to be a stalemate in Europe. On the eve of the fall of France, the United States Army still numbered less than 250,000 men, and the National Guard, now undergoing more intensive training, about 235,000. Perhaps the main impact of the initial phase of the European war on American military strength was the stimulus that British, French, and Finnish purchases had given to production of munitions, particularly aircraft.[8]

It was in this situation of military weakness at home and suddenly looming peril from abroad that President Roosevelt, in an address at Charlottesville, Virginia, on June 10, 1940, proclaimed his government's determination to pursue two parallel courses of action:

> We will extend to the opponents of force the material resources of this nation; and at the same time we will harness and speed up the use of those resources in order that we ourselves in the Americas may have equipment and training equal to the task of any emergency and every defense.[9]

To proclaim these goals was to state the problem. With France out of the running, Great Britain facing imminent invasion, and prospects that Japan might move southward or eastward, or both, possibly with Soviet connivance, Roosevelt's military advisers, Army Chief of Staff General George C. Marshall and Chief of Naval Operations Admiral Harold R. Stark, urged him on June 24 to concentrate on the more attainable goal of defending the hemisphere, for which task alone, they declared, "the concerted effort of our whole national life is required." The British would have to wait.[10]

Roosevelt yielded, but not all the way. For the immediate future, he agreed, rearmament and mobilization must have top priority, but limited aid to Great Britain would continue "if [as General Marshall reported his decision] the British displayed an ability to withstand the German assault, and it appeared that a little help might carry them through to the first of the year . . . ."[11] Within two weeks events began to vindicate Roosevelt's decision. With the destruction or neutralization of the bulk of the French fleet by the British on July 3–4, the threat of a rapid expansion of German naval power evaporated. The air assault on the British Isles began a few days later, but in September the battered Luftwaffe finally recoiled in defeat, and the menace of an early invasion receded. From then on American military planners could think in terms of a prolonged struggle with British survival a possible, even probable eventuality. In this perspective continued material aid to the British could be realistically viewed as a long-term contribution to American security.

The decisions of June, 1940, were crucial in the emergence of America's "arsenal" role in the anti-Axis coalition. By maintaining a trickle of war material to nations already fighting the Axis at a time when it seemed least likely to influence the course of events and conflicted most sharply with the immediate and desperate needs of American forces, these decisions firmly established foreign aid as an essential feature of the total strategy of rearmament, mobilization, hemisphere defense, and, eventually, victory in a global war. Thenceforth, discussion and disagreement over foreign aid revolved about the specifics of amounts, kinds, recipients, and methods; the principle was not seriously challenged.

It is also worth noting, for it was vital to the success of the policy, that Roosevelt's chief military advisers loyally supported the decisions of June, 1940. General Marshall especially played a key role, not merely because most military aid in 1940 consisted of Army-type materiel, but also because on June 28 a Congress, dubious of the President's intentions, ruled that any material sold or exchanged to foreign governments must be certified by the Chief of Staff as surplus to the defense needs of the United States. Marshall managed to steer a careful middle course during the months that followed, in certifying transfers to the British and other recipients of the obsolescent weapons and ammunition from Army stocks which made up the bulk of military aid in 1940. The release of more than a million old Enfield rifles to the British by February, 1941, for example, did not then seriously impair the Army's expanding training program—though its impact was felt after Pearl Harbor when the pace of expansion quickened—but the release of 188 million rounds of small-arms ammunition was a calculated risk in view of the serious ammunition shortage which continued well into 1942. Between June, 1940, and the following February, Marshall permitted no releases of field artillery at all, because of lagging production of the new 105-mm howitzer, and for similar reasons he resisted transfers of tanks and bombers.[12]

The amounts of American war material sent to Great Britain in 1940 were not large, relative to the total need, and they were, of course, infinitesimal compared with the deluge that followed American entry in the war.[13] They did, however, contribute significantly to Great Britain's defense posture against the immediate threat of invasion, and the fifty overage destroyers transferred in September, in exchange for the lease of Atlantic bases, greatly strengthened Britain's vital sea communications.[14] All this was a prelude to the passage of the lend-lease act on March 11, 1941, which, after the crucial decisions of the preceding June, stands as the most conspicuous landmark in the evolution of the arsenal policy. This historic legislation removed, at one stroke, the legal and financial obstacles to the flow of war material to the nations fighting the Axis, and, nine months before Pearl Harbor, provided a legal basis for the swelling tide of munitions that continued without interruption as the United States moved closer to, and finally over the brink of war. Above all, in the words of the Army's official history, the lend-lease act "put the stamp of Congressional approval on the President's policy of dividing American resources between rearmament of the United States and the anti-Axis nations abroad, and promised that aid to these nations would continue so long as they showed any ability to resist." [15]

III

Not until the middle of 1941, however, a full year after the first commitment to a policy of aid to the anti-Axis nations, and, significantly, after the German invasion of Russia had transformed the whole scale and outlook of the conflict, did American policy-makers examine the implications of this policy in terms of a rational division of resources and effort in an all-out coalition war. The vehicle for this examination was the "Victory Program," as it came to be called, in which the military staffs first attempted to calculate the ultimate requirements and costs of defeating the Axis powers.[16]

This undertaking was prompted by an order from the President to the secretaries of the Army and Navy on July 9, 1941, to explore "the overall production requirements required to defeat our potential enemies," on the explicit assumption that the total production of the United States and its allies must "exceed by an appropriate amount that available to our potential enemies." He did not have in mind, he pointed out,

> a detailed report, but one which, while general in scope, would cover the most critical items in our defense and which could then be related . . . into practical realities of production facilities. It seems to me we need to know our program in its entirety even though at a later date it may be amended.[17]

Manifestly, Roosevelt thought of American mobilization as, at bottom, an industrial effort and the production of munitions as the key to eventual victory. The assumption tied in neatly with his conception of America as the "arsenal of democracy" in the present conflict, with its hopeful implication that the Axis powers could be defeated by a combination of American industrial might and allied manpower. The idea had deep roots in American experience in

World War I and the Civil War. A further assumption of the President, expressed in a supplementary letter to Secretary of War Henry L. Stimson a few weeks later, was that "the reservoir of munitions power available to the United States and her friends is sufficiently superior to that available to the Axis to insure defeat of the latter." [18]

The military planners sharply disagreed with this approach. "It would be unwise to assume," wrote the Army's chief planner, General Leonard Gerow, to Assistant Secretary of War John J. McCloy, "that we can defeat Germany simply by outproducing her. One hundred thousand airplanes would be of little value to us, if these airplanes could not be used because of lack of trained personnel, lack of operating airdromes in the theater and lack of shipping to maintain the squadrons." Munitions must be translated into effective military power, and this required shipping, trained soldiers, expert leadership, and sound plans. Production capacity had to be defined in terms of proper balance among the types of weapons produced, and balance, in turn, could only be defined in terms of the strategy which determined how armies were employed. Wars were won, General Gerow argued, "by sound strategy implemented by well-trained forces which are adequately and effectively equipped." The determination of requirements accordingly must be approached in this order: first, a basic strategy and strategic plans to implement it; second, forces sufficient to execute the plans; and, last, production capacity sufficient to arm the forces.[19]

The military staffs worked during most of the summer of 1941 on the application of this formula to the task of calculating the ultimate "victory requirements" in production capacity requested by the President. The Army projected a strategy of full-scale American participation in the war, on the assumption that Soviet resistance would crumble by mid-1942, but that Germany would require a year to repair her own losses, restore order in Europe, and begin to exploit the conquered lands to the east and southeast. Mid-1943 was thus a crucial date. As the Army strategists saw it, hope for Allied victory hinged on the ability of the United States and Great Britain to weaken Germany by air bombardment, limited peripheral offensives, and blockade in 1942, while preparing to launch a decisive attack in mid-1943. In the Far East, meanwhile, they would have to remain on the defensive. Army planners counted on the deterrent power of their new heavy bomber, the B-17 "Flying Fortress," numbers of which were about to be dispatched to the Philippines within striking range of Formosa and Japan's home islands. In the last resort, the Allies might have to trade space for time in this theater, arming Chinese manpower on a large scale to offset Japan's over-all preponderance. Ultimately the United States Pacific Fleet would fight its way back to the Philippines. But Germany must be defeated first.[20]

Army and Navy strategists were generally in agreement on this basic strategy. But significant divergences appeared among the advocates of ground, air, and sea power both between and within the service staffs, on the nature of American participation. Ground force proponents in the Army asserted that "as an almost invariable rule wars cannot be finally won without the use of land armies"; sea and air power were contributory but not decisive. They proposed to mobilize an American Army of great "destructive power and mobility," heavily accoutered with armor, motor transport, antitank and antiaircraft artillery, together with a strong air force—almost 8.8 million men in all, of whom five million would be used to invade the European continent.

> We must prepare to fight Germany by actually coming to grips with and defeating her ground forces and definitely breaking her will to combat . . . . Air and sea forces will make important contributions, but effective and adequate ground forces must be available to close with and destroy the enemy within his citadel.[21]

To this Clausewitzian vision, Navy planners opposed a less heroic concept of American participation based on sea and air power and much heavier reliance on allied manpower. Their estimate of American overseas deployment, for example, totaled only 1.5 million men, of whom a third would be sent to Latin American areas. They argued that

> . . . since the principal strength of the Associated Powers is at present in naval and air categories, the strategy that they should adopt should be based on the effective employment of these forces, and the employment of land forces in regions where Germany cannot exert the full power of her land armies.[22]

The Army Air Corps staff, finally, emphasized the potential role of strategic air bombardment of the German homeland in destroying the sources of Germany's military power and breaking her will to resist.[23]

But on the whole the Army point of view was dominant in the completed program submitted to the President at the end of September, 1941. The Navy's limited-liability approach, while reflected in some of the accompanying statistics, tended to be submerged in a broad strategy built on the expectation of developing crushing superiority in all arms, but mainly in ground and strategic air forces. As a corollary, the program also constituted an unequivocal statement of professional military opposition to the President's "arsenal" policy as a basis for eventual participation in the war. Allied armies would need American arms—particularly in the Far East where Chinese manpower was the only barrier to Japan on the Asiatic continent—but the United States would necessarily have to assume the main burden in the total military effort against the Axis. And if the latter were to be defeated, full-scale American entry into the conflict could not be long delayed. Speaking for both military departments, Secretary Stimson warned the President that ultimate victory depended on the early participation of the United States "in an avowed all-out military effort" against Germany. Mere extension of the current policy of "munitions, transport, and naval help" would not suffice. Without such an effort, Stimson bluntly asserted, "the British and their allies cannot defeat Germany, and . . . the resistance of the United Kingdom cannot continue indefinitely, no matter what industrial effort is put forth by us." [24]

Yet it is interesting, in retrospect, to note how far the military planners, for all their insistence on an all-out American *military* effort, had actually moved over to the President's view that it would be, at bottom, an *industrial* effort. Ostensibly, the "strategy-forces-munitions" formula for determining requirements made strategy the arbiter of both the size of the armed forces and of the industrial mobilization needed to support them. According to General Gerow this was in fact the approach used: from the broad strategic concept described above, the staff supposedly determined "in a general way" the pattern of expected operations, translated these into a force structure, and this in turn into requirements for critical items of munitions. These, together with marginal requirements submitted by the British and extrapolations from the other lend-lease programs, constituted the total requirement to be placed on American industry. The obvious tenuousness of the link between strategy and force structure in this process was glossed over, but it drew critical comment from the British, who were accustomed to calculate their requirements theater by theater, with fairly detailed accounting for factors peculiar to each theater, such as port and rail capacity, power facilities, expected enemy strength, and intensity of combat. The Americans rejected this approach, arguing that "the only safe assumptions concerning theaters of operations are that they may develop in any part of the globe, and that the Atlantic and European area will be the decisive theater." [25]

Indeed, the American planners appear to have rejected much more. The staff officer responsible for calculating the Victory Program troop basis, Major (later Lieutenant General) Albert Wedemeyer, testified years later that what he had in fact done was to obtain from the civilian manpower and production agencies estimates of the number of men that the armed services could expect to be allotted in a fully mobilized economy in mid-1943. From this figure he deducted Navy requirements for 1.25 million men and an additional 3.5 million as a cushion against unforeseen war economy expansion. The remainder, 8,795,658, was assumed to be the ceiling on the Army's expansion.[26]

This was a far cry from the strategy-forces-munitions approach to determining requirements, and it served to bring the Victory Program estimates, in substance, somewhat closer to the President's "arsenal" policy than appeared on the surface. Wedemeyer's method of fixing the ultimate limits of the armed forces' expansion was calculated to ensure that the expansion of industry would not be held back by lack of manpower; the reserve of 3.5 million men for unforeseen war economy requirements emphasized this aim.

Some military planners, to be sure, felt that with armed forces of over ten million men to be supported, along with substantial foreign aid requirements as well, "the load to be placed on both industry and raw materials in the United States will tax its maximum capacity." [27] Before Pearl Harbor the military tended to take a conservative view of the expansive capacity of American industry, in marked contrast to their tendency after that date to overestimate it. With a still half-trained and ill-equipped army of only 1.6 million to show for more than a year of feverish mobilization, a goal of 8.8 million looked very large indeed in the fall of 1941. Even at maximum capacity American industry might not produce enough of a surplus to provide the kind of arsenal the President appeared to have in mind.

Nevertheless, expansion of production to an unspecified maximum was a goal that the President and the military alike could applaud, and to some if not all of the latter it was more important at the moment than either a settled strategy or fixed force goals. "The plan for material," observed the War Department Defense Aid Director, Colonel Henry S. Aurand, in November, 1941, "need await neither a strategic concept nor a determination of troops to accomplish this objective. It is sufficient to know that maximum production of military equipment must be obtained in this country at the earliest possible date." [28] In any event, American industry was to confound the pessimists by supporting an even larger mobilization of United States forces, and far more allied forces, than the Victory Program had contemplated.[29]

As a blueprint for full participation in the war, the Victory Program could not, of course, affect American policy during the remaining weeks of neutrality before the Japanese attack. During those weeks, the United States was, to be sure, moving inexorably toward deeper involvement, as American warships patrolling the North Atlantic convoy routes clashed with German submarines and relations with Japan reached a crisis stage. But the nature of the involvement evidently envisaged by the President bore little resemblance to the full mobilization, large deployments, and major operations pictured in the Victory Program. It was more along the lines of the small task-force movements, base occupations, and line-of-communications protection outlined in the military staff agreements concluded with the British in March, 1941. For the present, moreover, the military establishment was in no condition to contemplate anything more ambitious, and an open British bid for American intervention at the Argentia Conference in August was emphatically rejected: "The weakness of our potential allies, the present inadequacy of production, the unreadiness of our forces, the lack of shipping at this time, and the two-ocean threat to our ultimate security, present a situation we are not prepared to meet as a belligerent." [30]

After mid-1941, in fact, American mobilization slowed down markedly. With a strength of almost 1.5 million in June, the Army absorbed less than two hundred thousand more men during the next five months, concentrating rather on improving its state of training and equipment. While most of the swelling output of munitions in 1941, as in 1940, continued to go to American forces, the proportion diverted to lend-lease steadily mounted. Of certain critical items, including aircraft, most current production was assigned to the British and the Soviet Union.[31]

In short, as mobilization leveled off and munitions production continued to mount, American policy in late 1941 was moving strongly toward fuller realization of the arsenal role. To the military leaders, a major shift of emphasis in this direction seemed dangerously premature, in view of the nation's continued unreadiness to face a really serious threat. Yet such a shift seemed imminent. Public and Congressional aversion to military involvement in the war was signalled by such indicators as the apathetic reactions to German submarine attacks on American destroyers, the one-vote extension of selective service, and continuation of the prohibition against sending selectees to serve in bases like Iceland outside the hemisphere. Public opinion polls confirmed the trend.[32] One manifestation of the drift was a strong sentiment for concentrating defense preparations on naval and air power while cutting back the ground army. In a widely discussed article in September, Walter Lippmann argued "the case for a smaller army" on the basis of the disappearance of the threat to British survival and the manifest security of the hemisphere. Continued expansion of the Army, he asserted, was "the cancer which obstructs national unity, causes discontent which subversive elements exploit, and weakens the primary measures of our defense, which are the lend-lease program and the naval policy." Lippmann believed that

America's proper contribution, if she were drawn into the war, should be one "basically of Navy, Air, and manufacturing."[33]

Shortly after this article appeared, Marshall was summoned to the White House to defend the Army's present strength and plans for expansion. In his vigorous defense, Marshall asserted that an Army cutback in order to increase aid to the British and Russians at this time would give Germany "positive indications . . . that they need not fear an eventual onslaught of [American] ground forces."[34] No cutback was ordered; indeed, Roosevelt denied that he had ever contemplated one. Nevertheless, an early major diversion of the flow of American munitions from home and hemisphere defenses to the nations fighting the Axis was clearly in prospect. Lend-lease allocation policy laid down at the end of September provided that, beginning the following March, the great bulk of American munitions output would go into lend-lease channels. As a corollary, the Army, still with only 70 per cent of its minimum training allowances of equipment, would be stabilized at substantially its existing strength.[35] Thus, on the eve of Pearl Harbor, Roosevelt's arsenal policy seemed about to come to fruition.

IV

With the Japanese attack and the German and Italian declarations of war immediately following, the United States found itself fully engaged in a struggle which removed limited-war options from the realm of practical consideration. The President lost no time in announcing his own expectations. Only five days after the Pearl Harbor attack he reported to the Congress:

> The world-wide strategy of the Axis powers must be met with equal strategy on the part of all the nations who are joined together in resisting their aggression. Accordingly we must use the weapons from the arsenal of the democracies where they can be employed most effectively. And that means we must let Britain, Russia, China and other nations, including those of this Hemisphere, use the weapons from that arsenal so that they can put them to most effective use. Too much is at stake in this greatest of all wars for us to neglect peoples who are or may be attacked by our common enemies.[36]

On January 3, he wrote the Secretary of War that the other nations fighting the Axis were near the limits of their resources and that ultimate victory would depend on "our overwhelming mastery in the munitions of war." He declared: "We must not only provide munitions for our own fighting forces, but vast quantities to be used against the enemy in every appropriate theater of war, wherever that may be." [37] It was the Charlottesville manifesto of June, 1940, translated into the larger setting of total war. Three days later, in his state-of-the-union message, he proclaimed to a listening nation some of the magnitudes of the production effort that would be called for—60,000 airplanes in 1942 and 125,000 in 1943; 45,000 tanks in 1942 and 75,000 in 1943; 20,000 anti-aircraft guns in 1942 and 35,000 in 1943; 6 million deadweight tons of shipping in 1942 and 10 million in 1943—and avowed his faith that they would be achieved. "Let no man say it cannot be done. It must be done—and we have undertaken to do it." [38]

Roosevelt's reaffirmation of his belief that American industrial power was the key to ultimate victory and his evident determination to use that power to supply allied forces on a massive scale did not precipitate the kind of confrontation with the military leaders that had occurred in June, 1940. There was now no question, as there had seemed to be then, of an "either-or" choice between arming American and arming allied forces. The Japanese attack and the sudden plunge into a two-front war had created a war psychology in which both alternatives, in their extreme form, were equally unthinkable. Only later, and then only in limited official circles, would the "arsenal" theory in something like its pre-Pearl Harbor form, receive serious consideration.[39] For the present the practical question was what priorities would govern the allocation of American industrial output to serve the needs of both the United States and its allies.

From the outset aid to the Soviet Union was treated as a separate and favored category. Allocations and shipments of war material to that country were governed by a series of annual protocols negotiated at the highest level—the first of these, covering the period through June, 1942, was signed at Moscow on October 1, 1941—and throughout the war the fulfillment of protocol commitments was treated as a matter of transcendant urgency reflecting both the vital strategic role of the Soviet Union and the delicacy of its relations with the Western allies. When Stimson and Marshall proposed soon after Pearl Harbor that Soviet protocol commitments be revised downward in view of the planned rapid expansion of United States armed forces, the President made his displeasure emphatically clear. "The whole Russian program is so vital to our interest," he wrote Stimson, "I know that only the gravest consideration will lead you to recommend our withholding longer the munitions our Government has promised to the U.S.S.R." He insisted that existing deficits in shipments be made good by April.[40]

Thereafter, in the unending process of "dividing deficiencies" among competing needs, military officials learned to expect, almost as a foregone conclusion, a Presidential veto on any reduction of Soviet claims. Indeed, the principal curb on American aid to the U.S.S.R., particularly during the first two years of the war, was the heavy cost levied by distance, weather, and enemy action on cargo movements to Russia. Despite these obstacles almost 2.5 million long tons of military cargo were shipped to the Soviet Union during 1942 (more than three hundred thousand tons were lost at sea), and the value of military lend-lease to the Soviets during the war came to $5.5 billion, about one-fourth of the total.[41]

The chief beneficiaries of American foreign aid during World War II were the British. To the British Empire (excluding Canada) went some $13.7 billion in Army lend-lease, more than half the total.[42] Because Britain was, from the first, both the principal and the intimate partner of the United States—and also because the special status of the Soviet Union, the only other major recipient, was not negotiable at levels below the President—debate over the arsenal policy after Pearl Harbor revolved mainly about its application to the British. To the latter, the form this policy would take following American entry into the war was a matter of pressing concern. With their own manpower and war economy almost fully mobilized, their forces deployed, their theater establishments and lines of communications manned and in operation, British leaders had waited patiently for the tapering off of the limited American mobilization in late 1941 that would permit diversion of the bulk of American munitions into lend-lease channels. In this expectation the British had allotted manpower to the armed forces at the expense of the war economy more generously than they would otherwise have dared to do. Now that America was in the war, not everyone, amid the general rejoicing, shared the optimism of Lord Beaverbrook, who was confident that "all the present statistics [of American production] would be surpassed and swept away . . . . [and] there would be enough for all." Churchill himself, along with many others, feared a vast, wasteful, endless mobilization that would soak up all the munitions American factories could produce.[43]

At the Arcadia Conference held in Washington soon after Pearl Harbor, the British leaders, with Roosevelt's cooperation, won substantial insurance against such an eventuality. They persuaded the American military to agree, first, that finished munitions produced by the two countries should be regarded as a common pool to be allocated in accordance with strategic needs without regard to the nationality of the forces using them; and, second, that allocations should be made by a system of combined, that is, United States–British, committees controlled and coordinated by a central board, the Munitions Assignments Board, organized in two sections sitting permanently in Washington and London, respectively. Churchill and Beaverbrook had hoped to make this a top-level political body responsible directly to the President and Prime Minister, but at the insistence of General Marshall (who threatened to resign over the issue) Roosevelt, at first favorable to the scheme, agreed that it should be subordinate to the newly established Combined Chiefs of Staff, who were charged with the coordination of coalition strategy. Churchill grudgingly conceded the point, on a trial basis, and the new board became in fact a permanent, and vital, part of the machinery of Anglo-American collaboration.[44]

The Munitions Assignments Board was one of a cluster of combined boards established, at British behest, within a few months following Pearl Harbor to coordinate munitions, food and raw materials allocation, production, and the use of shipping. Unlike the MAB, the other boards were responsible to the President and the Prime Minister, to whom they served as advisory bodies in their respective functional areas rather than as effective allocating agencies.[45] Whether the MAB, if established at the same level as Churchill had proposed, would have assumed a similar character, or, conversely, would have severed the vital link between strategy and munitions allocation and extended British influence back into the American war effort, as General Marshall evidently feared, are, to use Roosevelt's word, "iffy" and therefore unanswerable questions.

In the MAB and its subordinate committees, at all events, American and British officials brought sharply opposing points of view to the task of allocating munitions. Their views differed not only because British mobilization and deployment were farther advanced than American, but, even more fundamentally, because the bulk of the common pool of munitions was American and the disproportion grew larger as the war progressed. For all practical purposes, British munitions were fully absorbed by the requirements of British Empire forces and those of protégés such as Turkey. The real problem in dividing the munitions pool was the problem to which this study is addressed, the degree to which American industrial power should be used to arm allied at the expense of American forces.

The central issue quickly came to the surface. Late in February, 1942, the Americans demanded in one of the assignments committees that all the minimum equipment needs of the entire United States Army then projected to the end of 1942—seventy-one divisions—must be met before any critical materiel could be assigned from United States production to other countries. The British objected that this would nullify the principle of assignment in accordance with need and the issue was taken up to the CCS. There the British countered with a proposal that first priority in allocating munitions should be given to the full requirements of troop units already in or about to proceed to an active war theater. As an American staff officer remarked, allocations on this basis would "consume all production for some time to come, and there will be nothing left for the needs of large forces that must be developed if we are going to win the war." [46]

A related issue was the British effort, in the Munitions Assignment Board and the Combined Resources and Production Board (one of the new boards mentioned earlier), to establish integrated long-range production requirements for both countries based on an agreed common strategy—requirements which presumably would become the basis for assignments of munitions through the MAB committee system. The debate sparked by this effort in the latter part of 1942 revived the old disagreement over the method of calculating military requirements—the British on the basis of projected deployments to specific theaters, the Americans on the over-all planned force structure—as well as the considerable gap between their respective maintenance and reserve scales of equipment. These differences, when translated into demands on American production, again raised the threat, in the minds of the American military, of an outpouring of American munitions to British forces overseas, including "such logistical vacuums as India," as one officer later remarked, that would cripple and delay the training of American forces at home.[47] How the British viewed the problem is well stated in their official history:

> The immense expansion of United States Army programmes . . . was threatening to engulf vast resources in the production of equipment which would not be required for years to come and which it might never be possible to ship overseas. Meanwhile, in the campaigns immediately ahead, the fighting forces of America and the British Empire were likely to find that they had been deprived of urgently necessary equipment through the waste of resources caused by misguided efforts to provide them with "the maximum of everything." [48]

The basic obstacle to meaningful long-range production planning, in any case—and this was as true at the national as at the coalition level—was the divergence in strategic outlook between the two allies which, except for a short-lived agreement in the spring of 1942 on a plan for invading Europe the following year, thwarted all efforts in that year to produce a common strategy.[49] Without such a strategy, theater deployments, orders of battle, and mobilization and training programs could only be based on educated guesses as to the needs that would ultimately have to be met. In one area—aircraft allocations—the Americans were able to accept projected theater deployments (though still at short range) as the common basis for determining requirements. This was embodied in the Arnold-Slessor-Towers Agreement of July 2, 1942, the first of a series of working-level pacts which governed the allocation of United States aircraft production to the British for the remainder of the war.[50] In other areas of military supply planning, however, the two allies went their separate ways as sovereign partners in a common enterprise. In the Weeks-Somervell Agreement—another working-level arrangement produced during the visit of the Lyttelton Mission to Washington in the fall of 1942—it was decided that military requirements on both sides would be determined unilaterally and without reciprocal scrutiny, but the acceptance of British stated requirements for inclusion in American production programs became a subject of bilateral horse-trading at the military level, the ultimate determination being made by the American supply agencies.[51]

Meanwhile, practical compromises emerged from the original confrontations in the actual assignments of equipment coming off American production lines: an equal priority with theater troops for United States troops in training (but only at 50 per cent of authorized equipment allowances); and, in 1943, the more selective allocation criterion of *employments,* that is, in specific CCS-approved operations, as opposed to total numbers of overseas *deployments.*[52] Understandably, these working compromises tended to favor American interests. In day-to-day committee operations, the United States Army history confesses, "the American members . . . managed in one way or another . . . to assure a certain continuing priority for U.S. Army needs" in the allocation of United States materiel.[53] It is true that the most urgent needs of the British were met during 1942. On the other hand, as will be seen presently, only about half of their *accepted* requirements for 1942 in the United States Army Supply Program of September, 1942, were actually delivered—a default which seriously strained relations and brought the Lyttelton Mission to Washington in October to negotiate new agreements on various aspects of the joint war effort. This was the price paid for an accelerated American mobilization which, by the end of 1942, had put some 5.4 million men in uniform and almost a million troops overseas.[54]

The common pool indeed retained little more than metaphorical meaning. A War Department study candidly admitted in 1943 that

> . . . the resources of the United States are applied primarily to equipping United States forces, and the resources of the United Kingdom are applied primarily to equipping British forces. Furthermore, the control of production facilities within each country remains in the hands of that country, as does the power to determine what and how much those facilities shall produce.[55]

And yet, if the compromises between American and British interests in the division of the American arsenal favored the former, they were compromises nonetheless—and this was an infinitely better outcome for both than if either had won its original case.

V

The crisis and turning point in the wartime arsenal policy came near the end of 1942. It was part of a more general crisis in the management of the whole American war effort, an effort that for almost a year had been running at high speed and with very little sense of direction. The President's grandiose production goals announced at the beginning of the year, for all their success in giving the nation a sense of power and purpose, left much to be desired as a framework for a balanced war production program. By the time the military services had filled in all the interstitial related and supplementary items, with the normal superstructure of reserve, maintenance, and pipeline allowances, the total had soared far beyond the most optimistic estimates of the nation's productive capacity. The President, on the advice of production officials, ordered the resulting programs cut back, but in balance. The effect was to precipitate a prolonged and confused wrangle within the military establishment over the distribution of the reductions and the assignment of priorities.[56]

Monthly production schedules, meanwhile, were shaped by factors that had little to do with long-range objectives: shortages of materials, facilities, and labor, and a still embryonic system of priorities and regulations for allocating these essential ingredients. Output soared, indeed. During the first half of 1942 American factories poured out more than twice as much materiel for the Army as during the six months preceding: almost a million hand

and shoulder weapons, 235,000 machine guns, 7,329 tanks, 285,-000 trucks, over 3 billion rounds of small arms ammunition, 212,-000 tons of aircraft bombs, and 18,060 aircraft. But advances were uneven and became more so after midyear, while alarming slowdowns developed in certain major lines, notably aircraft and machine guns. In September, total output showed only a 10 per cent gain over that of August, as contrasted with monthly increases of 20 per cent during the spring; in October the increase over September was only 4 per cent.[57]

Production officials watched these developments with growing concern. In September the Planning Committee of the War Production Board, the top level interagency body responsible for coordinating production, forced a showdown by transmitting to Lieutenant General Brehon B. Somervell, chief of the Army's Services of Supply, a report challenging the feasibility of both the 1942 and the 1943 goals of the current war production programs. The report, prepared by Simon Kuznets, a distinguished economist and specialist in national income analysis, predicted that war production in 1942 would fall short of objectives by about $15 billion —a remarkably accurate prediction, as it turned out—and asserted that 1943 goals were even less attainable. He recommended a drastic curtailment of military programs and the establishment of a superboard to reconcile military strategy with production capabilities.[58]

For the military leaders the attack on their supply programs came at a critical time. The first limited offensives against the Japanese were under way on Guadalcanal and in northern New Guinea. Detailed plans and preparations were in full swing for large-scale combined landings in French North Africa with the British in October or November, an operation proposed by Prime Minister Churchill and forced on the reluctant American chiefs of staff by the President. The administrative turmoil attendant on this sudden change in allied strategy from the plan for an invasion of northern France in the spring of 1943 was heightened by corollary reorientations of American deployments, current and planned, to the Pacific and Middle East. In September and October, moreover, the mounting volume of troop and cargo movements in the United Kingdom in preparation for the North African landings was accompanied by an ominous upsurge in shipping losses to German submarines in the North Atlantic. In November the toll of Allied merchant shipping was to reach such alarming proportions as to raise doubts whether large-scale American deployment overseas could continue to be supported. At home, meanwhile, the armed services' far-reaching plans for expansion were coming under public and Congressional criticism.[59]

Apart from these pressures and distractions, opinion within the military was divided on the technical aspects of the feasibility question. General Somervell himself was a firm believer in incentive goals as a spur to production in wartime, and discounted the risks of disruption resulting from inflated objectives. In any case he was skeptical of dollar value estimates of national productive capacity. But his civilian superior, Undersecretary of War Robert P. Patterson, disagreed with him and urged compromise. After some preliminary skirmishing, Somervell backed down and suggested that the chiefs of staff be asked for guidance in determining which parts of the 1943 program could be deferred with least damage. This move served to neutralize the superboard proposal, preserved the principle that the military should determine military supply requirements, and, perhaps most important, avoided a showdown in the White House, the results of which no one could predict. The chairman of the War Production Board, Donald Nelson, accepted the proposal and the Joint Chiefs were asked to reduce the total 1943 program, amounting to about $98 billion including a residual deficit from 1942, to between $75 and $85 billion in munitions and war-related facilities and construction, over and above the minimum needs of the civilian economy.[60]

The resulting supply program for 1943 proposed by the Joint Chiefs in November totaled a little more than $80 billion, which, with some reservations, the WPB declared "within the realms of possible accomplishment." [61] In absolute terms the deepest cuts were made in ground force programs, which were reduced by about 21 per cent; Navy programs were cut in about the same proportion. Large reductions were imposed on military construction, war housing, and industrial facilities for the end items involved in the Army and Navy munitions programs. Military lend-lease programs were slashed by more than a fifth, overall, but the Soviet protocol program of $2.7 billion was left intact—clearly in deference to the President's known, or explicitly stated, desires. The merchant shipping program emerged unscathed (indeed, it had recently been expanded), and antisubmarine vessel construction was touched only lightly, testifying to the serious concern over the crisis in the North Atlantic. Aircraft construction was reduced by only 10 per cent.

Overall, the 1943 war production program was reduced by about 14 per cent, the chief victims being the ground army, the navy, the British, and the smaller lend-lease recipients. There was no attack on the "arsenal" policy as such, no attempt to pass on a disproportionately large share of the required reductions to lend-lease programs. British claims on the American supply programs were reduced roughly in the same proportion and in the same categories as those of the armed forces of the United States. Thus British ground forces suffered equally with the American, while the Royal Air Force shared with the United States Army Air Forces the relatively light reductions in aircraft programs. The feasibility crisis coincided with the presence in Washington of the Lyttelton Mission, bringing already scaled-down requests for 1943 allocations of ground force munitions in the more critical categories, for which the British, disturbed by the late 1942 allocation shortfalls, hoped to obtain a definite American commitment. In the Weeks-Somervell Agreement which emerged from the negotiations, these requests were further reduced by some 21 per cent in an over-all reduction of about 25 per cent imposed on British approved requirements in the current United States Army supply program, but the British got their definite commitment.

In subsequent negotiations, moreover, compensating increases were accepted in some of the less critical categories, with the remarkable result that the total British ground force requirements reflected in the February, 1943, United States Army supply program for 1943 were approximately the same as those in the original unreduced program of September, 1942. In effect, the severe shortfalls in deliveries to the British during the latter half of 1942, for which no explicit compensation was offered, were largely absorbed into the 1943 program.[62] As a British official history summed up the outcome:

On the face of it, therefore, the outcome was very much the maintenance of the status quo. In broad terms, the shortfall on assignments in 1942 had to be considered as a dead loss, but the British had averted any further cut in the total value of ground munitions being procured for them in 1943. The final provision for the two years represented only two-thirds of their original request [made in June 1942], but well over four-fifths of the more searchingly examined requirements put forward at the end of 1942. This was by no means an unsatisfactory outcome.[63]

When the untouched Soviet protocol program is brought into this equation, therefore, the *net* result of the feasibility crisis of late 1942 was a measurable shift in the general employment of American industrial power toward a more thoroughgoing arsenal policy. The two major beneficiaries of that policy, engrossing three-fourths of the total military aid program, emerged with their allotments from American production virtually intact, at least in aggregate totals. Reductions in American supply programs, on the other hand, were not only severe, but bore especially hard on the ground forces. All of which, even though the general magnitudes were still those of history's most "total" war, faintly recalled the emphases of Walter Lippmann's limited-war philosophy of late 1941.

The corollary of these developments was a corresponding cutback in the military services' manpower goals. The attack on military supply programs in the summer and fall of 1942 had been paralleled by mounting criticism, in Congress and in the various home-front agencies, of both the vastness and the vagueness of the armed forces' mobilization goals. The Army's revised "Victory Program" troop basis, issued soon after Pearl Harbor, aimed at a total of ten million men under arms by mid-1944—admittedly an impressionistic estimate—and a firmer mobilization objective of 3.6 million for 1942. As labor shortages began to develop in the summer of 1942, manpower waste in the armed services came under increasing criticism and investigating committees in both houses of Congress took the whole manpower problem under scrutiny. In mid-September Paul V. McNutt, chairman of the War Manpower

Commission, proposed a joint military-civilian commission to establish the ultimate manpower needs of industry, agriculture, and the armed services.[64]

The President himself, up to this time, appeared to be no more concerned over ultimate limitations on the nation's manpower supply than over those on its productive capacity. At the end of September, he told the services, in effect, to continue to expand toward their present goals for the end of 1943—8.2 million men for the Army, 2.7 million men for the Navy—with a good expectation of further increases later. But in October the War Production Board's Planning Committee, coincidentally with the attack on the military supply programs, sharply questioned the capacity of the economy to support so heavy a drain of manpower from productive pursuits and challenged the Army's ability to transport overseas the vast numbers of troops it planned to mobilize. The Committee warned against the accumulation of "a stagnant pool of manpower, contributing neither to the defense of the country in a military sense nor to its productive output." [65]

Evidently shaken, the President ordered a review of military manpower goals. In November the controversy reached a climax in a clear confrontation of antithetical views which posed the issue of the arsenal policy in starker terms than had been heard since the fall of 1941. Pressing its attack, the Planning Committee of the WPB declared:

> . . . the United States could contribute more toward a successful termination of the war by producing and shipping to our Allies the great quantities of munitions needed, than by shipping and supplying large numbers of American troops, which would interfere with our munitions production . . . . Although foreign labor cannot be brought in to relieve our industrial manpower shortage, foreign soldiers can be substituted for American soldiers in many of the theaters of war. A true combined strategy of the United Nations would free shipping and rationalize the use of manpower.[66]

This "fallacious and humiliating proposition," as General Marshall's staff characterized it, stung the Army chief of staff to a ringing reaffirmation of the Victory Program credo of September, 1941. The war would be ultimately won on the ground, he told the President, and large *American* armies would be needed to do the job. "The morale of the hostile world must be broken not only by aggressive fighting but, as in 1918, by the vision of an overwhelming force of fresh young Americans being *rapidly* developed in this country." [67] Against the possibility of insufficient transport to deploy American forces overseas, Marshall boldly argued that the risks of underexpansion were far greater. "It would be far better," he declared publicly about this time, "to have more trained men than we could ship than to have empty bottoms for which there were no trained troops, to support commanders whose forces might be wiped out for lack of them." [68]

By then the question had been settled. Late in November the President reaffirmed the Army's 1943 objective of 8.2 million men in an armed forces total of a little less than eleven million—but with an emphatic warning that further expansion was highly unlikely. His decision was undoubtedly made easier by the assurance he now had from the Joint Chiefs that the reduced supply programs they were about to recommend would support a force of that size. Army leaders were not displeased. Much could happen before 1944 and, if larger forces were really needed, the country could be expected to make them available. Moreover, as Marshall's deputy, Lieutenant General Joseph T. McNarney, privately admitted, the Army still had plenty of residual fat which could, if necessary, be rendered into additional combat power.[69] For the present, the President's warning would be heeded: "we should stop talking," commented an assistant chief of staff late in November, "about increases beyond this figure [8.2 million]"—and the Joint Chiefs of Staff decided a few days later to relegate to the back files a subcommittee plan envisaging ultimate force levels of 17.5 million men.[70] There, for the duration, it remained.

VI

There are two ways of looking at the American arsenal policy in World War II: in terms of the division of effort between the provision of American armed forces and the arming of allied forces, and in terms of the proportionate contributions made to the coalition in armed American manpower and in production of munitions.

In the largest and most summary view, American lend-lease aid throughout the war represented 14 per cent of the total defense expenditures of the United States—$43.6 billion out of $304.4 billion.[71] Defense expenditures, to be sure, embrace many activities only indirectly related to the provision and support of armed forces, but if one narrows the focus to War Department expenditures alone, the proportion accounted for by lend-lease is the same, 14 per cent.[72] Not surprisingly, both the scale of foreign aid and the proportion of the whole military effort that it represented increased as the emphasis shifted progressively from mobilization and training of forces at home to their deployment and use in major campaigns overseas. In 1941 lend-lease munitions accounted for only 2.6 per cent of the $7.3 billion of War Department expenditures, though considerable larger amounts of materiel were exported under direct purchase by foreign countries, mainly Great Britain. In 1940, of course, the entire export of United States munitions was by purchase, consisting mainly of United States Army stocks released as "surplus." How large a proportion of current production and existing stocks of munitions in the United States was diverted from American rearmament to foreign aid is difficult to determine, but it was almost certainly less than in the years following.[73]

In 1942 the floodgates opened, and the War Department allocated $3.2 billion, or 11 per cent of its total expenditures, to lend-lease. In 1943, following the cutback in supply and manpower goals at the end of 1942, the figure rose to $6.6 billion (14 per cent) and in 1944 to $7.2 billion (15 per cent). These two years brought into being a larger French army equipped with American materiel, which played a significant role in the campaigns in North Africa and Europe as part of the increased emphasis on the arming of foreign manpower. In the last year of the war, cutbacks in lend-lease supply after the defeat of Germany brought War Department lend-lease allocations down to $3.1 billion, representing 9 per cent of total expenditures in that year.[74]

During this period the mobilization of American manpower remained substantially within the outside limits ordered by the President in November, 1942, even in 1944 and early 1945 when the competing demands of a two-front war and an unexpected prolongation of the European campaign drained away the last trained reserves. In this context the sudden collapse of Germany in the spring of 1945 has been well named a "photofinish." [75] The corollary of the compact and barely adequate ninety-division American army in World War II was the air and sea power which, at a lower cost in manpower diverted from the production of munitions, helped to bring the nation's immense industrial strength to bear against the Axis.

It is interesting, in retrospect, to contrast the weapon that the United States Army fashioned out of the manpower allotted to it with the expectations of the Army planners in the summer of 1941. The aggregate size of the force envisaged in the Victory Program (8.8 million) was not much larger than the peak strength actually attained (8.3 million).[76] Its composition, however, bore little resemblance to the World War II army. The Victory Program envisaged 215 divisions, including sixty-one armored and fifty-one motorized, with half a million men in antiaircraft units. In the event, only sixteen armored and no motorized divisions were organized, and the antiaircraft component was only about half as large. Instead of the armor, mechanization, and specialization of the Victory Program army, the actual challenges of World War II produced a standardized, multipurpose, primarily infantry-artillery army with adequate armor, ample firepower, generous supply and transport services, and strong air support. The Victory Program planners greatly underestimated the number of troops who, in a modern war, never get near the front lines: the "division slice" of the 1941 plan was forty-one thousand, that of the 1945 army was ninety-one thousand men.[77]

These mistakes in forecasting were not surprising. They grew from the planners' failure to predict developments which in 1941 were not susceptible to scientific prediction, but which decisively shaped the whole course of the war: the successful resistence of the Russians and the errors in German strategy which helped to bring disaster and not merely setbacks to German arms on the Eastern front, thus quite probably averting a stalemate in Europe; Japan's swift aggression and the direction of her initial strokes; the series of mischances which made the Japanese attacks on Pearl Harbor and the Philippines the brilliant tactical successes that they were; the almost complete collapse of Allied power in the Far East in the early weeks of the war. In other words, the effort to estimate ultimate munitions requirements on the basis of long-range strategic predictions and plans proved unsound.

The United States mobilized about 12 per cent of its continental population in World War II, a percentage that compared favorably with Russia's 13, Germany's 14, and Japan's 13, and matched that of the United Kingdom. The sixteen million men put into uniform represented about a quarter of the forces mobilized by the major powers of the coalition, including China's seventeen million and India's 2.4 million, relatively few of whom saw action.[78] The comparison between this 25 per cent contribution to the armed manpower of the coalition and the 50 per cent provision of its munitions is one measure of the impact of the American arsenal policy.[79] Events neatly reversed the expectations of the American planners in 1941 regarding the role that would be played by allied manpower. In Europe the great reservoir of Russian manpower, discounted in the Victory Program, in the end overwhelmed the Wehrmacht; while on the other hand China's teeming millions, which had been counted on to wear down Japan until help could come from the West, actually played a minor role. American losses were, of course, much lower than those of the other allies—less than three hundred thousand military deaths, against 557,000 for Great Britain, 2.2 million for China, and 7.5 for the Soviet Union. This disparity was mainly a consequence of the late American entry and slow deployment to the fighting fronts: the Army reached a strength of eight million only in mid-1944, two and a half years after Pearl Harbor, and its overseas strength did not exceed five million until early in 1945, reaching a peak of 5.5 million that spring. Attrition forced the Soviet Union to mobilize twenty-two million soldiers in order to attain a peak strength of 12.5 million, a level which the United States almost reached with a total mobilization of only 16.1 million.[80]

In general, the full weight of American manpower was felt in the active theaters of war only from mid-1944 on. At the end of the war in Europe, American forces on hand in that sector (3.6 million) comprised about a fifth of the seventeen million Soviet, British, and other Allied forces arrayed against Germany. When

Japan collapsed a few months later, the two-million-odd American ground, air, and naval forces deployed against her probably constituted roughly the same proportion of the Allied total, if the entire mobilized strength of India and of China (Communist as well as Nationalist) is taken into account.[81] The effective contribution of American forces to the war against Japan was, of course, vastly greater than these figures would suggest.

On balance, it is fair to say that America's major and decisive contribution to the defeat of the Axis powers was, as Roosevelt had anticipated, the supply of munitions to its allies. The response to Churchill's plea in 1941 to "give us the tools, and we'll do the job," though sluggish at first, nevertheless served to stiffen Allied forces in the field long before American fighting men could make their own contribution effective. But the role of "arsenal of democracy" was in no sense, as many had hoped in 1941, a substitute for full-scale participation. As already noted, the American contribution in armed manpower represented a levy on the total population of the United States as heavy as that of most of the other major belligerents, and was on a scale wholly commensurate with the dimensions of twentieth-century "total" war. The supply of Allied forces on an unprecedented scale was superimposed on this "normal" mobilization of manpower.

Yet even this phenomenal performance was not the most remarkable feature of the American role in World War II. What most disconcerted the hard pressed allies was the ease with which the industrial giant across the Atlantic accomplished the miracle. The point is best illustrated by comparing the use of manpower in the United States with that of its closest partner, the United Kingdom. In the latter country in June, 1944, 55 per cent of the total labor force was either serving in the armed forces or engaged in war-related work. In the United States the corresponding figure was only 40 per cent. Many factors accounted for this disparity, but the meaning in terms of total war effort is clear. If the war had gone on longer, or if the threat had been more dire, the United States could have mustered even larger armed forces and supported even greater industrial expansion.[82]

Yalta Viewed From Tehran

William M. Franklin

DIRECTOR, HISTORICAL OFFICE, DEPARTMENT OF STATE *

The documents on the Yalta Conference of 1945 were released by the Department of State in 1955, setting off journalistic tremors that shook the front pages of every consequential newspaper around the globe.[1] In 1961 the Department published the documentation of the Tehran Conference of 1943,[2] and the only repercussions were the usual quiet reviews in the learned journals. This difference in public reaction surprised no one, for the notoriety appeal of the Yalta Conference remained unchallenged among all the summit meetings of World War II. The reasons for this sensational aura are not hard to find: the nature and number of the secret agreements signed at Yalta and revealed in successive shocks for two years thereafter; the President's haggard appearance at Yalta and his sudden death only two months later; the presence of Alger Hiss at the Conference; the insistent party-political charges and countercharges that made the very name of Yalta a household word for a decade; and last of all, the dramatic and unconventional manner in which the Yalta papers were released by the Department of State.

* The views here expressed are those of the author and do not necessarily reflect any official attitude on this subject by the Department of State.

Obviously the Tehran Conference, with none of these "notorious" characteristics, could not be expected to rival Yalta in general public interest, but even among scholars it has not received all the attention that it merits. The Tehran Conference was, after all, a major affair and the only other occasion on which Franklin D. Roosevelt, Winston S. Churchill, and Josef V. Stalin conferred in person. Vital decisions of the most fundamental nature and widest scope were reached at Tehran. Roosevelt held secret talks with Stalin at Tehran which were as long and detailed as those at Yalta. In this connection it is interesting to note that since Yalta had been so thoroughly covered in the memoir literature, it turned out that the official publication on Tehran was actually more "revealing" than the one on Yalta.

The discussions at Tehran, in addition to their own intrinsic importance, have a unique collateral value in the light that they throw on Yalta, and particularly on Roosevelt. For there was, as we shall see, a surprising amount of Yalta in Roosevelt's policies at Tehran. By comparing the positions taken by F.D.R. at both conferences, we get new perspectives on the goals and methods of that complex personality. For Roosevelt at Tehran was in excellent health and very much on his own. A large State Department delegation accompanied the President on his trip to Yalta, but there was none for Tehran. Only Secretary of State Cordell Hull and a few higher officers even knew where Roosevelt was going in November, 1943. No "Black Books" or "Position Papers" were prepared in State for Roosevelt's guidance on this trip as was done rather elaborately for the Yalta Conference.[3] The Tehran documents thus give us a remarkably clear picture of the true Roosevelt, and when this picture is superimposed on that of F. D. R. at Yalta, an interesting stereoscopic effect is produced. The following pages constitute an effort to give this kind of perspective to five subjects that concerned both conferences.

I. *Choice of Conference Site.* It has been a subject for speculation and criticism that Roosevelt agreed with relatively little argument to go all the way to Yalta to confer with Stalin in the winter of 1945. The reason was, according to Harry Hopkins, that "there was not a chance of getting that meeting outside of the Crimea."[4] Hopkins did not say so, but it was the negotiations for the conference at Tehran that proved his point. On that occasion Roosevelt and Churchill had vigorously employed every art of persuasion to induce Stalin to come to any one of a dozen spots closer to the United States or the British Isles, but all to no avail. He was finally persuaded to come out of Russia only as far as Tehran where he was protected by Russian military forces and where his lines of communication were entirely under Soviet control.[5]

Incidentally the Tehran experience was made even more conclusive by the fact that Roosevelt and Churchill had tried in vain to persuade Stalin to come to the Casablanca Conference in January, 1943. Stalin had said then that he could not (or would not) go out of the Soviet Union.[6]

Whether it was really necessary for Roosevelt and Churchill to confer personally with Stalin in February, 1945 is a separate question; but if such a conference was felt to be required, then it had to be held in the Union of Soviet Socialist Republics.

It is interesting to note that at Tehran the Russians raised the alarm of Nazi agents on the prowl and so induced F.D.R. to move from the American Legation to the Russian Embassy where the Conference meetings took place.[7] This may well have been a wise precaution, and certain it is that the Russians did all they could to make the President comfortable. The interesting fact remains that at both Tehran and Yalta Roosevelt lived in quarters where the Russians could easily have contrived to hear everything that went on in the President's suite.

II. *Entry of the Soviet Union into the War Against Japan.* It is well known that Stalin, on the occasion of the Moscow Meeting of Foreign Ministers, just before the Tehran Conference, promised Secretary of State Hull that the U.S.S.R. would enter the war against Japan. In his memoirs, Hull pointed out that this promise was made without any strings attached, the implication being that Roosevelt was unnecessarily generous at Yalta in making concessions to get Stalin to do what he had already promised to do.[8]

It will be recalled that these "concessions" consisted of a promise from Churchill and Roosevelt (1) to restore to Russia certain of those rights and possessions that had been taken from her by the Japanese in 1905; (2) to maintain the *status quo* (independence from China) of Outer Mongolia; and (3) to hand back to Russia the Kurile Islands (which Russia had traded for Sakhalin in 1875).[9]

Whatever one may think of these concessions, they were not hastily dreamed up at Yalta. They were in fact largely discussed and agreed upon at Tehran, as Ambassador W. Averell Harriman pointed out many years ago.[10] Apparently Mr. Hull thought that Stalin's promise was for free, but he seems to have been the only person of consequence who so assumed. Obviously Stalin would not discuss the *quid pro quo* with Hull, since Hull was not the man to make such decisions and in any case Stalin was going to see the President himself in less than a month after Hull left Moscow.

The minutes of the Tehran Conference make it clear that both Roosevelt and Churchill had been thinking about some concessions to induce Stalin to come into the war against Japan sooner rather than later, that is, soon enough to do the Western Allies some real good in the assault on Japan. But first they wanted to make sure that they had Stalin's explicit agreement to the Cairo Declaration which promised to restore to the Chinese what the Japanese had taken from them in 1895.[11] Stalin's agreement was obtained at the luncheon meeting on November 30, after which Churchill began to talk sympathetically of Russia's postwar need for "access to warm water ports." Stalin observed that it might be well to relax the regime of the Turkish Straits, but that question could wait. When Roosevelt began a disquisition on some kind of free-zone status for the German Hanseatic ports and international control over the Kiel Canal, Stalin cut him short with the gruff query as to "what could be done for Russia in the Far East." [12]

Roosevelt, anticipating this question, had just gotten Generalissimo Chiang Kai-shek at the Cairo Conference to agree that Dairen might be used by the Soviets as a free port—in return for Stalin's support of Chiang and the Cairo Declaration.[13] F.D.R. was thus in a good position to offer Stalin Dairen as a free port, with the assurance that Chiang would have no objection.

Neither the American minutes nor those published by the Soviets [14] indicate any further specific discussion at Tehran of those Russian political desires in the Far East that figured in the Yalta deal on the entry of the Soviet Union into the war against Japan.

But strangely enough both Roosevelt and Stalin later enumerated other specific items. In his report to the Pacific War Council on January 12, 1944, President Roosevelt said that at Tehran they had discussed not only Dairen but also the Manchurian railroads, Sakhalin, and the Kurile Islands.[15] In F.D.R.'s account there is no mention of Port Arthur or Outer Mongolia, but Stalin, in a conversation with Ambassador Harriman in December, 1944, said that all these items, except Outer Mongolia, had been mentioned by him at Tehran.[16]

Although these accounts all vary a bit, there is no doubt that the whole subject was thoroughly explored at Tehran, where agreement was reached on the general lines as indicated above. The Tehran discussion did not work up to an agreement because Stalin was not anxious to negotiate seriously until he was a lot closer to victory in Europe. But when the subject came up again in December, 1944, it required only some verbal "tidying up" before being committed to paper at Yalta.[17] Insofar as generosity may have played a part in prompting the agreement on the Anglo-American side, that consideration was best expressed not at Yalta but at Tehran and not by Roosevelt but by Churchill when he concluded the discussion with the thought that the nations who were to govern the world after the war "should be satisfied and have no territorial or other ambitions." They should be "in the position of rich, happy men." [18]

III. *Polish Boundaries.* The Yalta agreement on Polish boundaries published at the end of the conference provided that Poland should accept the Curzon Line in the East (with some digressions in favor of Poland), in return for which Poland was to receive "substantial accessions of territory in the north and west," the final delimitation to be made at the peace conference.[19] Behind the scenes, however, Roosevelt and Churchill at Yalta tentatively accepted the line of the Oder River as Poland's Western boundary.[20]

The agreement on the Curzon Line (with small digressions in favor of Poland) was reached at the Tehran Conference, and those "in the know" were aware of it long before Yalta. That Churchill had favored the Curzon Line for several years before the Tehran Conference was public knowledge. Roosevelt's position was not known until the Prime Minister of the Polish Government in London, Stanisław Mikołajczyk, heard (with a "shock of surprise") from Molotov in a discussion on October 13, 1944, that Roosevelt had also accepted the Curzon Line.[21]

The acceptance had taken place at Tehran in a private conversation with Stalin on December 1, 1943. Since Churchill had taken the initiative at Tehran in proposing the Curzon Line (with accessions for Poland in the north and west), F.D.R. felt called upon to explain his silence to the Soviet leader. Speaking as one hardheaded politician to another, the President pointed out to Stalin that he might have to run again in 1944 and that he did not wish to lose the votes of "six to seven million Americans of Polish extraction." For this reason he could not take any public position on the matter at that time, although privately he would like to see Poland's "Eastern border moved further to the west and the Western border moved even to the River Oder." [22]

On this subject the Tehran minutes appear not to have been as detailed as the actual discussion. In October, 1944, Stalin recalled that Roosevelt in this Tehran conversation had agreed to the Curzon Line but with Lwow (Lemberg) going to Poland.[23] Since this was exactly the position that Roosevelt later voiced at Yalta and since Stalin himself opposed the cessation of Lwow, there is reason to believe that F.D.R. probably used this precise phrase in talking with Stalin at Tehran.[24] Unfortunately the Tehran documents published by the Soviets (which are riddled with huge deletions) leave out this entire discussion. From the sources cited, however, it is clear that Roosevelt's (and Churchill's) agreement on Polish boundaries was reached orally at Tehran and needed only to be written down at Yalta.

IV. *The Suggested Dismemberment of Germany.* The Protocol of the Yalta Conference provided that Article 12(a) of the draft surrender terms for Germany should read as follows:

> The United Kingdom, the United States of America and the Union of Soviet Socialist Republics shall possess supreme authority with respect to Germany. In the exercise of such authority they will take such steps, including the complete disarmament, demilitarisation and the dismemberment of Germany as they deem requisite for future peace and security.[25]

When this Protocol of 1945 was published in March, 1947, it was the oldest official document that revealed Roosevelt as favoring dismemberment. By chronology it followed directly on the heels of the Morgenthau Plan, and would appear to have been influenced by it.[26] In fact, however, Roosevelt had been an earnest advocate of dismemberment long before Henry Morgenthau's Plan came onto the scene in September, 1944.

At the Tripartite Political Meeting at Tehran on December 1, Roosevelt opened the problem of Germany by saying that the question was whether to split or not. Stalin promptly stated that he favored dismemberment. The American minutes then read as follows:

> The President said he had a plan that he had thought up some months ago for the division of Germany into five parts. These five parts were:
> 1. All Prussia to be rendered as small and weak as possible
> 2. Hanover and Northwest section
> 3. Saxony and Leipzig area
> 4. Hesse-Darmstadt
>   Hesse-Kassel and the area South of the Rhine
> 5. Bavaria, Baden, and Wurtemburg [Württemberg]
>
> He proposed that these five areas should be self-governed and that there should be two regions under United Nations or some form of International control. These were: 1. The area of the Kiel Canal and the City of Hamburg. 2. The Ruhr and the Saar, the latter to be used for the benefit of all Europe.[27]

It was this plan that Roosevelt reported at Yalta, giving it a bit more flexibility by saying that it provided for Germany to be broken down "into five or seven states." [28] While the Big Three at Yalta could not agree on the exact lines of division, they did agree on the principle of dismemberment and so added it (as we have seen) to the draft surrender terms.

Although the writing down of this agreement took place at Yalta, it is an odd fact that there was more enthusiasm for the subject at Tehran. The idea had always been supported primarily by the Big Three personally. The Department of State had never favored the idea; [29] Foreign Secretary Anthony Eden was increasingly skeptical;[30] and by the time of the Yalta Conference, Churchill was definitely dragging his feet though he went along with his more enthusiastic colleagues.[31] With the death of Roosevelt and the last minute substitution of a different surrender instrument,[32] the idea died, in principle, although it survived in fact through the division of Germany by the Soviet's Iron Curtain, subsequently reinforced by the Berlin Wall.

V. *The Concept of a United Nations Organization.* With respect to the concept of a postwar United Nations organization, it cannot be maintained that Yalta reflected Tehran. On the contrary, as far as Roosevelt's policy was concerned the difference was striking, and a comparison becomes quite revealing.

F.D.R.'s very personal concepts on this subject were expressed at Tehran, to which he went without benefit of State Department advice and to which he took no prepared proposals on the subject. The President obviously spoke from the heart when he talked to Stalin about his concept of the "Four Policemen" (the U.S., U.K., U.S.S.R., and China) who would keep the peace of the world after the war. To be sure, there would be an assembly of all members of the UN organization, and an executive committee of some ten members; but real power would be in the hands of the Four Policemen.[33] Indeed, Roosevelt was only being realistic: three of the Four Policemen did emerge with overwhelming power and the fourth (China) would have so emerged if the war against Japan had been fought as anticipated to a victorious conclusion from a liberated China rather than from across the Pacific. F.D.R.'s instinctive insight told him that the unity of the powerful was the bedrock of world peace.

Between Tehran and Yalta the President was prevailed upon to study more deeply the question of United Nations organization, despite his impatience with administrative matters. From the Dumbarton Oaks Conversations of 1944 and from Department of State studies, Roosevelt came to understand the need for a central, worldwide organization, a precise formula for voting in the Security Council, and a general conference of all the victors to work out the exact language of a United Nations charter.

On these subjects at Yalta Roosevelt spoke rather little, leaving it largely up to Secretary of State Edward R. Stettinius to present the views of the United States.[34] The President supported his Secretary at Yalta, and there is no doubt that F.D.R. was intellectually convinced of the value of the organizational work being done. If, however, one compares the color of the President's remarks on this whole subject at Tehran and at Yalta, it becomes evident that he was most enthusiastic about the postwar needs and prospects for that intimate club of the Four Policemen that would keep the peace. To a marked degree this attitude reflected F.D.R.'s realistic sense of power values; it was also his way of trying to make the postwar international security organization look attractive to the hard-boiled Soviet dictator. Churchill understood, and in an argument with Eden at Yalta he expressed the thought "that everything depended on the unity of the three Great Powers[35] and that without that the world would be subjected to inestimable catastrophe; anything that (preserved) that unity would have his vote."[36]

The five subjects considered in the preceding pages in their respective Tehran and Yalta aspects are offered only as examples, not as a complete list of the topics that ran through both of these summit meetings. The examples, however, will suffice to show that Tehran deserves more attention than it has been given. Whether one is inclined to blame, praise, or excuse Roosevelt at Yalta, it is demonstrably necessary to take Tehran into simultaneous calculation.

Reginald Charles McGrane
A Selected Bibliography

Compiled by Harry R. Stevens

I. BOOKS

Ed. *The Correspondence of Nicholas Biddle Dealing with National Affairs, 1807–1844.* Boston and New York: Houghton Mifflin Company, 1919. Pp. xix, 366.

The Panic of 1837: Some Financial Problems of the Jacksonian Era. Chicago: University of Chicago Press, 1925. Pp. vii, 260.
Republished: Phoenix Books. Chicago and London: University of Chicago Press. First Phoenix Edition, 1965.

William Allen: A Study in Western Democracy. Columbus: Ohio State Archaeological and Historical Society, 1925. Pp. 279.

Foreign Bondholders and American State Debts. New York: The Macmillan Company, 1935. Pp. vii, 410.

The Economic Development of the American Nation. Boston: Ginn and Company, 1942. Pp. vii, 691.
Second edition. Boston: Ginn and Company, 1950.

The Facilities and Construction Program of the War Production Board and Predecessor Agencies May 1940 to May 1945. War Production Board, Historical Reports on War Administration Special Studies. Washington, D.C., 1945. Pp. 246.

Reissued 1946.

Cincinnati Doctors' Forum. Cincinnati: Academy of Medicine of Cincinnati, 1957. Pp. vii, 389.

The University of Cincinnati: A Success Story in Urban Higher Education. New York: Harper, 1963. Pp. xiii, 364.

II. OTHER PUBLICATIONS

1913

"The Evolution of the Ohio-Erie Boundary," *Ohio Archaeological and Historical Quarterly*, XXII (April, 1913), 326–339.

"Documents Relating to Zachariah Cox," edited with Isaac Joslin Cox, *Historical and Philosophical Society of Ohio Publications*, VIII (April–September, 1913), 29–114.

1914

Ed. "William Clark's Journal of General Wayne's Campaign," *Mississippi Valley Historical Review*, I (December, 1914), 418–44.

1917

"Speculation in the Thirties," *Ohio Valley Historical Association Proceedings*, X (1916), included in *Indiana Historical Society Publications*, VI, No. 1 (1917), 22–42.

"The Veto Power in Ohio," *Mississippi Valley Historical Association Proceedings*, IX, No. 1 (1917), 177–89.

1920

"The American Position on the Revolution of 1848 in Germany," *Historical Outlook*, XI (December, 1920), 333–39.

1921

"The Rise and Fall of the Independent Treasury," *Historical Outlook*, XII (May, 1921), 158–64.

"The Bane of Our Colleges," *School and Society*, XIV (September 10, 1921), 161–63.

1925

"Ohio and the Greenback Movement," *Mississippi Valley Historical Review*, XI (March, 1925), 526–42.

1926

"The Panic of 1837 and the Subtreasury Bills," University of Chicago *Abstracts of Theses, Humanistic Series*, II, 181–85. Chicago: University of Chicago Press, 1926.

1928–1936

Dictionary of American Biography. For a list of biographies see below.

1929–1950

The Encyclopedia Americana. Several articles, including those on *Vice Presidency, Speaker of the House of Representatives, Andrew Johnson, James Monroe,* and *Zachary Taylor*.

1933

"Some Aspects of American State Debts in the Forties," *American Historical Review*, XXXVIII (July, 1933), 673–86.

1935

"The Apologia of American Debtor States," *Essays in Honor of William E. Dodd, by His Former Students at the University of Chicago*, ed. by Avery Craven. Chicago: University of Chicago Press, 1935, pp. 86–98.

1940

Dictionary of American History, ed. by James T. Adams. 5 vols. New York: Charles Scribner's Sons, 1940. Several articles.

1953

"Orator Bob and the Right of Instruction," *Historical and Philosophical Society of Ohio Bulletin*, XI (October, 1953), 251–73.

1954

"Jacksonian America as Seen by the British Minister," *Historical and Philosophical Society of Ohio Bulletin*, XII (July, 1954), 194–208.

"William Allen: 1874–1876," *The Governors of Ohio*. Columbus: Ohio Historical Society, 1954, pp. 101–104.

1955

"George Washington: an Anglo-American Hero," *Virginia Magazine of History and Biography*, LXIII (January, 1955), 3–13.

"The Cincinnati College of Pharmacy," *Historical and Philosophical Society of Ohio Bulletin*, XIII (January, 1955), 25–37.

1960

"Nicholas Longworth," *Museum Echoes*, XXXIII (August, 1960), 59–62.

1961

"Beverley Waugh Bond, Jr.," *Historical and Philosophical Society of Ohio Bulletin*, XIX (April, 1961), 159–60.

"Recent History," edited with Walter C. Langsam, *The American Historical Association's Guide to Historical Literature*. New York: The Macmillan Company, 1961, pp. 790–804.

Contributions to *Dictionary of American Biography*.

1928–1936

Christy, David (b. 1802)
Cist, Charles (1738–1805)
Cist, Charles (1792–1868)
Clarke, Robert (1829–99)
Cox, George Barnsdale (1853–1916)

Edgerton, Alfred Peck (1813–97)
Elder, William Henry (1819–1904)
Ellis, John Washington (1817–1910)
Ewing, Hugh Boyle (1826–1905)
Ewing, Thomas (1789–1871)
Ewing, Thomas (1829–96)
Faran, James John (1808–92)
Findlay, James (1770–1835)
Foraker, Joseph Benson (1846–1917)
Force, Manning Ferguson (1824–99)
Gage, Lyman Judson (1836–1927)
Galloway, Samuel (1811–72)
Greenwood, Miles (1807–85)
Guilford, Nathan (1786–1854)
Gunther, Charles Frederick (1837–1920)
Hammond, Charles (1779–1840)
Hovey, Charles Edward (1827–97)
Ingalls, Melville Ezra (1842–1914)
Langston, John Mercer (1829–97)
Lawrence, William (1819–99)
Leaming, Jacob Spicer (1815–85)
Leavitt, Humphrey Howe (1796–1873)
Lytle, William Haines (1826–633)
McLean, John (1785–1861)
Pattison, John M. (1847–1906)
Pendleton, George Hunt (1825–89)
Springer, Reuben Runyan (1800–84)
Thurman, Allen Granberry (1813–95)
Warden, Robert Bruce (1824–88)
Zimmerman, Eugene (1845–1914)

Notes

"A Fair Field and No Favor":
The Structure of Informal Empire

1 George F. Kennan, *American Diplomacy, 1900–1950* (Chicago, 1952), pp. 25–42. *See also* A. Whitney Griswold, *The Far Eastern Policy of the United States* (New York, 1938), pp. 36–86. Parts of this essay have appeared in another form in my *China Market: America's Quest for Informal Empire* (Chicago, 1967).

2 Charles S. Campbell, Jr., *Special Business Interests and the Open Door Policy* (Baltimore, 1951), pp. 45–49. Other general works that cover the Open Door notes include Tyler Dennett, *John Hay: From Poetry to Politics* (New York, 1934), pp. 284–96 and A. L. P. Dennis, *Adventures in American Diplomacy, 1896–1906* (New York, 1928), pp. 170–214. Interesting though sometimes romanticized Chinese-American views of the Open Door can be found in Joshua Bau, *The Open Door Doctrine in Relation to China* (New York, 1923); Tsung-Yu Sze, *China and the Most-Favored-Nation Clause* (New York, 1925); and Shutaro Tomimas, *The Open Door Policy and the Territorial Integrity of China* (New York, 1919). Less dated and more realistic, albeit stridently so at times, is Sheng Hu, *Imperialism and Chinese Politics* (Peking, 1955).

3 William McKinley, *Speeches and Addresses of William McKinley, from March 1, 1897 to May 30, 1900* (New York, 1900), p. 135.

4 Brooks Adams, "The New Struggle for Life among Nations," *The Fort-Nightly Review,* LXXI (1899), 280.

5 Quoted in Campbell, *Special Business Interests,* p. 91.

6 *Bankers' Magazine,* LXI (Sept., 1900), 341.

7 Patrick O'Hare to John Hay, Feb. 14, 1900, Hay MSS, Library of Congress.
8 Joseph Wheeler to William McKinley, Jan. 14, 1900, McKinley MSS, Library of Congress.
9 William W. Rockhill to John Hay, Oct. 19, 1899, Hay MSS.
10 *American Trade,* III (1899), 39.
11 *The Nation,* LXXII (May 9, 1901), 369.
12 Cushman K. Davis to Whitelaw Reid, April 20, 1899, Reid MSS, Library of Congress.
13 Chicago *Inter-Ocean,* Aug. 19, 1899, p. 5.
14 Notes on China (undated), Worthington C. Ford MSS, Library of Congress.
15 John Hay to Charles Dick, Sept. 11, 1899, Hay MSS.
16 Department of Commerce and Labor, *Exports of Manufactures from the United States and Their Distribution by Articles and Countries, 1800–1906* (Washington, D.C., 1907), pp. 32–33, 59.
17 *Senate Document No. 230,* 56th Cong., 1st Sess., pp. 6–7.
18 Horace Porter to William McKinley, Nov. 14, 1899, McKinley MSS.
19 NA, RG 59, *Russia Despatches* 54, No. 259, Herbert D. Pierce to Hay, Feb. 25, 1899 (notation by A. A. Adee); NA, RG 59, *China Instructions* 5, No. 126, Hay to Edwin H. Conger, Feb. 2, 1899; William R. Thayer, *The Life and Letters of John Hay II* (Boston, 1915), p. 241.
20 *See* NA, RG 59, *Germany Despatches* 69, No. 1037, Andrew D. White to Hay, Sept. 29, 1899. Therein, White summarizes the Spanish-German Treaty of February 12, 1899 on the Carolines and the Ladrones, as well as the American reaction to it.
21 Charles H. Allen, acting secretary of the navy, to Hay, Aug. 3, 1899, Hay MSS. On the subject of the Amoy settlement, *see* NA, RG 59, *Consular Despatches* 13, No. 38, A. B. Johnson to David J. Hill, Jan. 12, 1899; NA, RG 59, *China Despatches* 106, No. 132, Conger to Hay, Jan. 20, 1899; telegram, Conger to Hay, March 23, 1899; No. 169, March 24, 1899; NA, RG 59, *Consular Instructions* 166, telegram, Adee to Johnson, March 9, 1899; NA, RG 59, *China Instructions,* cipher telegram, Hay to Conger, March 24, 1899.
22 NA, RG 59, *Russia Despatches* 54, No. 259, Pierce to Hay, Feb. 25, 1899.
23 NA, RG 59, *China Despatches* 106, No. 219, Conger to Hay, June 16, 1899; cipher telegram, June 16, 1899; 107, No. 248, Aug. 10, 1899.
24 *Ibid.,* 106, cipher telegram, March 1, 1899; No. 167, March 16, 1899; New York *Times,* March 4, 1899, p. 7; March 13, 1899, p. 6; Chicago *Inter-Ocean,* March 11, 1899, p. 6. *See also* Joseph, *Foreign Diplomacy in China,* p. 390 and Campbell, *Special Business Interests,* p. 52.
25 Tomimas, *The Open Door Policy,* pp. 19–20; Joseph, *Foreign Diplomacy in China,* p. 390.
26 *See* New York *Times,* April 30, 1899, p. 18.
27 Joseph, *Foreign Diplomacy in China,* pp. 382–83.
28 New York *Times,* Feb. 2, 1899, p. 7.
29 *See* NA, RG 59, *China Despatches* 106, No. 237, Conger to Hay, July 15, 1899; 107, No. 278, Nov. 25, 1899; NA, RG 59, *China Instructions* 6, telegram, Hay to Conger, July 14, 1899; No. 191, July 15, 1899; No. 224, Jan. 19, 1900.

30 The New York *Times,* quoting presumably from Rockhill, noted official administration ambivalence on partitioning: that while it might be undesirable if it led to trade discrimination, on the other hand it might "break down Chinese conservatism and open up vast markets." *See* New York *Times,* Nov. 5, 1899, p. 12; Nov. 9, 1899, p. 4.

31 New York *Times,* March 4, 1899. p. 7. On Jan. 12, 1899, the American consul wrote the Department of State that in his opinion "the United States should be a preferred nation in Amoy owing to the fact that this is the chief port in China for the Philippines . . . . This is one port we must preserve if we make of our new possessions in the Orient what is now anticipated." And on May 9, 1899, he approached Chinese officials about the possibility of an American concession on Kulangsu Island. *See* NA, RG 59, *Consular Despatches* 13, No. 38, Johnson to Hill, Jan. 12, 1899; No. 48, May 9, 1899.

32 In late summer, the Department of State informed the American consul in Amoy that it could not "give unqualified endorsement of your course"; that he had "misunderstood the Department's" instructions. NA, RG 59, *Consular Instructions* 166, No. 51, Cridler to Johnson, Sept. 5, 1899.

33 Hay rejected this alternative, "for the present," in early 1899 when he wrote Paul Dana that "our best policy is one of vigilant protection of our commercial interests without formal alliances with other Powers interested." Thayer, *Life and Letters of John Hay II,* p. 241.

34 Hay to Rockhill, Aug. 7, 1899, Rockhill MSS.

35 Archibald R. Colquhoun to Hay, Jan. 12, 1899, Hay MSS.

36 Archibald R. Colquhoun, *China in Transformation* (New York and London, 1899), pp. ix–x, 155–57, 235, and 366–67.

37 Lord Charles Beresford, "China and the Powers," *The North American Review,* CLXVIII (May, 1899), 530; Beresford, *The Break-up of China* (London and New York, 1899), pp. 7, 63, and 416.

38 *Ibid.,* pp. 426 and 431–32.

39 Chicago *Inter-Ocean,* Feb. 20, 1899, p. 6.

40 *Journal of the American Asiatic Association,* I (March 11, 1899), 29; Beresford, *The Break-up of China,* p. 429.

41 *Ibid.,* p. 432.

42 *The Nation,* LXVIII (March 30, 1899), 236.

43 *Atlantic Monthly,* LXXXIV (Aug., 1899), 279–80.

44 John R. Proctor, "Saxon or Slav?—The Eastern Question," *Harpers Weekly Magazine,* XLIII (Nov. 25, 1899), 1179; John Barrett, "The Paramount Power of the Pacific," *North American Review,* LXXXIX (July, 1899), 168–69.

45 *Bankers' Magazine,* LXI (Sept., 1900), 341; *Journal of Commerce and Commercial Bulletin* (March 21, 1899), p. 4; Rockhill to Hay, Oct. 19, 1899, Hay MSS; Everett Frazer to Hay, Nov. 24, 1899; Campbell, *Special Business Interests,* p. 50.

46 New York *Times,* Nov. 3, 1899, p. 9.

47 "Foreign Policy of the United States: Political and Commercial," *The Annals of the American Academy of Political and Social Science Supplement* (Philadelphia, 1899), pp. 90–91; 163–64.

48 Griswold, *Far Eastern Policy,* p. 70.

49 New York *Times,* March 6, 1899, p. 1; March 7, 1899, p. 2.

50 Clipping from London *Times,* May 28, 1899, Albert J. Beveridge MSS.
51 NA, RG 59, *China Despatches* 107, No. 290, Conger to Hay, Dec. 9, 1899. *See also* the remarks and citation in footnote 32.
52 *See especially* NA, RG 59, *Germany Despatches* 68, No. 714, Andrew D. White to Hay, Jan. 25, 1899; No. 706, Jan. 21, 1899.
53 NA, RG 59, *Russia Despatches* 54, No. 81, Charlemagne Tower to Hay, Aug. 23, 1899.
54 New Orleans *Picayune,* Aug. 18, 1899, p. 4.
55 New York *Times,* Aug. 22, 1899, p. 6.
56 Hay to Rockhill, Aug. 24, 1899, Hay MSS.
57 The meat of the Rockhill-Hippisley arguments and efforts is reflected in the following correspondence: Alfred E. Hippisley to Rockhill, July 25, 1899, Rockhill MSS; Rockhill to Hay, Aug. 3, 1899, Hay MSS; Hippisley to Rockhill, Aug. 16, 1899, Rockhill MSS; Rockhill to Adee, Aug. 19, 1899, Hay MSS. *See also* Paul A. Varg, *Open Door Diplomat: W. W. Rockhill* (Urbana, Ill., 1952), pp. 26–36.
58 Griswold, *Far Eastern Policy,* p. 73.
59 Hay to Rockhill, Aug. 24, 1899, Hay MSS.
60 Rockhill to Hippisley, Aug. 29, 1899, Rockhill MSS.
61 Rockhill to Hay, Aug. 28, 1899, Hay MSS.
62 NA, RG 59, *England Instructions* 33, No. 205, Hay to Joseph Choate, Sept. 6, 1899.
63 Rockhill Memorandum, Dec. 19, 1899, Hay MSS.
64 W. W. Rockhill, "The United States and the Future of China," *The Forum* XXIX (May, 1900), 330.
65 Hay to Wu Ting-fu, Nov. 11, 1899, Hay MSS; Hay to Choate, Nov. 13, 1899; NA, RG 59, *China Instructions* 6, No. 217, Hay to Conger, Nov. 20, 1899.
66 Rockhill to Hay, Aug. 28, 1899, Hay MSS. This view is advanced by numerous historians, including Dennett, *John Hay* (*see* citation in Bau, *The Open Door Doctrine,* p. xix); Parker T. Moon, *Imperialism and World Politics* (New York, 1926), p. 341; and Earl H. Pritchard, "The Origins of the Most-Favored-Nation and the Open Door Policies," *The Far Eastern Quarterly,* I (Feb., 1942), 171.
67 Rockhill to Hay, Aug. 28, 1899, Hay MSS.
68 Choate to Hay, Nov. 1, 1899, Hay MSS.
69 NA, RG 59, *Russia Despatches* 55, No. 104, Tower to Hay, Sept. 20, 1899.
70 Choate to Hay, Nov. 1, 1899, Hay MSS; Hay to Choate, Nov. 13, 1899, Letterbook, Hay MSS.
71 NA, RG 59, *France Despatches* 118, No. 559, Porter to Hay, Nov. 10, 1899; Porter to McKinley, Nov. 14, 1899, McKinley MSS.
72 NA, RG 59, *Japan Instructions* 4, No. 263, Hay to Alfred S. Buck, Nov. 13, 1899.
73 Rockhill Memorandum, undated, Rockhill MSS.
74 Hay to Choate, Nov. 13, 1899, Letterbook, Hay MSS.
75 NA, RG 59, *England Despatches* 198, No. 216, Choate to Hay, Dec. 1, 1899.
76 *Ibid.,* telegram, Dec. 11, 1899; Hay to Choate, Dec. 4, Letterbook, Hay MSS.

77 NA, RG 59, *Germany Despatches* 71, telegram, John B. Jackson to Hay, Dec. 4, 1899.
78 NA, RG 59, *England Instructions* 198, telegram, Hay to Choate, Dec. 8, 1899.
79 NA, RG 59, *France Despatches* 118, No. 589, Porter to Hay, Dec. 15, 1899.
80 *Ibid.*, No. 579, Dec. 1, 1899.
81 *Ibid.*, telegram, Dec. 14, 1899.
82 *Ibid.*, telegram, Dec. 18, 1899.
83 *Ibid.*, No. 594, Dec. 21, 1899.
84 Andrew Malozemoff, *Russian Far Eastern Policy, 1881–1904* (Berkeley and Los Angeles, 1958), pp. 116–17.
85 NA, RG 59, *Russia Despatches* 55, No. 156, Tower to Hay, Nov. 23, 1899.
86 *Ibid.*, No. 167, confidential, Dec. 11, 1899.
87 *Ibid.*, No. 172, Dec. 26, 1899.
88 Rockhill Memorandum, Dec. 19, 1899, Hay MSS.
89 Hay to Henry White, April 2, 1900, Letterbook, Hay MSS.
90 NA, RG 59, *Russia Despatches* 55, No. 172, Tower to Hay, Dec. 26, 1899.
91 *Ibid.*, No. 174, Dec. 28, 1899.
92 *Loc. cit.*
93 *Ibid.*, No. 176, Jan. 2, 1900.
94 Rockhill to Hippisley, Jan. 16, 1900, Rockhill MSS.
95 *Loc. cit.*
96 Tower to Hay, Feb. 9, 1900, Hay MSS; Feb. 12, 1900.
97 For example, *see* NA, RG 59, *France Instructions* 24, No. 746, Hay to Porter, March 20, 1900.
98 Even a cursory perusal of the Hay MSS and of major American newspapers quickly persuades one of the almost unqualified approval given the Open Door notes by Americans of the day.
99 New York *Times*, Jan. 6, 1900, p. 7; Griswold, *Far Eastern Policy.*
100 Dennett, *John Hay*, p. 317.

William Howard Taft and the Ohio Endorsement Issue, 1906–1908

1 New York *Times*, Dec. 12, 1907.
2 Theodore Roosevelt to William A. White, July 30, 1907, Theodore Roosevelt MSS., in the Library of Congress; Herman H. Kohlsaat, *From McKinley to Harding* (New York, 1923), p. 161; Oscar K. Davis, *Released for Publication* (Cambridge, 1925), p. 54.
3 Philip C. Jessup, *Elihu Root* (2 vols., New York, 1938), II, 123–26; Henry L. Stoddard, *As I Knew Them* (New York, 1927), pp. 322–24; William H. Taft to Mrs. Alphonso (Louise) Taft, Aug. 16, 1907, William H. Taft MSS., Library of Congress; Davis, *op. cit.*, p. 54.
4 *See* Roosevelt to William H. Taft, Aug. 19, 1891, in Elting E. Morison, ed., *The Letters of Theodore Roosevelt* (8 vols., Cambridge, 1951–54), I, 258–59.
5 Roosevelt to Taft, July 15, 1901, April 22, 1903, III, 121–22, 464.
6 Roosevelt to Taft, May 22, 1903, III, 478.

7 Roosevelt to Charles W. Eliot, April 4, 1904, IV, 770.
8 Roosevelt to George Otto Trevelyan, May 13, 1905, IV, 1175.
9 Roosevelt to Trevelyan, June 19, 1908, Roosevelt MSS.
10 Henry F. Pringle, *The Life and Times of William H. Taft* (2 vols., New York, 1939), I, 134–38.
11 Mrs. William H. (Helen) Taft, *Recollections of Full Years* (New York, 1914), pp. 263–70, 304.
12 *See* Mrs. W. H. Taft to Taft, March 29, 1907, Taft MSS.; Kohlsaat, pp. 161–62.
13 Pringle, I, 315; Taft's letter and Mrs. Taft's visit are discussed in Roosevelt to Taft, March 15, 1906, in Morison, V, 183–86; George E. Mowry, *The Era of Theodore Roosevelt, 1900–1912* (New York, 1958), p. 234.
14 Everett Walters, *Joseph Benson Foraker, An Uncompromising Republican* (Columbus, 1948), pp. 256–72; Harold Zink, *City Bosses in the United States* (Durham, 1930), pp. 265–67; Reginald C. McGrane, "George Barnsdale Cox," *Dictionary of American Biography,* IV, 473–74.
15 Frederic L. Paxson, Review of Joseph B. Foraker's *Notes of a Busy Life, Mississippi Valley Historical Review,* III (Sept., 1916), 249.
16 An illuminating report on the early relations between Hanna and Foraker may be found in a memorial address delivered on April 7, 1904 by Foraker. *See Congressional Record,* 58 Cong., 2 Sess., XXXVIII, 4414–16. *See also* Steffens, "Ohio: A Tale of Two Cities," *McClure's Magazine,* XXV (July, 1905), 293–311; Herbert D. Croly, *Marcus Alonzo Hanna, His Life and Works* (New York, 1912), p. 138; Walters, *Foraker,* pp. 49–207.
17 James L. Harrison, comp., *Biographical Directory of the American Congresses, 1774–1949* (Washington, 1950), pp. 1081–82.
18 Walters, pp. 208, 227–28.
19 Elbert J. Benton, "Theodore H. Burton," *Dictionary of American Biography,* suppl. I, p. 141; "Harry M. Daugherty," *Who's Who in America 1922–1923* (Chicago, 1922), pp. 860–61. Roosevelt was well aware of political conditions in Ohio. He told Senator Henry C. Lodge that he knew the Burton faction wanted to "down both Dick and Foraker." Roosevelt to Lodge, Aug. 6, 1906, Morison, *Roosevelt Letters,* V, 347.
20 Steffens, "Ohio," p. 297.
21 Walters, pp. 201, 261.
22 Quoted in Pringle, *Taft,* I, 269.
23 It may not have been Taft's statement which defeated Herrick. Instead, it may have been the fact that Herrick was the first governor of Ohio to have the veto power. His use of that power had alienated several segments of the electorate. Harlow Lindley, *Ohio in the Twentieth Century* (Columbus, 1943), p. 7.
24 Cincinnati *Enquirer,* Aug. 17, 24, 27, 1906.
25 *Ibid.,* Sept. 9, 1906.
26 *Ibid.,* Sept. 12, 1906; Dayton *Journal,* Sept. 12, 1906; Columbus *Evening Dispatch,* Sept. 11, 1906.
27 Cincinnati *Enquirer,* Sept. 13, 1906.
28 *Loc. cit.;* Joseph B. Foraker, *Notes of a Busy Life,* 2 vols. (Cincinnati, 1916), II, 377; *Outlook,* LXXXIV (Sept. 22, 1906), 149.

29 Cincinnati *Enquirer,* Nov. 8, 1906.
30 McGrane, "G. B. Cox," p. 474.
31 Roosevelt to Taft, March 15, 1906, in Morison, V, 183–86.
32 Roosevelt to Benjamin I. Wheeler, July 3, 1906, V, p. 329.
33 Roosevelt to James Wilson, Sept. 11, Roosevelt to Taft, Sept. 17, Roosevelt to Lodge, Oct. 1, Roosevelt to Taft, Nov. 8, 1906, V, pp. 403–404, 414–15, 436–37, 491–92.
34 Mrs. Taft, *Recollections,* pp. 304–305.
35 Roosevelt to Taft, Nov. 5, 1906, Morison, V, 486–87; Mrs. Taft, p. 305.
36 Cincinnati *Times-Star,* Dec. 29, 1906.
37 *Loc. cit.*
38 Charles P. Taft to Taft, Dec. 29, Henry W. Taft to Taft, Dec. 30, 1906, Taft MSS; Cincinnati *Times-Star,* Dec. 29, 1906.
39 Taft to Charles P. Taft, Jan. 1, 1907, Taft MSS.
40 Charles P. Taft to Taft, Dec. 29, 1906, Taft MSS.
41 Emma Lou Thornbrough, "The Brownsville Episode and the Negro Vote," *Mississippi Valley Historical Review,* XLIV (Dec., 1957), 469–93. *See also* Walters, *Foraker,* pp. 232–47; Henry F. Pringle, *Theodore Roosevelt* (New York, 1931), pp. 458–64; James A. Tinsley, "Roosevelt, Foraker and the Brownsville Affray," *Journal of Negro History,* XLI (Jan., 1956), 43–65.
42 Walters, pp. 235–38.
43 Pringle, *Taft,* I, 326.
44 Joseph B. Bishop, *Theodore Roosevelt and His Times Shown in His Own Letters,* 2 vols. (New York, 1920), II, 29–30.
45 Arthur W. Dunn, *Gridiron Nights* (New York, 1915), chapter XIX; Foraker, *Notes,* II, 249–257; Stoddard, *As I Knew Them,* pp. 330–331; Walters, *Foraker,* pp. 238–240.
46 "Arthur I. Vorys," *Who's Who in America, 1910–1911* (Chicago, 1910), p. 1985.
47 Charles P. Taft to Taft, Dec. 29, 1906, memorandum for Secretary Taft, *ca.* Feb. 26, Taft to Charles P. Taft, March 22, 1907, Taft MSS.
48 Walters, p. 265.
49 Cincinnati *Enquirer,* March 27, 1907.
50 Cincinnati *Times-Star,* March 30, 1907.
51 *Current Literature,* XLII (May, 1907), 469–72.
52 Attempts to produce a compromise between Taft and Foraker were made by Elmer Dover, secretary of the Republican National Committee, George B. Cox, Arthur I. Vorys, and Senator Murray Crane of Massachusetts. *See* Cincinnati *Enquirer,* March 29 and 30, 1907; Joseph B. Foraker to Charles W. F. Dick, July 24, 1907, Joseph B. Foraker MSS., in The Cincinnati Historical Society; Taft to F. L. Dustman, May 4, Taft to Charles P. Taft, May 11, Taft to Arthur I. Vorys, July 20, Taft to Roosevelt, July 23, 1907, Taft MSS.; Herbert S. Duffy, *William Howard Taft* (New York, 1930), p. 206; Walters, *Foraker,* p. 261.
53 Roosevelt to Nicholas Longworth, April 11, Roosevelt to Kermit Roosevelt, April 23, 1907, Roosevelt MSS; Cincinnati *Enquirer,* April 10, 1907; *American Monthly Review of Reviews,* XXXV (May, 1907), 539.
54 Charles P. Taft to Taft, April 20, May 6, 20, 1907, Taft MSS.

55 Charles P. Taft to Taft, May 6, 20, 1907, Taft MSS.
56 Charles P. Taft to W. H. Taft, May 6, Taft to Charles P. Taft, May 8, 1907, Taft MSS.
57 Taft to Charles P. Taft, May 11, 1907, Taft MSS.
58 Walters, *Foraker,* pp. 261–62.
59 Taft to Arthur I. Vorys, July 2, Taft to Roosevelt, July 23, 1907, Taft MSS.
60 Foraker, *Notes,* II, 383–87.
61 Charles P. Taft to Rudolph K. Hynicka, July 23, Charles P. Taft to August Herrmann, July 23, 24, 1907, Taft MSS.
62 Cincinnati *Enquirer,* July 30, 1907; Cincinnati *Times-Star,* July 30, 1907; Foraker, *Notes,* II, 387.
63 Cincinnati *Times-Star,* July 31, 1907.
64 Cincinnati *Enquirer,* July 31, 1907.
65 *Loc. cit.*
66 Cincinnati *Times-Star,* July 30, 1907.
67 Walters, *Foraker,* pp. 264–65. *See also* Foraker's speech in Franklin, Ohio, on July 19, 1907, in Foraker, *Notes,* II, 401–403.
68 Joseph B. Foraker to Edmund Carleton, Aug. 27, 1907, Foraker MSS.; Walters, *Foraker,* p. 265.
69 Taft to Mrs. Taft, Aug. 15, 1907, Taft MSS.
70 Cincinnati *Enquirer,* Aug. 20, 1907; Taft to Mrs. Alphonso Taft, Aug. 21, Taft to Charles P. Taft, Aug. 21, 1907, Taft MSS.
71 Cincinnati *Enquirer,* Aug. 22, 1907.
72 Taft to Charles P. Taft, Aug. 18, 21, 1907, Taft MSS.
73 *See,* for example, Roosevelt to Taft, Sept. 3, Taft to Charles P. Taft, Sept. 11, Taft to Roosevelt, Sept. 11, 12, 1907, Taft MSS.
74 Taft had urged Burton to run against Johnson; Taft to Charles P. Taft, Sept. 11, 1907, Taft MSS.; *American Monthly Review of Reviews,* XXXVI (Dec., 1907), 656.
75 Cincinnati *Enquirer,* Nov. 21, 1907.
76 Foraker to William H. Holt, Nov. 23, 1907, Foraker MSS.; Cincinnati *Enquirer,* Nov. 30, 1907.
77 Cincinnati *Times-Star,* Nov. 30, 1907.
78 Foraker, *Notes,* II, 394.
79 Cincinnati *Enquirer,* Dec. 10, 1907.
80 *Ibid.,* Jan. 3, 4, 1908.
81 *Loc. cit.*
82 *Ibid.,* Jan. 29, 1908.
83 The Bronson Primary Law may be found in State of Ohio, *General and Local Acts Passed and Joint Resolutions Adopted by the Seventy-sixth General Assembly* (Springfield, 1904), pp. 439–42. The court cases of 1908 were: *The State,* ex rel. *Welty* v. *Marsh et al.* and *The State,* ex. rel. *Webber* v. *Felton et al.,* reported in Emilius O. Randall, reporter, *Reports of Cases Argued and Determined in the Supreme Court of Ohio* (Springfield, 1908), 554–93.
84 Foraker to William S. Cappeller, Jan. 24, 1908, Foraker MSS.
85 Cincinnati *Commercial Tribune,* Feb. 2, 1908; Cincinnati *Times-Star,* Feb. 12, 1908; Cincinnati *Enquirer,* Feb. 13, 1908. *See also Literary Digest,* XXXVI (Feb. 22, 1908), 249–50.

86 Cincinnati *Enquirer,* March 4, 5, 1908.

87 The entire platform may be found in the Cincinnati *Times-Star,* March 4, 1908.

88 Symbolic of the complete victory won by the Taft forces at the Columbus convention was the election of a new State Central Committee, which was now unanimous in supporting Taft. Cincinnati *Commercial Tribune,* March 4, 1908.

89 The Cincinnati *Enquirer* estimated that by March 16 Charles P. Taft had spent $750,000 for the expenses of his brother's campaign. Not all of this sum, however, had been spent in Ohio (Cincinnati *Enquirer* March 16, 1908). Several days later, the Sandusky *Register* reported that Charles P. Taft had spent $800,000. "It begins to dawn upon the people of the country," the paper observed, "that there is quite an expensive conspiracy organized to nominate Secretary Taft" (Sandusky *Register,* March 22, 1908). By April the story of heavy expenditures by Charles P. Taft had traveled outside the state. *See* Henry L. West, "American Politics," *Forum,* XXXIX (April, 1908), 447.

George W. Goethals and the Problem of Military Supply

1 Thomas Goethals to George W. Goethals, Nov. 10, 1916, G. W. Goethals to T. Goethals, May 20, 1917, in the Papers of George W. Goethals, at the Library of Congress; hereinafter cited as Goethals Papers. Known throughout the world as the "Genius of the Panama Canal," Goethals had a reputation for efficiency and success. Of Dutch heritage, he had been born in New York City in 1858. After attending City College of New York, he won an appointment to West Point, where he was graduated second in a class of fifty-two in 1882. Goethals made a reputation for daring and precision while working with Corps of Engineers flood control projects on the Cumberland and Tennessee rivers. In 1903, he was appointed a member of the War Department General Staff and was chosen a little later by President Theodore Roosevelt to superintend construction of the Panama Canal. His success as engineer and administrator in that venture made him a national hero and one of the best known Americans of his day. The General was a partisan Republican with little sympathy for President Woodrow Wilson or his domestic program. Previous experience had led Goethals to expect little but interference from the Democratic administration. Goethals resigned as director of the Emergency Fleet Corporation in July, 1917, following a conflict over steel and wooden ships with Chairman William Denman of the War Shipping Board. But Goethals knew when to obey an order as well as when to give one and never publicly criticized the President or his administration. Goethals' response when John J. Pershing rather than Leonard Wood was selected to command the AEF was characteristic of the man. "Pershing is a good man and in it I see another blow to Wood. Well, he has himself to blame, for he hasn't been loyal to the administration." During the autumn Goethals had helped develop the war-time organization of the New York Port Authority, and it was from New York that he was summoned to Washington. The best discussion of Goethals' career is Charles D. Rhodes, "George W. Goethals," in the *Dictionary of American Biography,* VII, 355–57. But

see also James Bishop, *George W. Goethals, Genius of the Panama Canal* (1930) and H. F. Hodges, "George W. Goethals" in the *Transactions of the American Society of Civil Engineers,* XCIII, 1928.

2 Goethals to Theodore Roosevelt, Dec. 23, 1917, Goethals Papers.

3 *War Department Annual Reports, 1919* (Washington, 1919), I, 340; NA, RG 92, Quartermaster Corps Historical Files, "Army Purchases and Their Administration," Jan., 1919; *ibid.,* "History of Demobilization Activities of the Storage Service" [1919]. One of the most significant needs was a common War Department system of nomenclature. In mid-1918 an order from the AEF for a considerable number of mufflers, olive drab, was forwarded to the Quartermaster's office. Officials there assumed logically that the order was for woven mufflers for enlisted men and sent the requisition to the clothing and equipage branch to be filled. It was not until after the order had been executed that it was found that the mufflers on that order were not for men but for motorcycles.

4 Goethals' approach, unlike that of the Ordnance Department, was based on the assumption that civilians in policy making positions could get more cooperation from the military if they remained civilians. Rank conferred precedence, and Thorne, for example, could accomplish little unless he held the rank of Brigadier General. As a civilian expert, Thorne as Goethals' associate, could move freely and effectively from one division of the Quartermaster Corps to another.

5 For Thorne's most important work, *see ibid.,* "Extracts from the Daily Progress Reports of Robert Thorne, March–July, 1918."

6 *War Department Annual Reports, 1919,* I, 417–26. For the details of the reduction of the Quartermaster Corps, *see* Erna Risch, *Quartermaster Support of the Army: A History of the Corps, 1775–1934* (Washington, OQMG, 1962), pp. 630–44.

7 The Office Diary of George W. Goethals, March 27, 1918, Goethals Papers; NA, RG 120, War Department Historical Files, "Extracts from Conferences on the Movement of Troops Abroad, March 14–21, 1918."

8 For a discussion of the evolution of the eighty-division plan, *see* Daniel R. Beaver, *Newton D. Baker and the American War Effort, 1917–1919* (Lincoln, Nebraska, 1966), pp. 157–59.

9 War Department General Order 5, Jan. 11, 1918. Pierce became a part of the regular General Staff organization by War Department General Order 14, Feb. 9, 1918, with the title of Director of Purchases and Supply, while Stettinius remained associated with the office of the Secretary of War.

10 For the best insight into Goethals' thinking during those critical March days, *see* Office Diary of Goethals, March 1–31, 1918, in the Goethals Papers.

11 The Papers of Benedict Crowell in some twenty boxes are at the Western Reserve University Library in Cleveland, Ohio. The most significant group, including some letters to President Wilson, are in Box 1. Crowell's massive history of War Department activities, 1917–21, *How America Went to War,* written with Robert F. Wilson and published by Yale University Press in 1921, claimed Army control of all military supply rested with his office and that he was ultimately Baker's civilian chief of staff for indus-

trial mobilization. Crowell was a figure of substantial significance, but the records indicate that he was concerned with ordnance, not general supply, and his attempts to control areas outside the munitions area met with rebuffs from Goethals and March.

12 Johnson served with Major General Enoch H. Crowder in the Judge Advocate General's office and helped superintend the selective service system. He later served on Pierce's staff in the Purchase and Supply Division of the General Staff and helped plan the April reorganization of Army supply.

13 NA, RG 165, General Staff Historical File, "Report of the Committee of Three," April 18, 1918.

14 War Department General Order 36, April 16, 1918.

15 Goethals to T. Goethals, April 14, 1918, Goethals Papers.

16 Goethals to S. W. Tillman, April 16, 1918, Goethals Papers.

17 *War Department Annual Reports, 1919,* I, 350–52.

18 The best discussion of early economic mobilization is Grosvenor Clarkson, *American Industry in the World War. The Strategy behind the Lines* (Boston, 1921), pp. 3–64. For Army-WIB relations, *see also* Daniel R. Beaver, "Newton D. Baker and the Genesis of the War Industries Board," *Journal of American History,* LII (June, 1965), 43–58.

19 "Report of the Committee of Three," April 18, 1918; *War Department Annual Reports, 1919,* I, 350.

20 *Ibid.,* p. 364. For the War Industries Board side of the story, *see* Clarkson, pp. 299–314, and Bernard M. Baruch, *American Industry in the World War* (Washington, D.C., 1921). The best study of Baruch is Margaret Coit, *Mr. Baruch* (Boston, 1957).

21 Goethals Diary, June 15, 1918, Goethals Papers. Thorne remained in the Quartermaster Corps with Major General Robert E. Wood. Swope assumed Thorne's former role as adviser and administrative trouble shooter for Goethals.

22 NA, RG 165, General Staff Historical File, Goethals to Peyton C. March, July 18, 1918. This is the famous July memorandum that set the stage for the consolidation of procurement in the Purchase, Storage, and Traffic Division.

23 Goethals Diary, July 19, 1918, Goethals Papers. For Goethals' difficulties with the bureau chiefs, *see* Goethals to T. Goethals, Aug. 5, 1918, Goethals Papers.

24 The reorganization was ordered in War Department General Order 80, Aug. 28, 1918. For the full documentary history of the Purchase, Storage, and Traffic Division, *see* Supply Bulletin 29, Nov. 7, 1918, National Archives. This was part of a general War Department reshuffle that consolidated control of the aircraft program in the office of Assistant Secretary of War John D. Ryan, transferred Stettinius to Europe as American representative on the Inter-Allied Supply Council, made Crowell Director of Munitions and turned questions of general supply and distribution over to Goethals.

25 Goethals Diary, Aug. 27, 28 and Sept. 4, 1918, Goethals Papers.

26 NA, RG 165, Colonel Fair's File, "History of the Purchase, Storage, and Traffic Division."

27 *Ibid.*

28 *Ibid.*
29 Meeting of the War Industries Board, Tuesday, July 16, 1918, in Bernard Baruch, *American Industry in the World War,* p. 380; NA, RG 61, War Industries Board Records, Meeting of Requirements Division, War Industries Board, July 23, 1918.
30 NA, RG 32, Shipping Board Records, Edward M. Hurley to Charles Schwab, July 18, 1918.
31 *Iron Age,* CI (April 18, 1919), 1016.
32 The so-called "industrial inventory" had been started by the Council of National Defense in late 1916 and continued during 1918 under the control of the WIB. It seems to have been of little short-run assistance, and the government relied on the War Service Committees of the United States Chamber of Commerce and later on the Resource Advisory Committees for industrial information.
33 NA, RG 61, War Industries Board Resources and Conversion File, Requirements Division, Franklin D. Crabb, regional adviser, Kansas City, to E. C. Gibbs, regional adviser, Cincinnati, Sept. 14, 1918.
34 NA, RG 61, War Industries Board Records, statement of Samuel Vauclain, Locomotive Committee, July 11, 1918.
35 Ickes' statement is quoted in Otto M. Nelson, *National Security and the General Staff* (Washington, 1946), p. 2.
36 Peyton C. March, *The Nation at War* (New York, 1932), p. 196.
37 For a discussion of traditionalist army views of the war's lessons and its attitude toward economic mobilization in the 1920's, *see* Albert A. Blum, "Birth and Death of the M-Day Plan," in Harold Stein (ed.), *American Civil Military Decisions, A Book of Case Studies* (Montgomery, Alabama, 1963), pp. 66–94.
38 *Everybody's Magazine* (June, 1918), vols. 376–78, p. 40.

British Labour Party and the Paris Settlement

1 Henry R. Winkler, *The League of Nations Movement in Great Britain* (New Brunswick, Rutgers University Press, 1952), pp. 167–98.
2 Carl F. Brand, *British Labour's Rise to Power* (Stanford, California, Stanford University Press, 1941), pp. 121–49; Austin Van Der Slice, *International Labour, Diplomacy, and Peace 1914–1919* (Philadelphia, University of Pennsylvania Press, 1941), pp. 218–31.
3 *Clarion,* October 4, 1918.
4 Bradford *Pioneer,* October 11, 1918.
5 *The Labour Party* (Labour Party Leaflet, unnumbered), 1918.
6 *Why Labour Supports a League of Nations* (Labour Party Leaflet, No. 17, new series), 1918; *Why I Shall Vote Labour, A Working Woman's Letter from "Blighty"* (Labour Party Leaflet, No. 26, new series), 1918; *Why Women Should Join the Labour Party and Vote for the Labour Candidates* (Labour Party Leaflet, No. 3, new series), 1918.
7 Francis Williams, *Fifty Years' March. The Rise of the Labour Party* (London, Odhams Press, 1950), pp. 285–87.
8 Advisory Committee on International Questions, Minutes, May 30, 1918 (Labour Party Library, Transport House, London). Present at the first

meeting were Sidney Webb, Leonard Woolf, G. Lowes Dickinson, H. Duncan Hall, G. D. H. Cole, Major Gillespie, C. Delisle Burns, and Arnold Toynbee.

9 Mimeographed "A League of Nations," Advisory Committee on International Questions (1918). Other mimeographed memoranda as the war drew to a close dealt with "The Freedom of the Seas," "Colonies," "The Reform of the Foreign Services," and, after the Armistice, "Intervention in Russia."

10 George N. Barnes, who had remained in the Coalition Cabinet after the affair of the Stockholm Conference, was a member of the British delegation, but Labour did not regard him as its representative.

11 Van Der Slice, p. 313.

12 Brand, esp. pp. 150–52.

13 H. M. Swanwick, *Builders of Peace: Being Ten Years' History of the Union of Democratic Control* (London, Swarthmore Press, 1924), pp. 114–18. Signatories were Fred Bramley, C. R. Buxton, F. Seymour Cocks, J. A. Hobson, F. W. Jowett, J. R. MacDonald, E. D. Morel, F. W. Pethick Lawrence, Arthur Ponsonby, Ethel Snowden, H. M. Swanwick, and Charles Trevelyan.

14 *Labour Leader,* January 9, 1919. Even when the Birmingham Trades Council warned against a "Capitalist" League, it went on to pass a resolution congratulating President Wilson for his support of the League idea. *Herald,* January 11, 1919.

15 *Herald,* January 18, 1919.

16 *Ibid.,* January 4, 1919.

17 *Forward,* October 5, 1918.

18 *Labour Leader,* January 9, 1919.

19 *Herald,* January 11, 1919.

20 *Labour Leader,* January 9, 1919.

21 Van Der Slice, pp. 309–42, gives a useful account of the Labour and Socialist Conference at Bern and its aftermath.

22 Mimeographed "Notes on Procedure at the International Labour Conference Proposed to be Held at the Same Time and Place as the Official Peace Conference," International Advisory Committee, No. 8 (November, 1918).

23 H. N. Brailsford, mimeographed "A Parliament of the League of Nations," International Questions Advisory Committee, No. 44 (January, 1919).

24 J. R. MacDonald in *Forward,* February 8, 1919.

25 *Report of the Nineteenth Annual Conference of the Labour Party* (1919), p. 18.

26 Van Der Slice, pp. 303–304.

27 *Report of the Nineteenth Annual Conference of the Labour Party* (1919), pp. 14, 196–97; Labour Party, *International Labour and Peace* (London, 1919), p. 4; *Herald,* February 15, 1919; Independent Labour Party, *International Socialism and World Peace,* new series, No. 1 (London, 1919), pp. 1–2. Wilson apparently considered very seriously the socialist project for minority representation, but his advisers could come up with no scheme which seemed practical. Charles Seymour, *The Intimate Papers of Colonel House,* IV (Boston, Houghton Mifflin Co., 1928), 313.

28 *Report of the Nineteenth Annual Conference of the Labour Party* (1919), pp. 197–98.
29 *See,* for example, *Herald,* January 25, 1919, which complained that "The first act of the preliminary Peace Conference has been to try to assure that the covenants of peace shall be not open and not openly arrived at . . . its decisions are being taken in secrecy without the knowledge of the people whose destinies are thus being settled for generations."
30 *Labour Leader,* February 20, 1919; *Herald,* February 8, 1919.
31 *New Statesman,* XII (February 2, 1919), 361; *Herald,* February 1, 15, 1919. See also Brand, pp. 151–52.
32 *New Statesman,* XII (February 22, 1919), 436–37 and (March 22, 1919), 540–41, but not without criticism of details; "Rob Roy" (Dr. J. Stirling Robertson), *Forward,* February 22, 1919. Robertson's views often differed from those of the editor of *Forward.*
33 *Labour Leader,* February 20, 1919; *Report of the Twenty-Seventh Annual Conference of the Independent Labour Party* (1919), pp. 37–41.
34 *Herald,* February 22, 1919.
35 *Forward,* February 22, March 1, 1919; Bradford *Pioneer,* February 21, 1919.
36 Swanwick, pp. 119.
37 W. Cyprian Bridge, "Pan-Anglo-Saxonism and the League of Nations," *Socialist Review,* XVI (April–June, 1919), 166–71. Earlier on February 1, 1919, the *Herald* had optimistically declared, "Our policy is the establishment of an international authority whose decrees would in practical fact never need to be backed by physical force."
38 *Clarion,* March 14, April 18, 1919.
39 *British Citizen and Empire Worker,* February 6, 20, 27, 1919.
40 Advisory Committee on International Questions, Minutes, March 4, 1919.
41 *Report of the Nineteenth Annual Conference of the Labour Party* (1919), pp. 23–25; *Herald,* April 3, 5, 1919; Trades Union Congress and Labour Party, *Amendments to the Covenant of the League of Nations to be Held at Central Hall, Westminster, London S.W. 1 on Thursday, April 3rd, 1919, 10:30 a.m.* (London, 1919), pp. 3–15.
42 *New Statesman,* XIII (May 3, 1919), 109.
43 Graubard, pp. 64–114.
44 For example, *Herald,* April 5, 8, 1919; *Labour Leader,* February 20, May 22, 1919. At the Independent Labour party's annual conference, the resolution calling for withdrawal of all Allied armies was introduced by the former Liberal, Arthur Ponsonby, who had recently joined the I. L. P., and was carried without discussion. *Report of the Annual Conference of the Independent Labour Party* (1919), pp. 73–74.
45 *Report of the Nineteenth Annual Conference of the Labour Party* (1919), p. 26.
46 *Ibid.,* pp. 17–18.
47 Van Der Slice, p. 335.
48 *Report of the Nineteenth Annual Conference of the Labour Party* (1919), pp. 206–11; Labour Party, *International Labour and Peace,* pp. 15–17.
49 Van Der Slice, pp. 343–75.

50 *Report of the Annual Conference of the Independent Labour Party* (1920), pp. 9–10.
51 *Report of the Nineteenth Annual Conference of the Labour Party* (1919), p. 216.
52 *Ibid.*, pp. 212–13; Labour Party, *International Labour and Peace*, pp. 19–20.
53 *Report of the Nineteenth Annual Conference of the Labour Party* (1919), p. 217.
54 W. W. Henderson, "Labour and the League of Nations" in Herbert Tracey, ed., *The Book of the Labour Party*, III (London, Caxton Publishing Co., 1925), pp. 91–94.
55 Advisory Committee on International Questions (May, 1919). There is no title on this memorandum, but a pencilled note at the top of the first page reads, "May, 1919. Peace Terms, Norman Angell."
56 *Ibid.* (n.d.) This is a typewritten, not mimeographed memo with no title, but with "Policy towards Germany" pencilled across the top.
57 There is no direct indication of who prepared Henderson's material, but the internal evidence makes the source quite clear.
58 Arthur Henderson, *The Peace Terms* (London, Labour Party, 1919), pp. 18–19.
59 Swanwick, pp. 121–22.
60 *Forward*, May 17, 1919.
61 *Labour Leader*, June 19, 1919.
62 *New Statesman*, XIII (May 10, 1919), 129.
63 *Herald*, May 17, 1919; Raymond Postgate, *The Life of George Lansbury* (London, Longmans, Green and Co., 1951), p. 192.
64 Philip Snowden at a meeting to protest the terms of peace held at Essex Hall, London, May 30. *Labour Leader*, June 5, 1919.
65 *Clarion*, May 23, 30, 1919.
66 The *New Statesman*, XIII (June 14, 1919), 249, however, thought that the modified peace terms were an improvement and hoped that the German Government would accept them quickly in order to pave the way for further revision.
67 An interesting sidelight on MacDonald's public emphasis on Germany's plight is provided by Sidney Webb. Writing to his wife from Southport, Webb noted: "Ramsay MacDonald is here, in his usual form. He says the socialists all over Europe, whilst hot against the Peace Treaty, are also indignant with the Germans, and wish to take a 'European' attitude about the peace terms, rather than a pro-German one, protesting against the Treaty on the grounds that it does not rebuild the economic life of the world, and provide for general industrial reconstruction. This is his usual good sense in council and in criticism. It is a pity he is not more constructive. . . ." Sidney Webb to Beatrice Webb, June 23, 1919, Webb Papers, British Library of Political and Economic Science. MacDonald himself had written publicly a few months before about "that terrible document of the League of Nations," the Draft Covenant, *Forward*, March 1, 1919.
68 *Report of the Nineteenth Annual Conference of the Labour Party* (1919), pp. 111, 139–42.

69 Tucker, p. 66; Brand, pp. 162–63.
70 *Report of the Nineteenth Annual Conference of the Labour Party* (1919), pp. 127–32; *Daily Herald,* July 23, 1919.
71 *Parliamentary Debates,* 5s., Commons, CXVII (July 3, 1919), 1232–34.
72 *Ibid.,* CXVIII (July 21, 1919), 959–64.
73 *Ibid.,* pp. 1031–33, 1118–19. The debate on the Anglo-French Alliance took place after the vote on the Treaty.
74 *Labour Leader,* July 31, 1919.
75 *New Statesman,* XIII (July 19, 1919), 382.
76 *Daily Herald,* June 28, 30, July 4, 1919.
77 "The New Triple Alliance," *Daily Herald,* July 2, 1919.
78 *Foreign Affairs,* July, 1919, pp. 1–2.
79 "The Peace Treaty," *Daily Herald,* June 30, 1919.
80 *Socialist Review* XVI (July–September, 1919), 200–201.
81 A letter to the editor of the Manchester *Guardian,* reprinted in the *Railway Review,* demonstrated how widely this feeling was shared. Subscribing to the view that "It is a settlement opposed to every ideal for which Labour stands," were, along with George Lansbury, C. T. Cramp of the National Union of Railwaymen, Robert Williams of the National Amalgamated Labourers' Union, Robert Smillie of the Miners' Federation of Great Britain, and John Brumley of the Locomotive Engineers. Cramp and Williams also served on the National Executive of the Labour Party, but it is clear that the leadership of the most powerful trade union groups in Great Britain were no less disillusioned by the peace settlement than the leaders of groups like the Independent Labour Party or Union of Democratic Control. *Railway Review,* July 4, 1919.
82 Labour Party, *Labour and the Peace Treaty. An Examination of Labour Declarations and the Treaty Terms* (London, Labour Party, 1919), pp. 13–14.
83 *Ibid.,* pp. 64–67. A much shorter pamphlet, also entitled *Labour and the Peace Treaty* (London, Labour Party, 1919), collected Conference resolutions, Party manifestos, and speeches in Parliament outlining the case against the Treaty.
84 I had an opportunity to read Arno J. Mayer's impressive *Politics and Diplomacy of Peacemaking. Containment and Counterrevolution at Versailles, 1918–1919* (New York, Alfred A. Knopf, 1967), only after this article had been edited and was on its way to the press.

Leopold Amery: Man against the Stars in Their Courses

1 *The Spectator,* CVC (September 23, 1955), 378.
2 The Commonwealth, he wrote in 1953, "potentially the richest and most powerful of all the nation groups, . . . is today the weakest. Its scattered units are none of them strong enough to defend themselves, let alone to give effective help to each other. And yet, developed as they might be, they could form an unbreakable girdle of peaceful strength encircling the globe." Leopold S. Amery, *My Political Life,* 3 vols. (London, 1953–1955), p. 17.

3 Amery, p. 34.
4 Henry Lunn, "Two British Statemen of Today," *Review of Reviews,* LXXI (March, 1925), 274.
5 Amery, I, 62.
6 *Ibid.,* pp. 72–73, 100–111; *The History of The Times,* 4 vols. (London, 1939, 1948, 1952), IV, pt. 1, 3–4.
7 *Ibid.,* pp. 3–4.
8 *Living Age,* CCCXXXIV (July, 1928), 996.
9 *History of The Times,* IV, 6.
10 These were the group of bright young men, the Kindergarten, whom Lord Milner had recruited to serve with him in the reconstruction of South Africa after the Boer War. Among them were Lord Lothian, Lionel Curtis, Geoffrey Dawson, and John Buchan, all brilliant intellects and all first-rate publicists. Technically Amery was not a member of the Kindergarten, for he was forced to decline an invitation to go out as Milner's secretary because of his previous commitment to do *The Times History of the War in South Africa.* Donald C. Watt, *Personalities and Policies* (London, 1965) pp. 29–30.
11 *Ibid.,* pp. 29–30; *History of The Times,* IV, 2–3. The neo-imperialists especially venerated Alexander Hamilton, but Amery regarded his views on centralization as too advanced for application to the existing British Empire which he believed should approach closer integration by means of free co-operation which Hamilton considered inadequate at the time for the formation of the American union. Amery, *Political Life,* I, 269.
12 Leopold Amery, *Union and Strength* (London, 1912), p. 2.
13 Watt, *Personalities and Policies,* p. 142; Alfred M. Gollin, *Proconsul in Politics: A Study of Lord Milner in Opposition and in Power* (London, 1964), p. 123.
14 Amery, *Political Life,* I, 253.
15 *Ibid.,* p. 254.
16 *Ibid.,* p. 255.
17 *Ibid.,* p. 307.
18 Randolph Churchill, *Lord Derby* (London, 1959), p. 78; Robert Blake, *The Unknown Prime Minister, the Life and Times of Andrew Bonar Law 1858–1923* (London, 1955), pp. 105–107.
19 Alfred G. Gardiner, *Portraits and Portents* (London, 1926), p. 240. A. J. P. Taylor unkindly characterizes him as "a long-winded bore." *English History 1914–1945* (New York and Oxford, 1965), p. 327.
20 *The Spectator,* CVC (September 23, 1955), 378. *See also, Living Age,* CCCXXXIV (July, 1928), 996.
21 Gollin, *Proconsul,* pp. 106–107, 607.
22 *Ibid.,* pp. 106–107, 109–112, 115–16.
23 Robert Blake, *The Unknown Prime Minister,* pp. 109–116; Gollin, *Proconsul,* pp. 169–70. For Amery, Bonar Law had the advantage that he eschewed the narrow protectionism of the average British business man, in contrast to Stanley Baldwin in the crucial episode of the 1923 election.
24 Hansard, *Parliamentary Debates, House of Commons,* 5th ser., XLI, col. 1443.

25 Gollin, *Proconsul,* pp. 377–78. Lloyd George wanted Milner as a political asset to secure the support of the diehard Tories and the aristocratic group that was close to Milner.
26 Taylor, *English History,* p. 82.
27 Gollin, *Proconsul,* pp. 395–96; Amery, *Political Life,* II, 91–92, 105. "The main idea which decided the Cabinet to make it a meeting of the War Cabinet and not a conference in the ordinary sense, was to lay emphasis on the full equality of status between the Dominion Prime Ministers and the Ministers here, and the right of the Dominion Ministers to have the fullest say, and to have it in good time, on the question of the terms of peace." Gollin, p. 396.
28 Robert M. Dawson, *The Development of Dominion Status, 1900–1936* (London, 1937), 23.
29 Amery, *Political Life,* II, 107.
30 Parliamentary (Command) Paper, Cmd. 8566, *Imperial War Conference, 1917: Minutes of Proceedings* (London, 1917), p. 5.
31 Dawson, *Development of Dominion Status,* pp. 25–27; Watt, *Personalities and Policies,* pp. 143–44.
32 Gollin, *Proconsul,* p. 397.
33 "Many people, particularly those living in Great Britain, felt and still feel that the war might easily have turned the Empire toward federalism; but at no time did this solution find more than a few adherents outside the United Kingdom." Dawson, *Development of Dominion Status,* pp. 127–28.
34 Rixford K. Snyder, *The Tariff Problem in Great Britain, 1918–1923* (Stanford University Publications: *History, Economics and Political Science,* Stanford, 1944), V, no. 2, 308–309.
35 *Ibid.,* pp. 12–14.
36 *Ibid.,* pp. 299, 306–307.
37 Hasard, *Debates, Commons,* 5 ser., CXV, cols. 194–95.
38 *Ibid.,* cols. 433–34.
39 *Ibid.,* cols 434–35.
40 Snyder, *Tariff Problems,* p. 323.
41 Amery, *Political Life,* II, 176–77.
42 Hansard, *Debates, Commons,* 5 ser., CXXXVIII, col. 1936.
43 For other aspects of his colonial program, *see ibid.,* CXVIII, cols. 2173–82; Amery, *Political Life,* II, 184–85.
44 *Ibid.,* II, 241.
45 Blake, *The Unknown Prime Minister,* p. 452. Although he does not mention the issue in this connection in his memoirs, Amery must have been impelled also by the strong Dominion revulsion to the Chanak crisis.
46 *Ibid.,* pp. 461–63; Amery, *Political Life,* II, 242; R. Churchill, *Lord Derby,* p. 460.
47 Blake, *Unknown Prime Minister,* pp. 345–46. *See also* the account of the ridicule poured on them, especially Amery, at a party at Balfour's home. Kenneth Young, *Arthur James Balfour* (London, 1963), p. 428.
48 Amery, *Political Life,* II, 241–42.
49 R. Churchill, *Lord Derby,* pp. 88, 177, 454.
50 *Ibid.,* p. 460.

51 *History of The Times*, IV, 794–95.
52 *See The Economist*, VC, (October 28, November 4, 11, 1922).
53 Amery, *Political Life*, II, 245; Blake, *Unknown Prime Minister*, p. 468.
54 *The Economist*, XC, 923 (November 18, 1922).
55 Amery, *Political Life*, II, 250.
56 For a careful analysis of the Singapore base as a catalyst of British political thinking between the wars, *see* Ronald L. Pollitt, "The Singapore Naval Base and British Politics," unpublished M.A. thesis, University of Cincinnati, 1961.
57 *H. of C. Deb.*, Hansard, *Debates, Commons*, 5 ser., CLXIII, cols. 1265 ff. and CLXVI, cols. 2559 ff.
58 *Ibid.*, vol. CLXVI, cols. 2541 ff.
59 Herbert G. Wells, *The New Machiavelli* (London, 1925), pp. 369–71; Amery, *Political Life*, II, 252–53; Gardiner, *Portraits and Portents*, p. 242.
60 Blake, *Unknown Prime Minister*, pp. 506–507.
61 The Marchioness Curzon of Keddleston, *Reminiscences* (London, 1955), p. 204.
62 Amery, *Political Life*, II, 299–300. "It was a disastrous appointment," in Amery's opinion.
63 See Robert M. Dawson, *William Lyon Mackenzie King, 1874–1923* (Toronto, 1958), pp. 401 ff. for an enlightening exposition of King's attitude. When King landed, September 29, he found fifty invitations to social events awaiting him. He was sure that this was a subtle plot to butter him up. See also Watt, *Personalities and Policies*, pp. 145–47.
64 Dawson, *Mackenzie King*, p. 463; Watt, *Personalities and Policies*, pp. 147–48.
65 Dawson, *Mackenzie King*, pp. 466–68; Amery, *Political Life*, II, 274.
66. *The Economist*, XCVII (September 29, 1923), 464–65.
67 *Ibid.*, XCVII (October 13, 1923), 547–48.
68 Dawson, *Mackenzie King*, pp. 479–80.
69 *The Annual Register* (London, 1923), pp. 116–17.
70 Amery, *Political Life*, II, 278–83.
71 *Ibid.*
72 The best exposition of this story is Randolph Churchill, *Lord Derby*, pp. 528–29. According to Churchill, his father was on tenterhooks during the week that Lloyd George was at sea and was being deluged with radiograms from Lord Beaverbrook urging him to outbid Baldwin. Winston met the ship at Southampton to catch Lloyd George before he met the press to hold him firmly to the free trade line. *See* also Frank Owen, *Tempestuous Journey, Lloyd George, His Life and Times* (London, 1954), p. 672. Owen had access to the Lloyd George papers. Also, Amery, *Political Life*, II, 278–83.
73 R. Churchill, *Lord Derby*, p. 523.
74 *The Annual Register* (1923), pp. 125–26.
75 Associated as he was with the iron industry, Baldwin was inclined to view tariffs from the narrow insular aspect of protecting the home market. He lacked Bonar Law's appreciation of their imperial significance.
76 *The Economist*, XCVII (November 17, 1923), 863. For its part, *The Economist* came out with a special supplement in this issue devoted to

the case for free trade. *See also,* Snyder, *The Tariff Problem,* pp. 413 ff.
77 *The Annual Register* (1923), p. 138.
78 R. Churchill, *Lord Derby,* pp. 541, 562.
79 Stanley Salvidge, *Salvidge of Liverpool* (London, 1934), p. 266.
80 Amery, *Political Life,* II, 290–91; R. Churchill, *Lord Derby,* p. 565.
81 Amery, *Political Life,* II, 291.
82 *Ibid.,* pp. 491–92.

An Illusion That Shaped History

1 Sumner Welles, *The Time for Decision* (New York, 1944), pp. 64 ff.; Winston Churchill, *The Gathering Storm* (Boston, 1948), pp. 251 ff.; Anthony Eden, *Facing the Dictators, 1923–1938* (Boston, 1962), pp. 621 ff.; Harold Macmillan, *Winds of Change 1914–1939* (New York, 1966), pp. 532 ff.
2 Churchill, pp. 254–55.
3 Herbert Butterfield, *History and Human Relations* (New York, 1952), p. 172.
4 The New York *Times,* August 26, 1936.
5 *Ibid.*
6 William E. Dodd, Jr. and Martha Dodd, eds., *Ambassador Dodd's Diary, 1933–1938* (New York, 1941).
7 *Ibid.,* pp. 344, 352, 388–89.
8 *Ibid.,* p. 380; Joseph E. Davies, *Mission to Moscow* (New York, 1941), pp. 9–10, 142, 153–54, 158–59.
9 Sumner Welles, *Seven Decisions That Shaped History* (New York, 1951), *see* below, pp. 9–10.
10 Welles, *Time for Decision,* pp. 64 ff.
11 *Ibid.,* pp. 67 ff.
12 Churchill, pp. 251 ff.
13 Arnold J. Toynbee, ed., *The World in March 1939* (New York, 1952), p. 39.
14 Keith Feiling, *The Life of Neville Chamberlain* (New York, 1946), pp. 222 ff.
15 *Ibid.,* p. 226. This was no passing sentiment on Chamberlain's part. In June, 1934, for instance, he wrote prophetically in his diary: "We ought to know by this time that U. S. A. will give us no undertaking to resist by force any action by Japan short of an attack on Hawaii or Honolulu." *Ibid.,* p. 253.
16 *Ibid.,* p. 325. For the text of the British proposal of July 20, 1937, and the polite American refusal one day later, *see Foreign Relations of the United States, 1937,* III (Washington, 1954), 226–27, 235–36.
17 Cordell Hull, *Memoirs,* I (New York, 1948), 546–47. Hull further revealed that "something similar to what Welles had in mind" had been proposed to Ambassador Davies by Dr. Hjalmar Schacht, in Berlin, in January, 1937. "When Davies commented that possibly the President would not be disposed to become entangled in such a matter unless there was some assurance of success, Schacht replied that the conference

should not be called unless an agreement had practically been reached in advance."

18 *Ibid.*, p. 547.

19 Elliott Roosevelt with Joseph P. Lash, eds., *FDR—His Personal Letters, 1928–1945* (New York, 1950), pp. 370, 383, 463, 472–73, 547, 555, 571, 648–49.

20 *Ibid.*, p. 606.

21 *Ibid.*, p. 649.

22 *Ibid.*, p. 702.

23 *Ibid.*, pp. 666–67, and *see below,* pp. 42–43. "The question of disarmament and other *political* issues," King wrote, "need not arise, or be drawn into the conference." What he had in mind was a "Permanent Conference on Economic and Social Problems," whose principal function would be to investigate the "economic and social injustices" that King thought were the roots of war, and thus rouse international opinion to do something about these problems before they led to new international conflicts.

24 Welles, *Seven Decisions,* ch. i.

25 William L. Langer and S. Everett Gleason, *The Challenge to Isolation, 1937–1940* (New York, 1952), pp. 31–32. For their impressively documented account of this whole episode, based on a wealth of unpublished materials, *see* pp. 10 ff.

26 Viscount Templewood [Sir Samuel Hoare], *Nine Troubled Years* (London, 1954), ch. xxii. "Rightly or wrongly," Hoare wrote, "we were deeply suspicious, not indeed of American good intention, but of American readiness to follow up inspiring words with any practical action" (p. 263). "The U. S. A. has drawn closer to us," Chamberlain wrote in his diary in mid-February 1938, "but the isolationists there are so strong and so vocal that she cannot be depended upon for help if we should get into trouble," Feiling, p. 322.

27 Hoare, pp. 267–68.

28 *Foreign Relations, 1937,* I (Washington, 1954), 638–41, 649–55.

29 *Ibid.*, p. 60.

30 *Ibid.*, p. 72.

31 *Ibid.*, pp. 84, 85.

32 *Ibid.*, p. 92.

33 *Ibid.*, p. 99. For Chamberlain's conversation with Norman H. Davis shortly thereafter, *see* below, pp. 37–38.

34 *Foreign Relations, 1937,* I, 132.

35 *Foreign Relations, 1938,* I (Washington, 1954), 121.

36 *Foreign Relations, 1937,* I, 103.

37 *Ibid.*, pp. 97–98.

38 *Foreign Relations, 1938,* I, 121 ff.

39 Welles, *Seven Decisions,* 15 ff.; *Foreign Relations, 1938,* I, 135–36.

40 *Ibid.*, p. 138.

41 Hoare, pp. 269 ff.; *Foreign Relations, 1938,* I, 122.

42 *Ibid.*, p. 124.

43 *Ibid.*, p. 125.

44 *Ibid.*, p. 127.
45 *Ibid.*, pp. 128–29.
46 *Ibid.*, pp. 128–29.
47 Welles, *The Time for Decision,* p. 68.
48 *Foreign Relations, 1938,* I, 130 ff.
49 *Ibid.*, p. 137.
50 *Ibid.*, p .135.
51 *Ibid.*, p. 121.
52 *Ibid.*, p. 146.
53 *Ibid.*, pp. 147–48.
54 *Feiling,* p. 325.
55 *Foreign Relations, 1938,* I, 428–29, 442 ff.; *Documents on German Foreign Policy, 1918–1945,* Series D, Vol. I (Washington, 1949), nos. 362, 391. Nor had the United States protested previous Nazi German treaty violations. *See Foreign Relations, 1936,* I (Washington, 1953), 218; *Documents on German Foreign Policy, 1918–1945,* Series C, Vol. III (Washington, 1959), no. 545, and Series C, Vol. V (Washington, 1966), no. 42. "In today's press conference," the German ambassador in Washington telegraphed his government on March 9, 1936, "the Secretary of State [Cordell Hull] said that, although he was keeping himself informed of events in Europe, he had no cause at all to concern himself with the Rhineland question."
56 *See,* for instance, Frederick Sherwood Dunn, *Peaceful Change—A Study of International Procedure* (New York, 1937).
57 *Foreign Relations, 1938,* I, 703. The most discerning assessment of the Munich conference came from the pen of Assistant Secretary of State George S. Messersmith [*Foreign Relations, 1938,* I, 704–07], a copy of which Hull passed on to President Roosevelt.
58 Lord Halifax, *Fullness of Days* (New York, 1957), pp. 195 ff.
59 The leading exponents of the new "anti-Munich" myths include Arthur M. Schlesinger, Jr., whose uninformed pronouncements on the subject are matched only by his supercilious contempt for those holding views different from his own. *See,* for instance, his *The Bitter Heritage—Vietnam and American Democracy, 1941–1966* (Boston, 1966), pp. 70 ff. But how little Schlesinger really knows about the Munich crisis and the role of the United States in that crisis is revealed in his account of New Deal diplomacy in John M. Blum, *et. al., The National Experience* (New York, 1963), pp. 685–87. "When it seemed," Schlesinger has written there, "as if Chamberlain were standing firm against Hitler, Roosevelt sent him an encouraging cable ("Good Man"). In fact, as has been known since the publication of Langer and Gleason's *The Challenge to Isolation* and the *Foreign Relations,* the situation is almost the opposite. Roosevelt sent Chamberlain the congratulatory message when he heard he was going to Munich and the outcome of the Munich conference was virtually certain. As for the President's reaction after Munich, there is his interesting comment in a letter to Ambassador Phillips in Rome, in mid-October—a letter published in 1950—"I want you to know that I am not a bit upset over the final result." Roosevelt and Lash (eds.), p. 818.

60 Iain Macleod, *Neville Chamberlain* (New York, 1961), p. 206.

61 The blindness of many British intellectuals (and members of the British Left) to the rise of Nazism remains an intriguing and largely unexplored subject. "We must not," declared Philip Snowdon, the Labour patriarch, in 1933, "allow our indignation with many of the things [Hitler] is doing . . . to blind us to the causes which have led to the placing of power in the hands of this attractive demagogue." In March, 1936, he sympathized with the remilitarization of the Rhineland, declaring that "the real danger comes from France trying to encircle Germany by making a pact with Russia." Colin Cross, *Philip Snowden* (London, 1966), pp. *Times* on August 12, 1937, that "Englishmen would do well to remember that the Nazi form of government is in large measure the outcome of Allied and British injustice at Versailles in 1919 . . . let us recognize and appreciate what is good and great in the other nation." And Arnold J. Toynbee returned from an interview with Hitler reportedly convinced of "Hitler's genuine desire for peace in Europe and 'close friendship with England.'" Martin Gilbert, *The Roots of Appeasement* (New York, 1966), pp. 167, 164. "The current habit of classifying countries by the type of political theory professed by their government" was unsound, E. H. Carr assured his readers in 1937. "There is little or nothing in common," so ran his version of "polycentrism" in those days, "between the ambitions of Germany and Japan, or of Italy and Japan. The present association between Italy and Germany seems particularly unstable; for both have interests in Central and South-East Europe which might at any time bring them into conflict." Carr, *International Relations Since the Peace Treaties* (London, 1937), pp. 258–59.

62 Macleod, p. 174.

63 *Ibid.*, p. 212.

64 *Ibid.*, p. 213.

65 Anthony Eden, *Full Circle* (Boston, 1960).

66 Eden, *Facing the Dictators*, pp. 595–96; Welles, *Seven Decisions*, pp. 25–26. "The leakage of confidential information from Downing Street in those days," Welles wrote later, "was notorious. If the British government had advance notice, there was every likelihood that the whole story would be in the press within forty-eight hours. In that case the proposal would be subject to every kind of misinterpretation before the President could explain it to the American people."

67 Eden, p. 599.

68 *Foreign Relations*, 1937, III, 159–60, 286–90, 455–56, 464–65.

69 Eden, pp. 608–13.

70 *Ibid.*, p. 615.

71 *Ibid.*, p. 618. On December 13, 1937, Herschel V. Johnson, the American chargé in London, telegraphed the State Department that the Foreign Office attached "great importance to the British and American action [in the Far East] being at least along synchronized parallel lines if it is to have any effect on the Japanese. What they really hope for . . . is that we will consent to joint action . . . they realize that our views as to the advisability of joint action in the past has been different from

theirs but . . . [feel] the circumstances of the present situation might perhaps cause us to reconsider this attitude." They did not. *Foreign Relations, 1937,* IV, 494–95.

72 Eden, p. 616.

73 Dorothy Borg, *The United States and the Far Eastern Crisis of 1933–1938* (Cambridge, Mass., 1964).

74 *See* Dorothy Borg, "Notes on Roosevelt's 'Quarantine' Speech," *Political Science Quarterly,* LXXII (September, 1957), 405–33.

75 Borg, *The United States and the Far Eastern Crisis,* p. 374.

76 *Ibid.*, p. 375, and *see* above, 13.

77 Borg, p. 375.

78 *Ibid.*, pp. 375–76.

79 *Ibid.*

80 *Ibid.*

81 *Ibid.*

82 *Foreign Relations, 1938,* I, 116. For the full text of Welles's memorandum to the President, see *ibid.*, pp. 115–17. "It is important to remember," Welles wrote, "that in the Hitler-Halifax conversations [in November, 1937], Hitler expressed his willingness to agree immediately to the elimination of offensive weapons. It is equally important to recall that Mussolini six months ago publicly suggested that the President take the leadership in a move for immediate limitation and eventual reduction of armaments." It is worth noting that—as Langer and Gleason have pointed out, p. 23—in October, 1937, Welles had argued even more explicitly that "a reference . . . to the probable need for readjustment of the settlements arrived at after the conclusion of the World War would, I think, almost inevitably create a favorable reaction on the part of Germany."

83 Langer and Gleason, p. 23.

84 For Eden's fulsome tribute to Welles, *see Facing the Dictators,* p. 645.

85 *The Times Literary Supplement,* November 23, 1962.

86 Janet Adam Smith, *John Buchan* (Boston, 1965).

87 *See* Smith, p. 9. Roosevelt seems quickly to have sensed Tweedsmuir's great interest in closer Anglo-American relations, and, as early as his visit to Quebec, in August, 1936, discussed with the new Governor General his ideas about a possible world peace conference. *See* Smith, p. 444.

88 Following his official visit to Washington in March, 1937, Tweedsmuir wrote to Stanley Baldwin that Roosevelt was "quite clear that in the event of another world war America could not stay out, and that her participation would probably mean something in the nature of a domestic revolution. He therefore feels that international peace is a bread-and-butter problem for his country, and no mere piece of idealism. His general idea is to make an appeal for a conference to deal with the fundamental economic problems, which are behind all the unrest. He believes that now is the right moment . . . he is determined to be present . . . and he believes he would have America wholeheartedly behind him." On May 29, 1937, Tweedsmuir wrote in similar vein to Chamberlain and received a notable reply some months later. Smith, pp. 444–45.

89 *Ibid.*, p. 475.

90 Roosevelt and Lash, pp. 664–68. "Collective security," King wrote in his memorandum to the President, "should not be identified with reliance upon force."
91 Ian Colvin, *None So Blind* (New York, 1965).
92 *Ibid.*, p. 117.
93 *Ibid.*, p. 118.
94 *Ibid.*, p. 119.
95 *Ibid.*, p. 140.
96 *Ibid.*
97 *Ibid.*, p. 141; *Foreign Relations, 1937,* I, 98 ff.
98 Colvin, p. 140. On the history of American neutrality legislation, *see* Robert A. Divine, *The Illusion of Neutrality* (Chicago, 1962), *passim.*
99 Colvin, p. 183.
100 Arthur Krock, *In the Nation, 1932–1966* (New York, 1966), p. 63. Krock's memory deserted him in two details: Hitler and Stalin met only in Low's unforgettable cartoon; and Henry A. Wallace was Secretary of Agriculture, not Labor.
101 *Documents on German Foreign Policy,* Series C, Vol. V (Washington, D. C., 1966).
102 *Ibid.*, no. 544.
103 *Ibid.*, no. 611.
104 *Ibid.*, no. 626.
105 *Foreign Relations, 1933,* I (Washington, 1950), 490 ff; Hull, I, 246 ff. For a record of Roosevelt's conversations with Schacht, *see Documents of German Foreign Policy,* Series C, Vol. II (Washington, 1957), nos. 214, 233. For Roosevelt's ideas on disarmament, see *Foreign Relations, 1933,* I, 145. "If all the nations," the President declared, "will agree wholly to eliminate from possession and use the weapons which make possible a successful attack, defenses automatically will become impregnable, and the frontiers and independence of every nation will become secure. The ultimate objective of the Disarmament Conference must be the complete elimination of all offensive weapons. The immediate objective is a substantial reduction of some of these weapons and the elimination of many others." In May, 1933, the President also told the German ambassador he "was willing, if others should do so, to subject America to supervision by an international commission with respect to her disarmament, in spite of misgivings about this within his own administration and in particular by the Hearst press. Such supervision would have to be made . . . without prior announcement." *Documents on German Foreign Policy,* Series C, Vol. II, no. 259.
106 Frank Freidel, *Franklin D. Roosevelt—The Triumph* (Boston, 1956), pp. 250 ff.
107 Hull, I, 546. "I am confident," the President wrote Mussolini in July, 1937, "that you share with me the desire to turn the course of the world toward stabilizing peace. I have often wished that I might talk with you frankly and in person because from such a meeting great good might come . . . P. S. This is your birthday and I send you wishes for many happy returns for the day." Neither presidential wish was fulfilled. Roosevelt and Lash, p. 700.

108 William E. Leuchtenburg, *Franklin D. Roosevelt and the New Deal, 1932–1940* (New York, 1963), pp. 229–30; Manfred Jonas, *American Isolationism, 1935–1941* (Ithaca, 1966), pp. 160 ff. The Ludlow Amendment, Dexter Perkins has written, "was the most extraordinary of all proposals of this extraordinary epoch." *The Age of Franklin Roosevelt, 1932–1945* (Chicago, 1957), p. 101.

109 Nicholas Clifford, *Retreat from China—British Policy in the Far East, 1937–1941* (Seattle, 1967), p. 164. "From the outset, Washington was suspicious of British efforts to involve her in the East; and from the outset, London felt that America was refusing to pull her own weight, allowing Britain to do the dirty work as spokesman for western interests against Japan. In retrospect, it might be added, each side had considerable justification for its estimate of the other." *Ibid.*, p. 19.

110 Borg, *The United States and the Far Eastern Crisis,* ch. xiv; Nicholas Clifford, "Britain, America, and the Far East, 1937–1941: A Failure in Cooperation," *The Journal of British Studies,* III (1963), 137–54.

111 "If the Axis refused to cooperate, nothing would be better calculated to convince the democracies that isolation and neutrality in the modern world could never insure their safety." Welles, *Seven Decisions,* p. 24.

112 "Not to ascertain in advance," Hull wrote later, "the opinion of Britain and France, at least, seemed unwise and unfair . . . [because] to 'spring' so ambitious a project on them without warning might seriously embarrass them." Hull, I, 548.

113 *See* above, p. 47.

114 *See* above, p. 35.

115 *Foreign Relations, 1937,* III, 583.

116 *Foreign Relations, 1938,* I, 147–48.

117 "I feel I should tell you," Édouard Daladier wrote the President on April 4, 1940, "that during the past two years when I was Prime Minister, Ambassador Bullitt always said to me that in case of a European conflict, France should make her decisions knowing that, according to the opinion of Ambassador Bullitt, the United States of America would not enter the war." On October 14, 1940, the President sent a copy of Daladier's testimonial to Bullitt, adding that it "should be accepted as indisputable proof that . . . this government [did not assure] the government of France that if France should become engaged in war in Europe, the United States would enter the war." Daladier to Roosevelt, October 14, 1940 (MSS., Franklin D. Roosevelt Library). *See also* Hans L. Trefousse, *Germany and American Neutrality, 1939–1941* (New York, 1951), pp. 50, 179; and Gordon Wright, "Ambassador Bullitt and the Fall of France," *World Politics,* X (October, 1957), 67.

118 Francis L. Loewenheim, ed., *Peace or Appeasement? Hitler, Chamberlain, and the Munich Crisis* (Boston, 1965), p. xvii; Hugh Thomas, *Suez* (New York, 1967), p. 38.

119 *See* above, p. 44.

120 *See* above, p. 51.

121 Richard Hofstadter, *The American Political Tradition and the Men Who Made It* (New York, 1948), p. 338.

122 Roosevelt and Lash, p. 555.

123 James MacGregor Burns, *Roosevelt—The Lion and the Fox* (New York, 1956), p. 262.

124 Francis L. Loewenheim, ed., *The Historian and the Diplomat—The Role of History and Historians in American Foreign Policy* (New York, 1967), pp. 42 ff.; Warren I. Cohen, *The American Revisionists—the Lessons of American Intervention in World War I* (Chicago, 1967), *passim.*

125 Jonas, 22–23.

126 "The Jeffersonian party," Charles A. Beard wrote in *Scribner's Commentator* in February, 1935, "gave the nation the War of 1812, the Mexican War, and its participation in the World War. The Pacific War awaits," and the following month he wrote to Raymond Moley: "As I have often said to you, I consider the foreign implications of our domestic policy and the hazards of a futile and idiotic war in the Far Pacific more important than old age pensions and all the rest of it." Leuchtenburg, p. 212. *See also* Jonas, pp. 33–34, 105–106, 152 ff.

127 "There was never much 'sanctity' in my opinion," Edwin M. Borchard of the Yale University Law School wrote to Assistant Secretary of State R. Walton Moore in March, 1935, "to such an uncivilized treaty as the Treaty of Versailles, and the further we keep away from it the better for the United States. . . . The Allies unfortunately disregarded the elementary conditions of peaceful organization of the peoples of Europe and have much to answer for in producing Hitler and any eventual war which may come from present conditions." Borchard to Moore, March, 1935 (MSS., Franklin D. Roosevelt Library). *See also* Jonas, pp. 56, 110, 117.

128 *Ibid.*, pp. 72 ff., 85, 120, 231, 249, 267, 270. Early in 1939 Norman Thomas told the House Foreign Affairs Committee that he was "convinced that the disorganization of Europe and the problems of Asia can no more be solved by new American participation in Europe's or Asia's wars than did we solve them by our participation in the World War." As late as January, 1941 he insisted that "if we show it is possible to improve and keep democracy and settle better than the dictatorships have ever settled the problems of jobs and the cries of poverty, no dictator could ever keep Europe under his thumb." Robert Maynard Hutchings wrote, in *Scribner's Commentator,* in April, 1941, "I believe that the American people are about to commit suicide."

129 These organizations included the Friends' Peace Group, American Youth Congress, American League Against War and Fascism, National Council of Methodist Youth, Inter Seminary Movement, Student League of Industrial Democracy, National Council for the Prevention of War, Committee on Militarism in Education, Women's International Congress for Peace and Freedom, and People's Mandate to Governments to End War.

130 "During the New Deal," Richard Hofstadter has written in *Anti-Intellectualism in American Life* (New York, 1963), p. 214, "the rapprochement between intellectuals and the public was restored. Never had there been such complete harmony between the popular cause in politics and

the dominant mood of the intellectuals." What this meant in practice has been pointed out by William E. Leuchtenburg, *Franklin D. Roosevelt* . . . pp. 197–98: "Opinion leaders publicly avowed their guilt for leading the country into war in 1917, and resolved that they would never again so abuse the trust people had placed in them."

131 Robert E. Sherwood, *Roosevelt and Hopkins* (New York, 1948), p. 130. "A cold appraisal of the American interest," wrote Walter Lippmann in the New York *Herald Tribune* in February, 1935, "seems to me to lead to the conclusion that we can contribute nothing substantially to the pacification of Europe today. . . . For the time being, therefore, our best course is to stand apart from European policies." Allan Nevins, ed., *Walter Lippmann—Interpretations 1933–1935* (New York, 1935), p. 350.

132 "The radical peace groups," Robert H. Ferrell has written, "had a profound effect upon American public opinion . . . through a maze of supporting peace groups and interlocking committees [they] were able to reach out to a total of between forty-five and sixty million Americans." "The Peace Movement," in Alexander DeConde, ed., *Isolation and Security—Ideas and Interests in Twentieth Century American Foreign Policy* (Durham, N.C., 1957), p. 101. It is well to point out that some of the most prominent surviving isolationist intellectuals and writers of the 1930's, including Robert Maynard Hutchings, Norman Thomas, and Walter Millis, have been among the leading critics of American foreign policy in the latter 1960's. As for the New Left's historical version of the 1930's, it is instructive to note the opinion of Carl Oglesby, a former president of the Students for a Democratic Society: "The Depression experience brought about a kind of social contract between the American people and the Government. The people said to the Federal Government that your No. 1 priority is to secure material prosperity. You've got to make jobs for us, and if you do that, you can do anything else you like, even provoke war with Japan. . . . O.K., Roosevelt, throw the oil embargo on that." Quoted in the Washington *Post*, July 9, 1967.

133 Roosevelt and Lash, pp 547, 716–17.

134 *Ibid.*, pp. 506–07.

135 Samuel I. Rosenman, comp., *The Public Papers and Addresses of Franklin D. Roosevelt, 1936* (New York, 1938), pp. 290–91.

136 Henry L. Stimson and McGeorge Bundy, *On Active Service in Peace and War* (New York, 1948), pp. 309 ff. "At every turn," Richard N. Current has written caustically, "the Elder Statesman called upon his country to do its part by imposing [upon Italy, Spain, Japan, Germany, and Russia] a Stimsonian peace." *Secretary Stimson—A Study in Statecraft* (New Brunswick, N.J., 1954), p. 131.

137 Robert W. Bingham to Roosevelt, July 21, 1937 (MSS., Franklin D. Roosevelt Library).

138 For assistance in the preparation of this essay, I am deeply indebted to the staffs of the Manuscripts Division of the Library of Congress, the National Archives, and the Franklin D. Roosevelt Library, and to my friends and former colleagues, Frederick Aandahl, G. M. Richardson Dougall, William M. Franklin, Harold D. Langley, and Howard McGaw

Smyth. But my greatest debt of all is to the distinguished and inspiring scholar-teacher who first introduced me to the study of American history between the World Wars—and to whom this essay is gratefully inscribed —Reginald C. McGrane.

American Arsenal Policy in World War II

1 Winston S. Churchill, *Their Finest Hour* (Boston, Houghton Mifflin, 1949), 7–8.
2 War Production Board, *The World Production of Munitions at the End of the War in Europe* (WPB *Document* No. 25, Washington, D.C., June 15, 1945), pp. 4, 5, 6, 12; Raymond W. Goldsmith, "The Power of Victory, Munitions Output in World War II," *Military Affairs,* X (Spring, 1946), 71–75. These two sources are concerned with "combat munitions," a term which they define rather carefully in order to ensure the validity of the intricate comparisons involved. The present article is focused, though not exclusively, on a roughly comparable category, military materiel produced for the United States Army and distributed through War Department lend-lease channels after March, 1941; Navy lend-lease materiel enters the discussion occasionally, but was a relatively small category. The two sources cited here differ somewhat in their estimates of relative output of combat munitions by the major belligerents, as a result of using different price levels and time series. The figures cited in the WPB document indicate that the United States produced 52 per cent of the munitions for the coalition during the period, 1938 to mid-1945; Goldsmith's figures for the period, 1935–44, indicate 49 per cent. The differences are not considered significant. *See also* H. Duncan Hall, *North American Supply* (London, Her Majesty's Stationery Office, 1955), pp. 419–24 for a similar analysis.
3 At the end of May, 1944, Germany had 7,130,000 foreign workers, including prisoners of war. See Alan S. Milward, *The German Economy at War* (London, Athlone Press, 1965), p. 113.
4 Stetson Conn and Byron Fairchild, *The Western Hemisphere: The Framework of Hemisphere Defense* (Washington, D.C., Department of the Army, 1960), pp. 41, 150–51. These authors cite polls published in Hadley Cantril, ed., and Mildred Strunk, comp., *Public Opinion 1935–46* (Princeton, N.J., Princeton University Press, 1951).
5 The phrase was used in his Charlottesville speech of June 10, 1940. U.S. Department of State, *Peace and War: U.S. Foreign Policy, 1931–41* (Pub. 1853, Washington, D.C., 1943), p. 76; Richard M. Leighton and Robert W. Coakley, *Global Logistics and Strategy 1940–43* (Washington, D.C., Department of the Army, 1955), p. 28; Conn and Fairchild, p. 36.
6 Robert W. Sherwood, *Roosevelt and Hopkins: An Intimate History* (New York, Harper & Bros., 1948), p. 226.
7 Conn and Fairchild, pp. 41–44; Leighton and Coakley, pp. 28–30; Mark S. Watson, *Chief of Staff: Prewar Plans and Preparations* (Washington, D.C., Department of the Army, 1950), pp. 95–96, 104–107, 168–82; R. Elberton Smith, *The Army and Economic Mobilization* (Washington, D.C., Department of the Army, 1959), pp. 126–33; War Department,

Annual Report of the Secretary of War 1941 (Washington, D.C., Government Printing Office, 1941), 50–53, 60–61; Civilian Production Administration, *Industrial Mobilization for War* (Washington, D.C., Government Printing Office, 1947), Part I, chapters 2–3; H. D. Hall, *North American Supply*, chapter V.

8 Leighton and Coakley, pp. 21–23, 27–28; Conn and Fairchild, pp. 14–25; Watson, pp. 64–69; Kent R. Greenfield and Robert R. Palmer, "Origins of the Army Ground Forces: General Headquarters, U.S. Army, 1940–42," in Greenfield, Palmer, and Bell I. Wiley, *Organization of Ground Combat Troops* (Washington, D.C., Department of the Army, 1947); Wesley F. Craven and James L. Cate, eds., *The Army Air Forces in World War II*, Vol. I, *Plans and Early Operations* (Chicago, University of Chicago Press, 1948), 104 ff.; *Biennial Report of the Chief of Staff of the U.S. Army, July 1, 1939 to June 30, 1941* (Washington, D.C., 1941).

9 *See* note 5.

10 Memo Marshall and Stark for Roosevelt, June 27, 1940, quoted in Leighton and Coakley, p. 28; Conn and Fairchild, pp. 38–39; Watson, pp. 107–11.

11 Informal memo, June 24, 1940, quoted in Leighton and Coakley, pp. 29–30.

12 *Ibid.*, pp. 34–36; Forrest C. Pogue, *George C. Marshall: Ordeal and Hope, 1939–42* (New York, Viking Press, 1966), 64–66.

13 From July, 1940, to December, 1941, the United States allocated to the United Kingdom 45 per cent of its output of combat aircraft, 31 per cent of its medium tanks, 61 per cent of its tank and antitank ammunition, and 56 per cent of its small arms ammunition. H. D. Hall and C. C. Wrigley, *Studies of Overseas Supply* (London, Her Majesty's Stationery Office, 1956), p. 177. See also Hall, *North American Supply*, chapter VI.

14 For the destroyer-bases deal, *see especially* Conn and Fairchild, pp. 51–62, and Hall, *North American Supply*, pp. 139–45.

15 Leighton and Coakley, pp. 44–45; Sherwood, pp. 221–29; Churchill, *Their Finest Hour*, pp. 558–67. War Department lend-lease shipments during 1941 totaled about $189,000,000. *See International Aid Statistics in World War II. A Summary of War Department Lend Lease Activities* (Washington, D.C., War Department, 1946), p. 9.

16 Accounts of the Victory Program can be found in Leighton and Coakley, pp. 126–40; Watson, chapter XI; Wm. Keith Hancock and Margaret M. Gowing, *The British War Economy* (London, Her Majesty's Stationery Office, 1949), pp. 384–88; Ray S. Cline, *Washington Command Post: The Operations Division of the General Staff* (Washington, D.C., Department of the Army, 1951); Maurice Matloff and Edwin Snell, *Strategic Planning for Coalition Warfare 1941–42* (Washington, D.C., Department of the Army, 1953), pp. 58–62; Smith, pp. 133–39; Pogue, pp. 157–61; Hall, *North American Supply*, pp. 322–35.

17 Quoted in Leighton and Coakley, p. 126.

18 Roosevelt to Stimson, August 30, 1941, quoted in *ibid.*, p. 127.

19 Ltr. Gerow to McCloy, August 5, 1951, quoted *ibid.*, p. 127.

20 *Ibid.*, p. 133; Matloff and Snell, pp. 58–62; Watson, chapter XI. The "Germany-first" decision had been taken in the United States-British staff conferences (ABC Conferences) of January–March, 1941, in Washington,

D.C. *See* Louis Morton, "Germany First: The Basic Concept of Allied Strategy in World War II," in *Command Decisions,* ed. K. R. Greenfield (Washington, D.C., Department of the Army, 1960).

21 War Department "Ultimate Requirements Study," September 11, 1941, quoted in Leighton and Coakley, p. 135.

22 Joint Board 355, Serial 707, September 11, 1941, title: *Joint Board Estimate of U.S. Overall Production Requirements,* quoted in *ibid.,* p. 137. The Navy did not oppose the Germany-first concept nor the strategy of engaging German military power on the European continent. Admiral Harold R. Stark, the Chief of Naval Operations, had been the first to propose this strategy in November, 1940. *See* Watson, pp. 119–23, and Morton, "Germany First."

23 Craven and Cate, pp. 131–32, 146–47.

24 Stimson to Roosevelt, September 23, 1941, quoted in Leighton and Coakley, p. 133.

25 Draft letter by McCloy, quoted *ibid.,* p. 132; memo, Gerow for Marshall, September 10, 1941, quoted *ibid.,* pp. 129–30.

26 Statement by Albert Wedemeyer to Mark S. Watson in 1948, cited in Watson, pp. 343–44. According to another active participant, James H. Burns, the staff simply figured military manpower "requirements" as 8 per cent of the nation's population—then about 130,000,000—in the continental United States. Interview with Burns, in Supporting Documents to Watson, Prewar Plans and Preparations file, Office, Chief of Military History, Department of the Army.

27 Staff memo, November 17, 1941, quoted in Leighton and Coakley, p. 132.

28 Memo, Aurand for Brig Gen Richard C. Moore, November 10, 1941, quoted *ibid.,* p. 132.

29 See Section VI of this article.

30 Memo, Joint Board, September 25, 1941, quoted *ibid.,* p. 120.

31 Conn and Fairchild, pp. 143–49; Craven and Cate, pp. 134–35; Leighton and Coakley, pp. 102–107.

32 Conn and Fairchild, pp. 150–51; Watson, pp. 358–66; Leighton and Coakley, pp. 138–39.

33 New York *Herald Tribune,* byline Walter Lippmann, September 20, 1941; Pogue, pp. 75–79.

34 Memo, Marshall for Roosevelt, September 22, 1941, quoted in Leighton and Coakley, pp. 139–40; Pogue, pp. 76–79.

35 Leighton and Coakley, pp. 138–40; Watson, pp. 358–66; William L. Langer and Everett S. Gleason, *The Undeclared War 1940–41* (New York, Harper & Bros., 1953), p. 735; Conn and Fairchild, pp. 143–49.

36 Quoted in Edward R. Stettinius, Jr., *Lend Lease, Weapon for Victory* (New York, Pocket Books, Inc., 1944), pp. 173–74.

37 Memo, Roosevelt for Stimson January 3, 1942, quoted in Leighton and Coakley, p. 198.

38 Address to Congress, January 6, 1942, quoted *ibid.,* p. 198; Smith, pp. 140–41.

39 *See,* in this connection, Lewis Richardson's study of war moods as analyzed by Anatol Rapoport in *Journal of Conflict Resolution,* I (1957), 282–93.

40 Roosevelt to Stimson, December 28, 1941, quoted in Leighton and Coak-

ley, p. 552; *see* also *ibid.*, chs. XX and XXI; Pogue, pp. 71–76; 239–40; Sherwood, ch. XVIII, and pp. 544–46, 551–52, 567–68, 570–72, 574–76, 636–41; R. W. Coakley, "The Persian Corridor as a Route for Aid to the USSR," in *Command Decisions*, ed. by Greenfield; Matloff and Snell, pp. 205–10.

41 Leighton and Coakley, App. D; *International Aid Statistics*, p. 18, table 7; military lend-lease to the U.S.S.R. was about half the total value of Soviet lend-lease; *see* Hancock and Gowing, p. 353.

42 *International Aid Statistics*, p. 18, table 7. Total lend-lease munitions transferred to the British Empire, including Canada, came to $15.5 billion, in a total of $30 billion for British lend-lease of all kinds. Hancock and Gowing, p. 353.

43 Churchill, *The Grand Alliance* (Boston, Houghton Mifflin, 1950), 641–43; Leighton and Coakley, p. 248; Hall and Wrigley, pp. 172–73.

44 Pogue, pp. 285–87; Sherwood, pp. 470–72; Hancock and Gowing, pp. 391–98; Hall and Wrigley, pp. 253–62; Hall, *North American Supply*, chs. VIII, IX, X; Leighton and Coakley, pp. 251–52.

45 Hall and Wrigley, chs. V and VI; S. McKee Rosen, *The Combined Boards of World War II* (New York, Columbia University Press, 1951); Leighton and Coakley, pp. 255–57; Hancock and Gowing, pp. 399–401.

46 War Department Operations Division notes for Combined Chiefs of Staff meeting March 3, 1942, quoted in Leighton and Coakley, pp. 271–72.

47 Memo, undated, Brig. Gen. P. H. Tansey, quoted in Leighton and Coakley, p. 282.

48 Hancock and Gowing, p. 399; Leighton and Coakley, pp. 277–82.

49 Richard M. Leighton, "Overlord Revisited: An Interpretation of American Strategy in the European War 1942–44," *American Historical Review*, LXVIII (July, 1963), 919–37; K. R. Greenfield, *American Strategy in World War II. A Reconsideration* (Baltimore, Johns Hopkins Press, 1963), chs. I and II; Matloff and Snell, chs. VIII–XII.

50 Leighton and Coakley, pp. 276–77; Craven and Cate, pp. 566–70.

51 Leighton and Coakley, pp. 282–84; Hancock and Gowing, p. 400; Hall and Wrigley, pp. 189 ff.

52 Leighton and Coakley, pp. 274, 285.

53 *Ibid.*, p. 274.

54 *Ibid.*, pp. 274–75; Matloff and Snell, ch. XVI and App. E. The 5.4 million strength at the end of 1942 was about 1.6 million more than had been projected at the beginning of the year.

55 War Department International Division Study, quoted in Leighton and Coakley, p. 285.

56 Leighton and Coakley, pp. 198–99; CPA, *Industrial Mobilization for War*, pp. 273–85; Smith, p. 142.

57 Leighton and Coakley, pp. 199–202, 602–3, and App. B; CPA, pp. 285–302; Smith, ch. I; David Novick, Melvin Anshen, and Wm. C. Truppner, *Wartime Production Controls* (New York, Columbia University Press, 1949), ch. V.

58 The "feasibility dispute," as it is usually called, is described in Smith, pp. 154–58; John E. Brigante, *The Feasibility Dispute* (Washington, D.C., Committee on Public Administration Cases, 1950); CPA, pp. 282–92;

Donald Nelson, *Arsenal for Democracy* (New York, Harcourt Brace & Co., 1946), pp. 376–81; Leighton and Coakley, pp. 602–4, 606–8. The chairman of the WPB Planning Committee was Robert Nathan, also a distinguished economist.

59 Leighton and Coakley, chs. XVI, XVII; Matloff and Snell, chs. XII–XV; K. R. Greenfield, *The Historian and the Army* (New Brunswick, N.J., Rutgers University Press, 1954), ch. III. *See also* note 49.

60 Brigante, pp. 100–5; Smith, pp. 156–57; CPA, pp. 284–89. A $5 billion carry-over from 1942 was included in the $98 billion program.

61 CPA, p. 290; Leighton and Coakley, pp. 606–7; K. R. Greenfield, R. R. Palmer, and B. I. Wiley, *The Organization of Ground Combat Troops,* p. 215; Greenfield, *The Historian and the Army,* pp. 64–65.

62 Hall and Wrigley, pp. 188–94; Leighton and Coakley, pp. 284–85.

63 Hall and Wrigley, p. 194.

64 Leighton and Coakley, pp. 196, 604.

65 Quoted *ibid.*, p. 605.

66 Minutes of the WPB Planning Committee, November 5, 1942, quoted *ibid.*, p. 611.

67 Draft memo Marshall for Roosevelt, November 7, 1942, quoted *ibid.*, p. 611.

68 *Time,* XL, no. 25 (December 21, 1942), p. 83.

69 War Department General Council Meeting, November 23, 1942, cited in Leighton and Coakley, p. 606.

70 Leighton and Coakley, p. 605; *see also* M. Matloff, "The Ninety Division Gamble," in *Command Decisions,* ed. K. R. Greenfield; Matloff, *Strategic Planning for Coalition Warfare 1943–44* (Washington, D.C., Department of the Army, 1959), 111–17; Greenfield, Palmer, Wiley, pp. 214–17; Bureau of the Budget, *The United States at War* (Washington, D.C., 1946), pp. 173–74, 445–46, 453; K. R. Greenfield, *The Historian and the Army,* ch. IV.

71 Smith, p. 4, table 1; Hancock and Gowing, p. 353.

72 *International Aid Statistics,* p. 18, table 7; Smith, p. 4, table 1.

73 *Ibid.*, p. 18, table 7; Hancock and Gowing, p. 373. In 1940 Britain obtained 5.6 per cent, and in 1941 9.1 per cent of her munitions through purchase in the United States.

74 *Ibid.*, p. 18, table 7.

75 Matloff, "The Ninety Division Gamble," in *Command Decisions,* p. 381.

76 *World Almanac 1967* (New York, Newspaper Enterprise Association, 1967), p. 706, citing Department of the Army sources. Peak strengths of all armed forces totaled 12,300,000 men.

77 Greenfield, Palmer, Wiley, pp. 194, 336–39; *Logistics in World War II. Final Report of the Army Service Forces* (War Department, Washington, 1947), pp. 140–49.

78 Wright, App. B.

79 *See* note 2.

80 Quincy Wright, *A Study of War,* 2d ed. (Chicago, U. of Chicago Press, 1965), App. B.

81 *Statistical Review, World War II. A Summary of ASF Activities* (Wash-

ington, D.C., Army Service Forces, no date), pp. 57, 198–99; *Selected Manpower Statistics* (Office, Secretary of Defense, Washington, D.C., 1 February 1963), p. 61.

82 Hancock and Gowing, p. 370.

Yalta Viewed from Tehran

1 *Foreign Relations of the United States. The Conferences at Malta and Yalta, 1945* (Washington, Government Printing Office, 1955); hereafter cited as *Malta and Yalta.*

2 *Foreign Relations of the United States. The Conferences at Cairo and Tehran, 1943* (Washington, Government Printing Office, 1961); hereafter cited as *Cairo and Tehran.*

3 Needless to say, Roosevelt did not always follow the Department's recommendations; *see,* for instance, how F.D.R. ignored the Department's recommendations on the western boundary of Poland in *Malta and Yalta,* pp. 233, 510, 776, and 792. Four State Department policy papers were made available to the President on the eve of Tehran, but none of these were prepared with the upcoming conference in mind. The four papers are in *Cairo and Tehran,* pp. 162, 167, 183, and 266.

4 Robert E. Sherwood, *Roosevelt and Hopkins* (New York, Harper and Brothers, 1948), p. 845.

5 *See* the long section of "Arrangements for the Conferences" in *Cairo and Tehran,* pp. 3 ff.

6 Winston S. Churchill, *The Hinge of Fate* (Boston, Houghton Mifflin Company, 1950), pp. 662–66.

7 *See Cairo and Tehran,* pp. 461–64.

8 Cordell Hull, *The Memoirs of Cordell Hull* (New York, The Macmillan Company, 1948), II, 1309–310.

9 The agreement is in *Malta and Yalta,* p. 984.

10 W. Averell Harriman, *Our Wartime Relations with the Soviet Union, Particularly as They Concern the Agreements Reached at Yalta* (Statement submitted to a Joint Senate Committee, August 17, 1951, privately printed, pp. 8–9). The statement also appears in *Military Situation in the Far East.* Hearings before the Committee on Armed Services and the Committee on Foreign Relations, U.S. Senate, 82 Congress, 1 session, part 5, pp. 3328–342.

11 For the text and negotiating history of the Cairo Declaration, *see Cairo and Tehran,* pp. 366, 399, 402–04, 448–49.

12 *Ibid.,* pp. 566–67.

13 *Ibid.,* pp. 366–67, 869, 891.

14 *See International Affairs,* published by the Soviet Society for the Popularisation of Political and Scientific Knowledge (July and August, 1961).

15 *Cairo and Tehran,* p. 869.

16 *Malta and Yalta,* p. 379.

17 *See Ibid.,* pp. 378–79.

18 *Cairo and Tehran,* p. 568.

19 *Malta and Yalta,* p. 974.

20 *Ibid.*, pp. 792, 869. Roosevelt and Churchill did not accept the Soviet proposal for the line of the Western Neisse River, *ibid.*, p. 716.
21 *Ibid.*, p. 205.
22 *Cairo and Tehran*, p. 594.
23 *Ibid.*, p. 885.
24 *Malta and Yalta*, p. 667.
25 *Ibid.*, p. 978.
26 *See* Henry Morgenthau's plan for partition of Germany in the frontispiece to his book, *Germany Is Our Problem* (New York, Harper and Brothers, 1945). *See also* the similar dismemberment proposal, also of 1944, in Sumner Welles, *The Time for Decision* (New York, Harper and Brothers, 1944).
27 *Cairo and Tehran*, p. 600. The editors of the Soviet documents on Tehran not only omitted this entire passage and every similar statement but they even baldly stated in their introduction that "The Soviet Government had always opposed the idea (of dismemberment), and while taking part in the discussion of those plans as a matter of course, it prevented any definite decision from being taken," *International Affairs* (July, 1961), p. 134.
28 *Malta and Yalta*, p. 614.
29 *Ibid.*, p. 187.
30 Lord Avon, *The Memoirs of Anthony Eden. The Reckoning* (Boston, Houghton Mifflin Company, 1965), pp. 338, 429, 432, 596–97.
31 *Malta and Yalta*, pp. 614–16.
32 *See* Forrest C. Pogue, *The Supreme Command*, in the series *United States Army in World War II* (Washington, Department of the Army, 1954), pp. 484–85.
33 *Cairo and Tehran*, pp. 530–31, 595, 622.
34 *See Malta and Yalta*, pp. 567, 661, 666, 735–36.
35 Churchill did not oppose China as the Fourth Policeman; he merely doubted that China would have the power to play the part.
36 *Malta and Yalta*, p. 590.

Contributors

Daniel R. Beaver, M.A., University of Cincinnati, 1954; Ph.D., Northwestern University, 1962; Associate Professor of History, University of Cincinnati.

William M. Franklin, M.A., University of Cincinnati, 1935; Ph.D., Fletcher School of Law and Diplomacy, 1941; Director, Historical Office, Department of State, Washington, D.C.

Richard M. Leighton, M.A., University of Cincinnati, 1937; Ph.D., Cornell University, 1941; Professor of National Security Affairs, Industrial College of the Armed Forces, Washington, D.C.

Francis L. Loewenheim, M.A., University of Cincinnati, 1948; Ph.D., Columbia University, 1952; Associate Professor of History, Rice University.

Thomas McCormick, M.A., University of Cincinnati, 1956; Ph.D., University of Wisconsin, 1960; Associate Professor of History, University of Pittsburgh.

Harry R. Stevens, M.A., University of Cincinnati, 1937; Ph.D., University of Chicago, 1946; Professor of History, Ohio University.

Alfred D. Sumberg, M.A., University of Cincinnati, 1951; Ph.D.,

University of Wisconsin, 1960; Staff Associate, American Association of University Professors.

C. William Vogel, M.A., University of Cincinnati, 1928; Ph.D., Harvard University, 1940; Professor of History, University of Cincinnati.

Henry R. Winkler, M.A., University of Cincinnati, 1940; Ph.D., University of Chicago, 1947; Dean of the Faculty of Liberal Arts and Professor of History, Rutgers University.

Index

Union of Soviet Socialist Republics. *See* Soviet Union

The manuscript was edited by Lewis Beeson and Marguerite C. Wallace. The book is designed by Peter Nothstein. The type face for the text is Linotype Caledonia, an original design by W. A. Dwiggins, cut in 1940. The display face is Weiss designed by E. R. Weiss.

The book is printed on S. D. Warren's Olde Style Antique paper and bound in Joanna Mills' Parchment vellum cloth over boards. Manufactured in the United States of America.